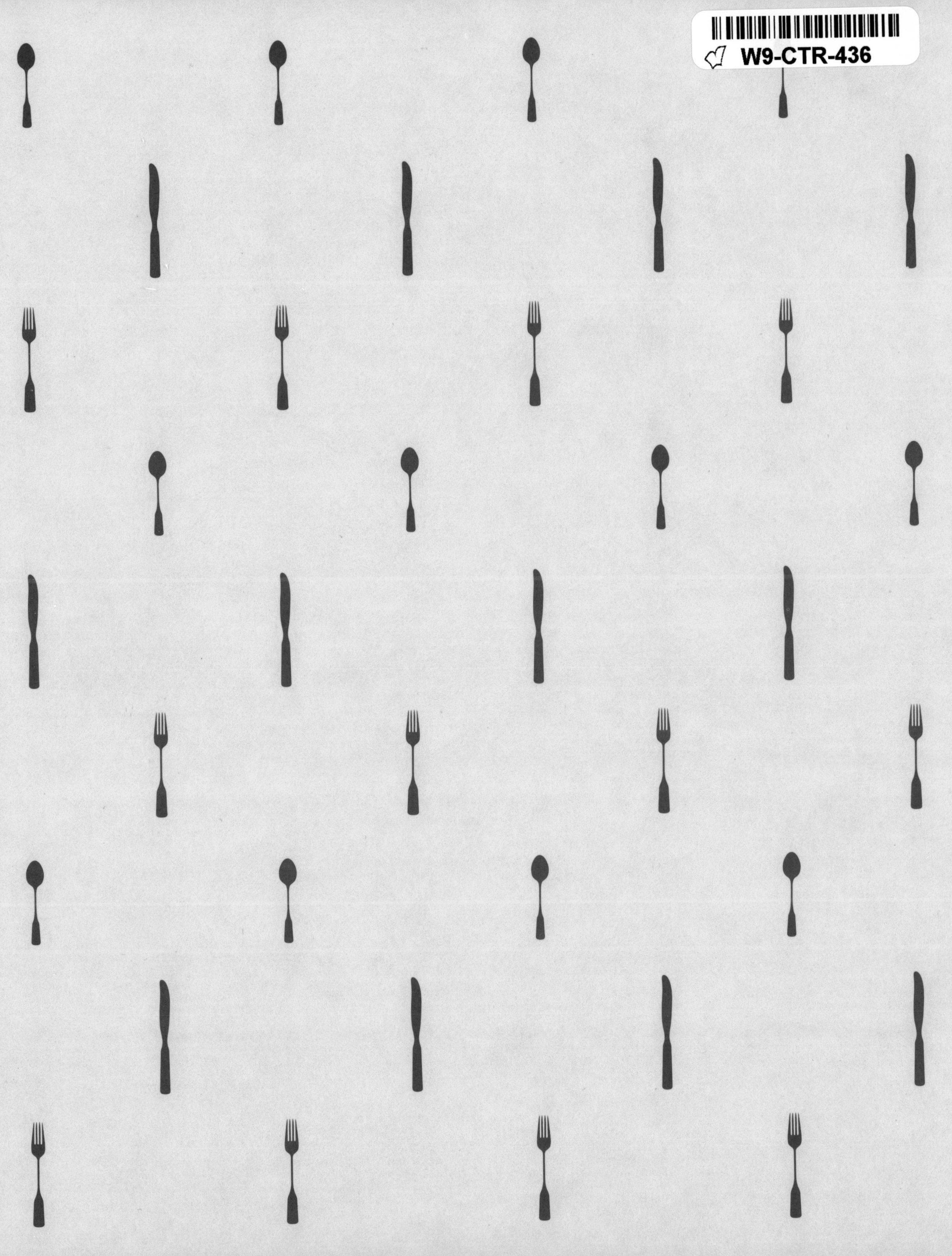

Fresh Ways with Lamb

Time-Life Books Inc.
is a wholly owned subsidiary of
TIME INCORPORATED

FOUNDER: Henry R. Luce 1898-1967

Editor-in-Chief: Jason McManus
Chairman and Chief Executive Officer: J. Richard Munro
President and Chief Operating Officer: N. J. Nicholas, Jr.
Editorial Director: Ray Cave
Executive Vice President, Books: Kelso F. Sutton
Vice President, Books: Paul V. McLaughlin

COVER
In this version of kabobs, cubes of lean lamb lightly coated with a fresh mint and oil-cured olive sauce are complemented by apples as well as the usual onions and green peppers (recipe, page 40). Broiled or grilled over charcoal and paired with a salad of lentils and onions as shown here, these lamb kabobs provide an exciting meal that is high in protein and low in saturated fat.

TIME-LIFE BOOKS INC.

EDITOR: George Constable
Executive Editor: Ellen Phillips
Director of Design: Louis Klein
Director of Editorial Resources: Phyllis K. Wise
Editorial Board: Russell B. Adams, Jr., Dale M. Brown, Roberta Conlan, Thomas H. Flaherty, Lee Hassig, Donia Ann Steele, Rosalind Stubenberg
Director of Photography and Research: John Conrad Weiser
Assistant Director of Editorial Resources: Elise Ritter Gibson

European Executive Editor: Gillian Moore
Design Director: Ed Skyner
Assistant Design Director: Mary Staples
Chief of Research: Vanessa Kramer
Chief Sub-Editor: Ilse Gray

PRESIDENT: Christopher T. Linen
Chief Operating Officer: John M. Fahey, Jr.
Senior Vice Presidents: Robert M. DeSena, James L. Mercer, Paul R. Stewart
Vice Presidents: Stephen L. Bair, Ralph J. Cuomo, Neal Goff, Stephen L. Goldstein, Juanita T. James, Hallett Johnson III, Carol Kaplan, Susan J. Maruyama, Robert H. Smith, Joseph J. Ward
Director of Production Services: Robert J. Passantino
Supervisor of Quality Control: James King

HEALTHY HOME COOKING

SERIES DIRECTOR: Jackie Matthews
Studio Stylist: Liz Hodgson
Editorial Assistant: Eugénie Romer

Editorial Staff for *Fresh Ways with Lamb:*
Editor: Neil Fairbairn
Researcher: Heather Campion
Designer: Mike Snell
Sub-Editor: Christine Noble
Indexer: Myra Clark

PICTURE DEPARTMENT:
Administrator: Patricia Murray
Picture Coordinator: Amanda Hindley

EDITORIAL PRODUCTION:
Chief: Maureen Kelly
Assistant: Samantha Hill
Editorial Department: Theresa John, Debra Lelliott

U.S. Edition:
Assistant Editor: Barbara Fairchild Quarmby
Copy Coordinators: Marfé Ferguson Delano, Colette Stockum
Picture Coordinator: Betty H. Weatherley

Editorial Operations
Copy Chief: Diane Ullius
Production: Celia Beattie
Library: Louise D. Forstall

Correspondents: Elisabeth Kraemer-Singh (Bonn); Maria Vincenza Aloisi (Paris); Ann Natanson (Rome).

THE COOKS

The recipes in this book were prepared for photographing by Pat Alburey, Allyson Birch, Jane Bird, Jill Eggleton, Joanna Farrow, Carole Handslip, Janice Murfitt, and Jane Suthering. *Studio Assistant:* Rita Walters.

THE CONSULTANT

PAT ALBUREY is a home economist with a wide experience in preparing foods for photography, teaching cooking, and creating recipes. She has written a number of cookbooks, and she was the studio consultant for the Time-Life Books series The Good Cook. She has created a number of the recipes in this volume.

THE NUTRITION CONSULTANT

PATRICIA JUDD trained as a dietician and worked in hospital nutrition before returning to college to earn her M.Sc. and Ph.D. degrees. She has since lectured in Nutrition and Dietetics at London University.

Nutritional analyses for *Fresh Ways with Lamb* were derived from McCance and Widdowson's *The Composition of Food* by A. A. Paul and D. A. T. Southgate, and other current data.

Library of Congress Cataloging in Publication Data
Fresh ways with lamb / by the editors of Time-Life Books.
p. cm. — (Healthy home cooking)
Includes index.
ISBN 0-8094-6045-9. ISBN 0-8094-6046-7 (lib. bdg.)
1. Cookery (Lamb)
I. Time-Life Books. II. Series.
TX749.5.L35F74 1988 641.6'63—dc19 88-39711
CIP

For information on and a full description of any Time-Life Books series, please call 1-800-621-7026 or write:
Reader Information
Time-Life Customer Service
P.O. Box C-32068
Richmond, Virginia 23261-2068

First printing. Printed in U.S.A.
Published simultaneously in Canada.
School and library distribution by Silver Burdett Company, Morristown, New Jersey 07960.

THE CONTRIBUTORS

JOANNA BLYTHMAN is a cook and recipe writer who owns a specialty food shop in Edinburgh, Scotland. She contributes articles on cooking to a number of newspapers and periodicals.

LISA CHERKASKY has worked as a chef at numerous restaurants in Washington, D.C., and in Madison, Wisconsin, including nationally known Le Pavillon and Le Lion d'Or. A graduate of The Culinary Institute of America at Hyde Park, New York, she has also taught classes in French cooking technique.

SILVIJA DAVIDSON studied at Leith's School of Food and Wine in London and specializes in the development of recipes from Latvia, as well as other international cuisines.

JOANNA FARROW, a home economist and recipe writer who contributes regularly to food magazines, is especially interested in decorative presentation of food. Her books include *Creative Cake Decorating* and *Novelty Cakes for Children.*

JENI WRIGHT is a freelance food writer and editor with wide-ranging culinary interests. Among the books she has written are *French Cooking, Midday Meals,* and *Entertaining with Friends.*

The following people also have contributed recipes to this volume: Maddalena Bonino, Heather Campion, Alexandra Carlier, Yvonne Hamlett, Carole Handslip, Pam Howe, Antony Kwok, Hilary Newstead, and Jane Suthering.

This volume is one of a series of illustrated cookbooks that emphasize the preparation of healthful dishes for today's weight-conscious, nutrition-minded eaters.

HEALTHY HOME COOKING

Fresh Ways with Lamb

BY

THE EDITORS OF TIME-LIFE BOOKS

TIME-LIFE BOOKS / ALEXANDRIA, VIRGINIA

Contents

Lamb and Broccoli Stir-Fry

Chilled Chops Coated with Mint Aspic

Moroccan Spiced Stew

Port Paupiettes

Salade Niçoise

Diced Lamb with Pink Grapefruit and Tarragon

A New Approach to Lamb

Over the millennia, no meat has more regularly graced the tables of mankind than lamb. It was some 10,000 years ago that tribes in Central Asia first domesticated sheep for their meat, milk, and wool. By 7,000 BC, the pastoral way of life had spread throughout the Middle East, where flocks of hardy sheep thrived despite punishing extremes of heat and cold. Little wonder that sheep are the first domestic animal mentioned in the Bible. Adam's son Abel, we learn, was a keeper of sheep, and when he made a sacrifice to God, he chose to offer up his newborn lambs.

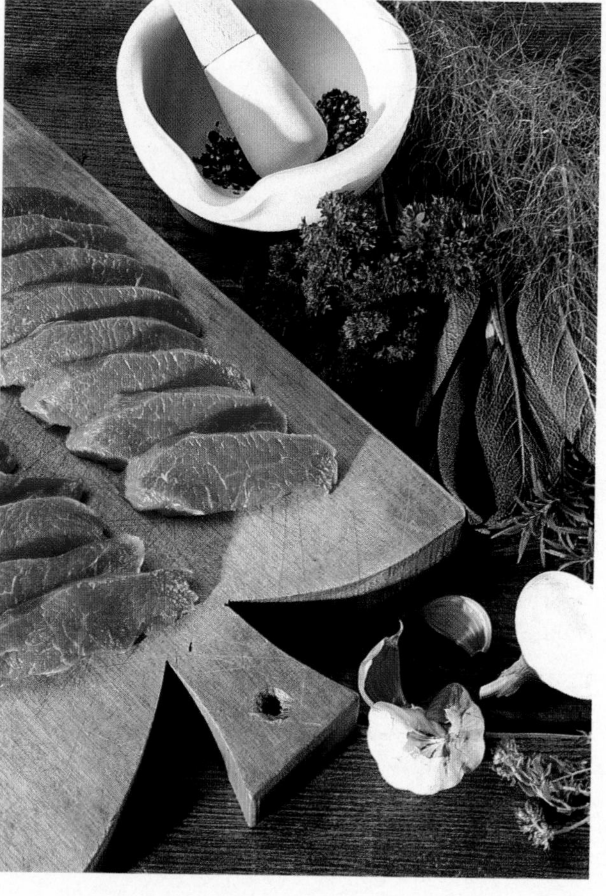

During its association with mankind, the sheep has evenhandedly fed both the rich and the poor. In many parts of the world, its meat has long been served not only for feasting and holy days but equally for everyday fare. In medieval Europe, the servant who carried the roasted saddle of lamb, crisp and golden, to the banquet table returned to the kitchen for his own bowl of mutton stew—not such an imposing dish as his master's, but just as nutritious and full of flavor. Throughout the Islamic Middle East, a whole roast of lamb still serves as the centerpiece of wedding feasts and other festivities, while lesser cuts of lamb play a central role in most ordinary meat dishes.

In other parts of the prosperous modern world, however, this most democratic of providers has lost its prized place in a large number of kitchens. Beef, poultry, and pork are all produced inexpensively enough to compete with lamb at the dinner table. A further blow to the prestige of lamb comes from health-conscious cooks who are wary of the fat content of red meats in general, and who regard lamb as having only a limited place in a healthful diet.

This volume of Healthy Home Cooking aims to restore lamb to its rightful place as a food for everyone. Reflecting its classless appeal, the 114 recipes offer inspiration for every kind of occasion. There are simple chops and cutlets, grand roasts, subtly flavored stews, assemblages of meat and vegetables, sautés, and salads. Devised by Time-Life Books' own team of chefs and nutritionists, these dishes have been prepared with a minimum of both fat and oil, allowing the most health-conscious of cooks to choose freely among them.

A nutritional profile

By any standards, lamb, like other red meats, is a highly nutritious food. A single 3-ounce serving of cooked lamb provides about ¾ ounce of valuable animal protein—one-third of the total daily intake recommended for adults. Just as beneficial is the range of vitamins present in red meat. Lamb is an important source of B vitamins, essential for healthy skin and the nervous system. A 3-ounce serving, for example, contains over 40 percent of the adult male's recommended daily intake of niacin and of vitamin B_{12}. Lamb is also rich in iron, in the form known as heme iron, which is not only easily absorbed by the body, but also promotes the absorption of iron from other foods.

The major drawback of lamb as part of a healthful diet is its high fat content. Most people are aware that we eat too much fat for our own well-being. Indeed, nutritionists urge us to cut our total fat consumption by about one-quarter—from nearly 40 percent of our daily energy intake to around 30 percent. They are especially insistent on the wisdom of cutting down on saturated fats—contained in animal fats—which promote the production of cholesterol in the body. Although cholesterol is produced naturally by the liver and in small amounts contributes to good health, excessive production stimulated by a diet high in saturated fats can, over a period of time, lead to heart disease.

Fortunately, lamb is a less fatty meat than it used to be. Farmers, encouraged by consumer demand, and in some countries by agricultural subsidies, are generally producing leaner lamb than was available a few years ago. In any case, most of the fat found in a cut of lamb can be easily trimmed off before cooking. But lean, uncooked lamb still contains about 9 percent intramuscular fat. This proportion is slightly higher than is found in pork and about twice as much as is present in lean beef. In other words, a certain intake of saturated fat cannot be avoided when you sit down to a dish of lamb. You would not want it otherwise, for fat in reasonable measure contributes to the flavor and succulence of meat; it is one of the reasons why lamb has been so highly regarded for such a long time.

The strategy adopted by the authors of this volume is to prepare the meat so that it is as free of fat as possible, and to eliminate all unnecessary fats from the cooking process, using the much more benign polyunsaturated or monounsaturated fats where necessary. An upper limit of 14 grams of total fat per 3-ounce serving of cooked lamb has been imposed as a reasonable guideline. These recipes also limit salt to no more than 400 milligrams per portion, since a high salt intake is also implicated in heart disease. At the same time, Time-Life Books' team of cooks and nutrition experts have in no way compromised the unique flavor and texture of lamb.

Choosing, buying, and storing

A first step in buying good-quality lean lamb is to seek the advice of a knowledgeable butcher. He or she should be able to tell you the age and origin of the animal—factors that influence the appearance, flavor, and fat content of the meat. As a general rule, the younger the lamb the paler and less fatty the meat. Lowland breeds are not inherently leaner than hill breeds, but they gain weight faster and are usually slaughtered at an earlier age. A fresh spring lamb of about six months has rose-pink flesh and white, firm fat; brittle, chalk-white fat suggests that the meat has been frozen. Certain hill breeds, however, have darker flesh than lowland strains, as does meat that has been hung. A useful indicator of a lamb's age is its bones; in a young animal they have a pinkish blue tinge, whereas in older animals they are white and less pliant.

There is no general agreement as to when lamb becomes mutton, for different breeds mature at different rates. It is safe to say, however, that an animal is no longer sold as lamb after it is a year old. Of course, mutton is now something of a rarity, being found mainly in butcher shops that cater to Asian or Middle Eastern communities.

Although the emphasis in this volume is on lean cuts, the recipes make use of cuts from most parts of the carcass. Not included are recipes for the breast and the neck, which have a very high fat content even after trimming. The liver, though a rich source of vitamin A, has a cholesterol content that exceeds the limit prescribed for healthful diets, and it should be eaten only occasionally. Shoulder of lamb appears infrequently in the recipes; full of flavor but also high in fat, it requires meticulous trimming before it is cooked.

The principal source of lean meat on a lamb is the sirloin end—the wide upper section—of the leg. Cuts from the sirloin can be cubed for stews and kabobs, ground for meat loaf, or sliced and pounded flat to create lamb's answer to the veal cutlet, ideal for quick broiling or flash-frying. The rib and the loin—adjacent cuts along the back of the carcass—yield smaller pieces of extremely tender lean meat. The rib, whether roasted whole as a rack or separated into individual chops, should be carefully trimmed of fat so that only the "eye" of lean meat along the backbone remains. Likewise, the loin can be cut into chops and trimmed of fat or boned to yield two strips of lean meat—the loin and the small but exquisitely delicate tenderloin *(page 134)*.

Several of the preparatory techniques illustrated on pages 134 to 136 are tasks routinely undertaken by a butcher, whose work is timesaving and usually free. You can order ready-to-cook noisettes, for example, or a boned leg or loin. Alternatively, buy the basic cuts and prepare them for cooking yourself; no doubt your own efforts will be slow, but you can take satisfaction in removing every piece of surplus fat. Likewise, the leanest and freshest ground meat is obtained by chopping by hand at home.

Stored in the coolest part of the refrigerator, fresh lamb will keep without spoiling for up to three days. Remove its wrapping and place the lamb on a rack set over a plate to encourage the circulation of air. Cover it with an upturned bowl to prevent its surface from drying out. Ground lamb should be eaten within two days of being refrigerated.

Lamb will keep in the freezer for six to nine months, ground lamb for four months. Freeze only fresh meat, extracting all air from the freezer bag or foil parcel before storing.

Appetizing flavors, healthful techniques

To keep fat and cholesterol levels within healthful limits, the recipes that follow call for skim milk in place of whole milk and polyunsaturated margarine rather than butter. Cheese is used only as a topping, never as a principal ingredient. To reduce both fat and calories, most of the gravies and sauces are thickened with cornstarch or arrowroot instead of the traditional roux made with flour and fat.

Far from limiting the variety and appeal of the recipes, these restrictions free a range of flavors that too often are suppressed by rich ingredients. Fiber-rich fresh vegetables and grains, dried fruits, and legumes are traditional partners for lamb, and this volume makes full use of them. The reduced level of salt permits fresh herbs and spices to assert their unique flavors with refreshing clarity.

Cooking techniques are also tailored to meet the dietary guidelines. In Healthy Home Cooking's test kitchens, heavy-bottomed pans are used to guard against burning the food when a small amount of oil is used. Nonstick pans brushed with the merest film of oil are perfectly adequate for browning meat and vegetables, as called for in many of the recipes. Safflower oil and virgin olive oil are favored for sautéing. Safflower is the oil of choice because

The Key to Better Eating

Healthy Home Cooking addresses the concerns of today's weight-conscious, health-minded cooks with recipes developed within nutritional guidelines.

The chart at right presents the National Research Council's Recommended Dietary Allowances of both calories and protein for healthy men, women, and children of average size, along with the council's recommendations for the "safe and adequate" maximum intake of sodium. Although the council has not established similar recommendations for either cholesterol or fat, the chart does include what the National Institutes of Health and the American Heart Association consider the maximum allowable amounts of these in one day's eating by healthy members of the general population.

Recommended Dietary Guidelines

		Average Daily Intake		Maximum Daily Intake			
		CALORIES	PROTEIN *grams*	CHOLESTEROL *milligrams*	TOTAL FAT *grams*	SATURATED FAT *grams*	SODIUM *milligrams*
Children	7-10	2400	22	240	80	27	1800
Females	11-14	2200	37	220	73	24	2700
	15-18	2100	44	210	70	23	2700
	19-22	2100	44	300	70	23	3300
	23-50	2000	44	300	67	22	3300
	51-75	1800	44	300	60	20	3300
Males	11-14	2700	36	270	90	30	2700
	15-18	2800	56	280	93	31	2700
	19-22	2900	56	300	97	32	3300
	23-50	2700	56	300	90	30	3300
	51-75	2400	56	300	80	27	3300

The volumes in the Healthy Home Cooking series do not purport to be diet books, nor do they focus on health foods. Rather, the books express a common-sense approach to cooking that uses salt, sugar, cream, butter, and oil in moderation while including other ingredients that also contribute flavor and satisfaction. The portions themselves are modest in size.

The recipes make few unusual demands. Naturally they call for fresh ingredients, offering substitutes should these be unavailable. (Only the original ingredient is calculated in the nutrient analysis, however.) Most of the ingredients can be found in any well-stocked supermarket; the occasional exceptions can be bought in specialty shops or ethnic groceries.

About cooking times

To help the cook plan ahead effectively, Healthy Home Cooking takes time into account in all its recipes. While recognizing that everyone cooks at a different speed, and that stoves and ovens may differ somewhat in their temperatures, the series provides approximate "working" and "total" times for every dish. Working time stands for the minutes actively spent on preparation; total time includes unattended cooking time, as well as time devoted to marinating, steeping, or soaking various ingredients. Because the recipes emphasize fresh foods, the dishes may take a bit longer to prepare than those in "quick and easy" cookbooks that call for canned or package products, but the difference in flavor, and often in added nutritional value, should compensate for the little extra time involved.

it is the most highly polyunsaturated oil generally available—and polyunsaturated vegetable fats are not only blameless in the cholesterol controversy, but they may actually reduce the blood-cholesterol level. A good second choice is sunflower oil, also high in polyunsaturated fats. Virgin olive oil is called for because it has a matchless fruity flavor and is high in monounsaturated fats, which are not linked to increased blood-cholesterol levels. Lesser grades of olive oil, such as pure, can be substituted for virgin, although they lack its incomparable bouquet.

When cooked slowly in a liquid, even the leanest of lamb will release a small amount of fat. If the cooking liquid is to be used for a sauce or gravy, skim off the fat with a ladle or a shallow spoon before serving. Alternatively, lay a paper towel flat on the surface, then lift it away immediately after it has absorbed the layer of fat. A stew that is prepared in advance can be chilled and then degreased even more thoroughly simply by lifting off the solid layer of fat that collects on the surface.

Keeping low-fat cuts of meat moist is a particular problem when sautéing, broiling, or roasting. Denied the traditional techniques of basting or ladling the meat with extra fat, the health-conscious cook must adopt different strategies. One such method is to stuff a roast or chop with a savory filling—such as the shoulder stuffed with wild rice and spinach on page 50 and the chops stuffed with walnuts and parsley on page 59—that moisturizes the meat from within as it cooks. Another technique, suitable for thin cuts of lamb, is to tenderize the meat in a marinade so that it cooks rapidly with a minimum wastage of moisture. Acidic marinades, made with vinegar, wine, or citrus juices blended with aromatics, will break down the meat's fibers while imparting their own distinctive flavors. Treated in this way, a slice of the leg flattened with a meat mallet will cook in very little time under a broiler—and will taste all the better for the marriage of flavors.

Whatever techniques you use to keep lamb moist, prolonged exposure to dry heat will eventually desiccate the meat. For this reason, the range of cooking times recommended in the recipes is for rare to medium meat. If lamb that is still pink in the middle is not to your liking, add a minute or two to the cooking time for small pieces and 10 to 15 minutes for roasts.

A choice of cooking methods

This book is organized in four main chapters, each one devoted to a different cooking method. Chapter 1 deals with dry cooking methods—sautéing, broiling, roasting—and covers the simplest and quickest ways of cooking tender cuts. It also includes those grand conversation-stopping roasts of old-fashioned dinner parties: the saddle, the crown, and the guard of honor. Chapter 2 describes moist cooking: braising, stewing, and poaching. These methods, traditionally used to tenderize tougher cuts of lamb, have been adapted to give superb results with leaner cuts. Chapter 3 features assembled dishes, in which lamb is variously used as a stuffing for pastry and pancakes, extended with grains, legumes, and pasta, layered with vegetables, or tossed in salads. Finally, Chapter 4 describes ways of preparing lamb dishes in a microwave oven, a quick and versatile cooking method.

Since many of the recipes call for unsalted brown stock or unsalted chicken stock, these preparations are given at the end of the book, together with a brief section on methods of readying lamb for low-fat cooking, as well as a glossary of culinary terms and ingredients.

The ingredient list for each recipe starts with lamb and continues with the other ingredients in order of use. And like other volumes in Healthy Home Cooking, *Lamb* presents an analysis of nutrients contained in a single serving of each dish, which includes approximate counts for calories, protein, cholesterol, total fat, saturated fat, and sodium. In order to simplify meal planning, most recipes list suitable accompaniments. These are suggestions only; cooks should let their imaginations be their guide to achieving an appealing and sensible balance of foods.

Cuts of Lamb for Healthful Eating

This diagram shows major, or primal, cuts into which a lamb carcass is commonly divided by butchers. It also identifies the retail cuts called for by recipes in this book. With careful trimming, most parts of a lamb can provide low-fat meals. Only the breast and the neck are unacceptably fatty.

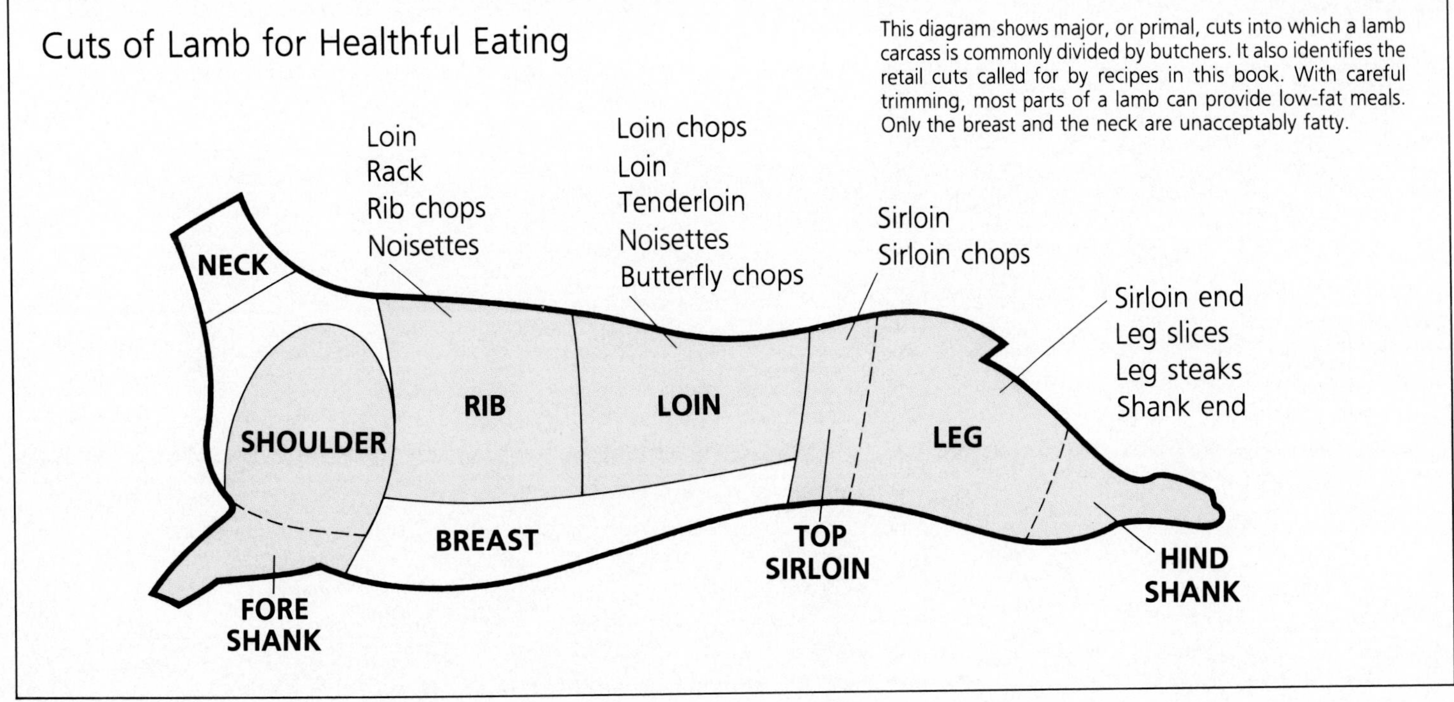

1 Lean strips of loin are stir-fried briefly in a wok with colorful fresh vegetables and a minimum of oil (recipe, page 22).

Updating the Classics

The first Stone Age person who seared chunks of meat over an open fire inadvertently discovered one of the best methods of cooking. Today, grilling and broiling are as valued as ever for cooking many kinds of meat, including lamb. The benefits of broiling are allied to those of roasting and frying. All of these dry-cooking techniques use high heat to sear the meat's surface, adding flavor and color. Together, they offer endless healthful, delicious ways of presenting lamb.

The choice of method depends partly upon the thickness and quality of the lamb. Tender strips of loin, stir-fried in a sauté pan or traditional Chinese wok, sear and cook through in little more than a minute. Thin cuts from the loin or rib are well suited to the intense surface heat of broiling or frying, as are chops, cutlets, and steaks from the leg; anything much thicker may char on the outside before the inside has cooked sufficiently. Large cuts, such as loin roasts, legs, or shoulders, are generally roasted in the less intense heat of the oven. The tougher shank end of leg requires relatively slow roasting.

Because the heat of a broiler, frying pan, or oven can dry out and toughen meat, traditional recipes often call for lamb to be smeared with oil and basted with fat. The recipes in this chapter use a minimum of oil yet still achieve succulent results. Steeped in a marinade or flattened with a meat mallet, slices of lamb become tender enough for rapid exposure to searing heat, while nonstick pans, brushed lightly with oil, help break up the unhealthful alliance between frying and fat. Large cuts, such as the boned leg on page 49, can be stuffed with vegetables, which release their moisture during roasting. A moist coating on the outside of a roast also makes for tender meat: The rack of lamb on page 54 is roasted in parsley marinade, which forms a protective, savory crust.

Low-fat dry cooking does not mean that the showy Sunday roast is a thing of the past. When carefully trimmed, as demonstrated on page 135, even the normally fatty rack of lamb finds a place on the health-conscious cook's menu. Well-trimmed racks can appear in traditional display pieces such as the guard of honor on page 55, while the crown roast on page 56 becomes a dish fit for a healthy king.

Several of the recipes that follow include sauces made from the meat's roasting juices. While you prepare the sauce, the meat should be loosely covered with foil and kept warm. This resting period of 10 or 15 minutes allows the juices that have concentrated in the center of the meat during cooking to flow back evenly throughout the roast, promoting firm, tender flesh and making carving easier.

Medallions of Lamb with Watercress Sauce

Serves 4
Working time: about 35 minutes
Total time: about 45 minutes

Calories **200**
Protein **25g.**
Cholesterol **90mg.**
Total fat **11g.**
Saturated fat **5g.**
Sodium **90mg.**

one 2¼-lb. lamb loin roast, trimmed of fat and boned (technique, page 134), cut diagonally into 12 slices, tenderloin reserved for another use

1¼ cups unsalted brown or chicken stock (recipes, page 137)

2 bunches watercress, washed

4 fresh sage leaves, or ⅛ tsp. dried sage

½ tsp. salt

ground white pepper

1 tbsp. apple jelly

1 tbsp. Worcestershire sauce, mixed with 1 tbsp. water

1 tbsp. sour cream

To make the watercress sauce, boil the stock until the liquid is reduced by half—5 to 10 minutes. Strip the leaves from the watercress, reserving 4 sprigs for garnish, and add the watercress and sage leaves to the reduced boiling stock. Cook the stock for one minute more, allow it to cool slightly, then liquidize it in a blender or a food processor. Transfer it to a small saucepan, season with half of the salt and some white pepper, and add the apple jelly. Stir the sauce over low heat until the jelly has melted, then remove the pan from the heat.

Season the lamb slices with the remaining ¼ teaspoon of salt and some white pepper. Brush a large, nonstick frying pan lightly with oil and cook six of the slices over high heat for one minute on each side. Lower the heat to medium, add half of the Worcestershire sauce and cook for 30 seconds to one minute more on each side for rare to medium meat. Transfer the meat to a platter and keep it warm. Cook the remaining slices in the same way.

Heat the watercress sauce through, then remove the pan from the heat and stir in the sour cream. Serve the lamb with the sauce, garnished with the reserved sprigs of watercress.

SUGGESTED ACCOMPANIMENT: *steamed mushrooms.*

Flambéed Chops with Stuffed Apricots

Serves 4
Working time: about 40 minutes
Total time: about 6 hours and 50 minutes
(includes soaking and marinating)

Calories **260**
Protein **31g.**
Cholesterol **75mg.**
Total fat **8g.**
Saturated fat **4g.**
Sodium **175mg.**

8 rib chops (about 3 oz. each), trimmed of fat
2 tbsp. coarsely chopped fresh ginger
2 garlic cloves, coarsely chopped
1 small onion, coarsely chopped
½ cup fresh orange juice
¼ tsp. virgin olive oil
¼ lb. mushrooms, finely chopped
¼ tsp. salt
freshly ground black pepper
8 dried whole apricots, soaked for 6 hours or overnight in water
2 tbsp. brandy
parsley for garnish (optional)

Place the chops in a single layer in a shallow dish or casserole. Blend together the ginger, garlic, half the chopped onion, and the orange juice in a food processor. Spoon the purée over the chops, cover them loosely, and let them marinate for at least six hours, or overnight, turning them once.

Heat the oil in a frying pan. Add the mushrooms and the remaining onion, season them with ⅛ teaspoon of salt and some freshly ground black pepper, and sauté over medium heat until the vegetables are soft—two to three minutes.

Dry the apricots on paper towels, and fill them with the mushroom and onion stuffing, enlarging the hole from which the pit was removed, if necessary.

Remove the chops from the marinade and pat them dry with paper towels; strain the marinade and reserve it. Preheat a nonstick sauté pan and sear the chops for one minute on each side. Add the brandy and light it with a match. When the flame dies down, arrange the stuffed apricots in the pan, pour in half of the marinade, and sprinkle the remaining salt over the apricots. Cover the pan with a tight-fitting lid and cook over low heat until the juices are still slightly pink when the chops are pierced with a knife—about 10 minutes.

Arrange the meat and stuffed apricots on a warm platter. Skim off any fat from the juices in the pan, then add the remaining marinade, bring it to a boil, and simmer for one minute. Spoon the sauce over the lamb and serve, garnished with parsley, if you are using it.

SUGGESTED ACCOMPANIMENTS: *green beans; steamed new potatoes.*

Medallions in Sweet and Sour Sauce

Serves 4
Working (and total) time: about 40 minutes

Calories **305**
Protein **26g.**
Cholesterol **85mg.**
Total fat **14g.**
Saturated fat **6g.**
Sodium **165mg.**

1 rack of lamb (about 1¾ lb.), boned (page 136, Steps 1 to 4), the fatty flap of meat that extends from the loin removed
1½ tbsp. unsalted butter
20 shallots, peeled
2 tbsp. red wine
2 tsp. honey
½ tsp. salt
freshly ground black pepper
chopped scallions for garnish

Sweet and sour sauce

4 small carrots, trimmed and peeled
7 oz. young pink rhubarb
one 3-inch piece fresh ginger
1 cup red wine
¼ cup finely chopped shallots
2½ cups unsalted brown stock (recipe, page 137)
1 tsp. honey

Start by preparing the ingredients for the sauce. Cut half of the carrots and rhubarb into 2½-by-⅛ inch sticks. Coarsely chop the remainder. Cut half the ginger into matchsticks and finely chop the rest. Blanch the carrot sticks in boiling water for one minute, refresh them immediately in cold water, and drain them.

Preheat the oven to 250° F. Put 1 tablespoon of the butter into a heavy-bottomed frying pan, and sauté the whole shallots until they begin to soften and become golden brown—four to five minutes. Pour in the 2 tablespoons of wine and the honey, increase the heat, and boil, stirring frequently, until the liquid reduces to a syrupy glaze. Place the shallots on a roasting pan in the oven.

Cut the lamb across the grain into 16 medallions. Season them with the salt and freshly ground pepper.

Melt the remaining butter in a frying pan over low heat. Sauté the ginger matchsticks for two to three seconds, add the carrot sticks, and sauté them for 10 seconds; then add the rhubarb sticks and sauté all the ingredients for 10 seconds more, stirring all the time. Remove the sticks with a slotted spoon, transfer them to a plate, cover them, and keep them warm.

Increase the heat to high and cook the medallions until they are browned—one to two minutes on each side. Put them on the roasting pan in the oven with the glazed shallots.

To finish making the sauce, pour off any fat from the frying pan. Put the pan over high heat, pour in the red wine, and bring it to a boil, stirring to dislodge any browned bits. Add the chopped shallots together with the chopped ginger, carrots, and rhubarb. Boil until only half the liquid remains, then add the stock and the honey, and continue boiling until the liquid is reduced by half again. Strain the sauce through a fine sieve into a clean saucepan. Add the carrot and rhubarb sticks and the ginger matchsticks, and heat them through.

Place four medallions of lamb on each warmed plate, pour the sauce around them, and garnish with the scallions. Serve with the glazed shallots.

SUGGESTED ACCOMPANIMENT: *boiled rice.*

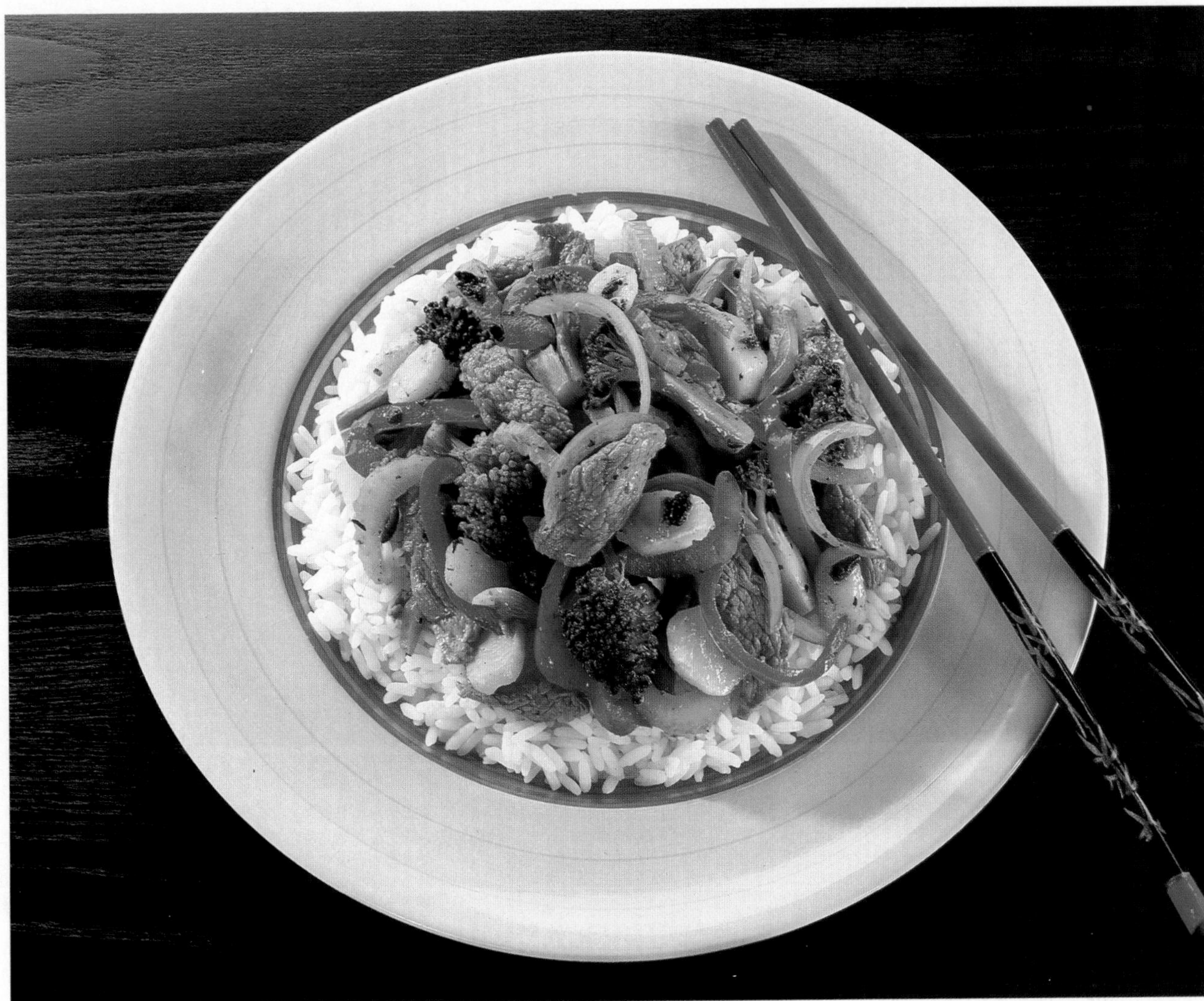

Lamb and Broccoli Stir-Fry

Serves 4
Working (and total) time: about 25 minutes

Calories **245**
Protein **22g.**
Cholesterol **50mg.**
Total fat **8g.**
Saturated fat **3g.**
Sodium **270mg.**

¾ lb. lean lamb (from the loin), cut into thin strips
4 tsp. safflower oil
¾ oz. fermented black beans (glossary, page 138), soaked in water for 5 minutes
½ tsp. sesame oil
1 onion, halved lengthwise and cut into strips
2 garlic cloves, finely chopped
one 1-inch piece fresh ginger, finely chopped
6 oz. broccoli, blanched, stalks peeled and julienned, flowers divided into florets
2 celery stalks, chopped
1 sweet red pepper, seeded, deribbed, and thinly sliced
1 tsp. low-sodium soy sauce
7 oz. fresh water chestnuts, peeled and boiled for 3 minutes, or 7 oz. canned water chestnuts, drained
3 tbsp. medium sherry

Heat 1 teaspoon of the safflower oil in a wok or a large, heavy-bottomed frying pan, and stir-fry half of the lamb over medium heat, tossing and stirring until it is browned—about two minutes. Remove the lamb from the wok and keep it warm. Heat another teaspoon of the oil in the wok, stir-fry the remaining meat, and add it to the first batch.

Drain the black beans and mash them in a small bowl with the sesame oil to make a coarse paste. Set the paste aside.

Put the remaining 2 teaspoons of safflower oil into the wok, and stir-fry the onion, garlic, and ginger for one minute. Add the broccoli, celery, red pepper, and soy sauce, and stir-fry for two minutes more. Add the water chestnuts, black-bean paste, and sherry, and return the lamb to the wok. Stir-fry over medium heat for two minutes more, so that all the ingredients are coated with the sauce and heated through.

Serve immediately.

SUGGESTED ACCOMPANIMENT: *boiled rice.*

Lamb Noisettes on Zucchini Pancakes

NOISETTES ARE SMALL, ROUND SLICES CUT FROM THE BONED LOIN.

Serves 4
Working (and total) time: about 30 minutes

Calories **235**
Protein **26g.**
Cholesterol **70mg.**
Total fat **9g.**
Saturated fat **4g.**
Sodium **295mg.**

one 2¼-lb. lamb loin roast, trimmed of fat and boned (technique, page 134)
3 tbsp. cut chives or finely chopped scallions for garnish

Zucchini pancakes

2 zucchini (about ¾ lb.), grated
1 carrot, grated
1 egg white
3 tbsp. freshly grated Parmesan cheese
2 tbsp. whole-wheat flour
2 garlic cloves, finely chopped
¼ tsp. salt
freshly ground black pepper
1 tsp. safflower oil

Cut the lamb loin into eight slices. With a meat mallet or the flat side of a heavy chef's knife, pound each slice of lamb between two sheets of heavy-duty plastic wrap or wax paper *(technique, page 24)* to a thickness of approximately ¼ inch. Set the noisettes aside.

Combine all the pancake ingredients but the oil in a bowl, and mix them well.

Heat a large, nonstick skillet over medium heat. Add the oil and spread it over the bottom with a paper towel. Drop four 2-tablespoon mounds of the pancake mixture into the skillet, allowing ample room between them. With a spatula, spread out each mound to form a pancake about 3 inches in diameter. Cook the pancakes until they are lightly browned—about three minutes per side. Transfer the pancakes to a cookie sheet and keep them warm in a very low oven. Cook four more pancakes the same way.

Increase the heat under the skillet to high. Add the noisettes to the skillet and cook them until they are browned—about two minutes per side.

Put two zucchini pancakes on each plate; top each pancake with a noisette. Sprinkle the noisettes with the chives or scallions, and serve at once.

SUGGESTED ACCOMPANIMENT: *tomato wedges with basil.*

Peppered Chops with Bean-Sprout Salad

Serves 4
Working (and total) time: about 40 minutes

Calories **260**
Protein **28g.**
Cholesterol **80mg.**
Total fat **12g.**
Saturated fat **4g.**
Sodium **330mg.**

4 boned lamb sirloin chops (about 4½ oz. each), trimmed of fat
2 tsp. black peppercorns
1 tbsp. virgin olive oil
3 tbsp. brandy
1¼ cups unsalted chicken stock (recipe, page 137)
1 tbsp. cornstarch
¼ tsp. salt
celery leaves for garnish

Bean-sprout salad

2 tsp. Dijon mustard
½ lemon, strained juice only
3 tbsp. sour cream
1 tbsp. chopped fresh parsley
¼ tsp. salt
freshly ground black pepper
6 oz. bean sprouts
one 4-inch piece cucumber, julienned
3 celery stalks, chopped
1 small sweet red pepper, seeded and thinly sliced

First, prepare the salad. Put the mustard, lemon juice, sour cream, and parsley into a salad bowl, season with the salt and some black pepper, and mix well together. Add the bean sprouts, cucumber, celery, and red pepper. Stir all the salad ingredients thoroughly, then cover the bowl and refrigerate while you cook the chops.

Coarsely crush the peppercorns with a mortar and pestle. Cut each chop into two neat pieces and coat both sides with the crushed peppercorns.

Heat the olive oil over medium heat in a large, heavy-bottomed frying pan. Add the chops and cook them for three to four minutes on each side for rare to medium meat. Using a slotted spoon, transfer the chops to a hot serving dish. Cover the chops and set them aside in a warm place.

Skim off any fat from the frying pan, then pour in the brandy. Heat it for a few seconds, then ignite it using a match. As soon as the flames subside, add the stock and bring the liquid to a boil, stirring and scraping the browned bits from the bottom of the pan into the sauce. In a small bowl, blend the cornstarch with a tablespoon of cold water, then stir it into the sauce, together with the salt. Bring the sauce to a boil, lower the heat, and simmer for two to three minutes, stirring frequently, until the sauce thickens.

Strain the sauce over and around the peppered chops. Garnish them with the celery leaves and serve immediately, accompanied by the bean-sprout salad.

SUGGESTED ACCOMPANIMENT: *small baked potatoes.*

Loin and Liver Cassis

Serves 4
Working time: about 30 minutes
Total time: about 40 minutes

Calories **175**
Protein **18g.**
Cholesterol **105mg.**
Total fat **8g.**
Saturated fat **3g.**
Sodium **355mg.**

10 oz. lean lamb (from the loin), trimmed of fat, thinly sliced, and flattened to about ⅛ inch thick (technique, page 24)
2 oz. lamb's liver, very thinly sliced
12 shallots, trimmed and peeled
½ tbsp. unsalted butter
2 tbsp. plus 1 tsp. crème de cassis
1½ tsp. black-currant vinegar or red wine vinegar
¾ tsp. salt
½ cup unsalted chicken stock (recipe, page 137)
2 tsp. unbleached all-purpose flour
freshly ground black pepper

Place the shallots in a heavy-bottomed, nonreactive saucepan with the butter, the teaspoon of crème de cassis, ½ teaspoon of the vinegar, ¼ teaspoon of the salt, and 3 tablespoons of water. Cover tightly, bring to a boil, and simmer until the shallots are tender—about 25 minutes. Remove the lid, increase the heat, and boil off the residual liquid to glaze the shallots, shaking the pan occasionally to prevent them from burning. Set the shallots aside and keep them warm.

Meanwhile, pour the stock and the remaining crème de cassis into a separate nonreactive saucepan. Boil rapidly until the liquid has reduced by about one-half—5 to 10 minutes. Set the reduced stock aside.

Sift the flour with some pepper and toss the liver in the seasoned flour until it is evenly coated. Brush a large, heavy-bottomed frying pan lightly with oil, place it over very high heat, and sear the slices of loin for 20 to 30 seconds on each side. Transfer them to a heated serving dish, sprinkle them with pepper, and keep them warm. Reduce the heat to low, brush the pan with a little more oil, and cook the floured slices of liver for 20 to 30 seconds, stirring constantly. Remove the liver and set it aside.

Increase the heat under the pan and add the remaining teaspoon of vinegar. Allow it to bubble for a few seconds, then add the reduced stock and the remaining ½ teaspoon of salt. Bring it to a boil, return the liver to the pan, and simmer for 30 seconds more before spooning the sauce and liver over the slices of loin. Serve with the glazed shallots.

SUGGESTED ACCOMPANIMENTS: *steamed snow peas; mashed potatoes sprinkled with chopped parsley.*

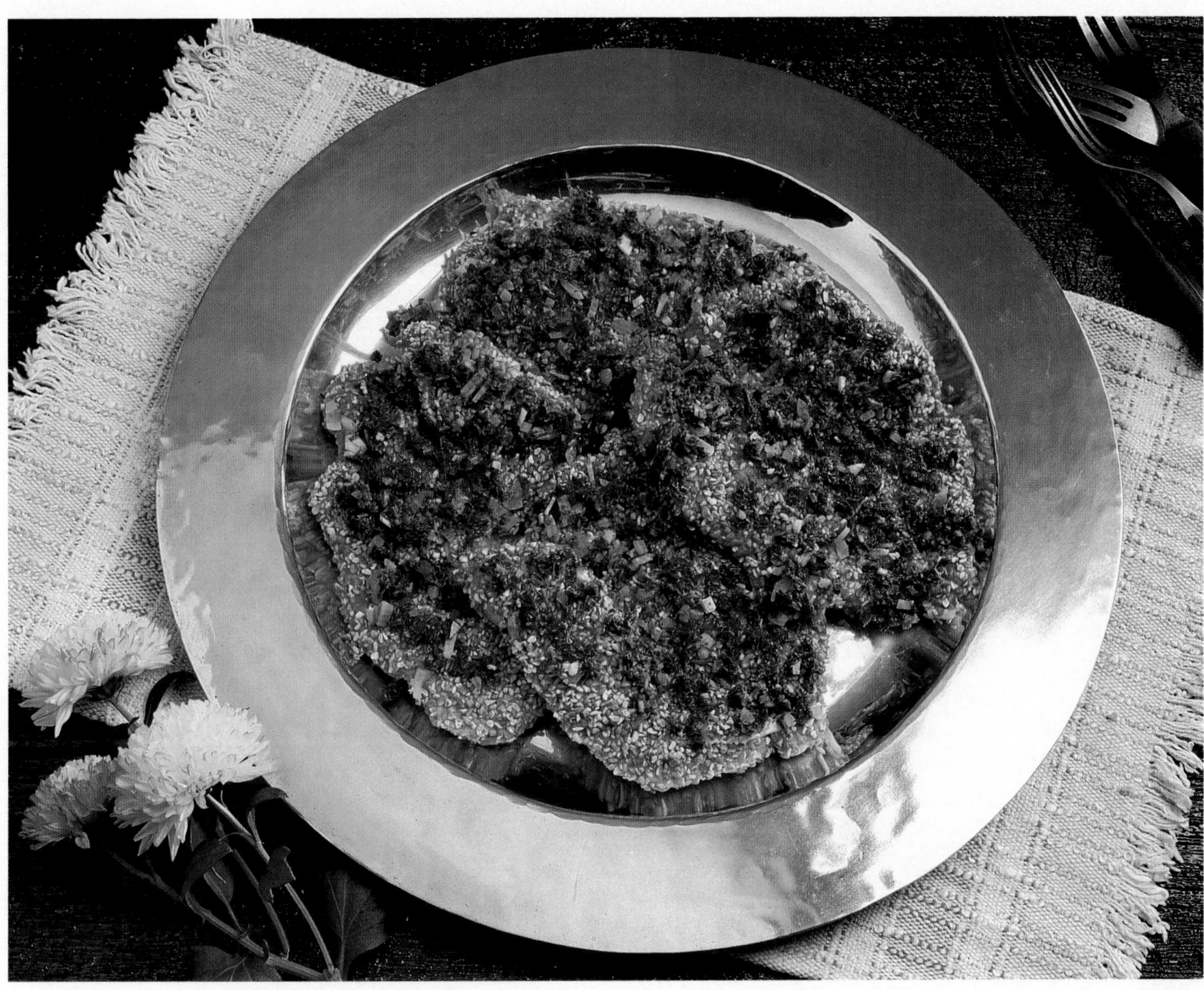

Kasha-Coated Lamb with Parsley-Garlic Sauce

Serves 4
Working (and total) time: about 20 minutes

Calories **410**
Protein **35g.**
Cholesterol **85mg.**
Total fat **14g.**
Saturated fat **5g.**
Sodium **75mg.**

4 lamb slices (about ¼ lb. each), cut from the loin end of the leg, trimmed of fat, and flattened to about ¼ inch thick (technique, page 24)
1 egg white
1 tbsp. fresh lemon juice
1 cup kasha (glossary, page 138)
¼ tsp. salt
freshly ground black pepper
1 tbsp. olive oil
½ tbsp. unsalted butter
1 shallot, finely chopped
1 garlic clove, finely chopped
½ cup chopped fresh parsley
1 ripe tomato, peeled, seeded, and puréed in a food processor or a blender

In a shallow bowl, whisk together the egg white and lemon juice. Spread the kasha on a plate. Sprinkle the lamb slices with the salt and some pepper. Dip a slice in the egg-white mixture, then dredge it in the kasha, coating both sides. Repeat the process to coat the remaining slices of lamb.

Heat the oil and butter in a large, nonstick skillet over high heat. Add the coated lamb slices and cook them until they are lightly browned on one side—about three minutes. Turn the slices and cook them for two minutes more to brown the second side. Transfer the slices to a warmed platter.

Add the shallot, garlic, and parsley to the skillet, and cook them for one minute. Stir in the tomato purée and some pepper. Cook the mixture for one minute more, then pour it over the lamb. Serve immediately.

SUGGESTED ACCOMPANIMENTS: *egg noodles; carrot purée.*

Lamb with Eggplant and Parmesan

Serves 4
Working time: about 40 minutes
Total time: about 1 hour

Calories **450**
Protein **34g.**
Cholesterol **80mg.**
Total fat **10g.**
Saturated fat **4g.**
Sodium **235mg.**

1 lb. lean lamb (from the leg or loin), cut into ½-inch cubes
½ lb. pasta shells
1 tsp. olive oil
½ lb. pearl onions, blanched in boiling water for 2 minutes and peeled
½ lb. small fresh mushrooms, wiped clean
¾ lb. eggplant, cut into ½-inch cubes
1 tsp. fresh thyme, or ½ tsp. dried thyme leaves
freshly ground black pepper
½ oz. Parmesan cheese, shaved with a vegetable peeler or grated (about ¼ cup)

Add the pasta to 3 quarts of boiling water with 1½ teaspoons of salt. Start testing the pasta for doneness after six minutes and cook it until it is *al dente.* Drain the pasta, rinse it under cold running water to prevent the shells from sticking together, and set it aside.

Heat a large, nonstick skillet over high heat. Add the pieces of lamb to the skillet and sauté them until they are browned on all sides—about three minutes. Lower the heat to medium and cook the lamb for three minutes more. Remove the lamb from the skillet and set the meat aside.

Add the olive oil and onions to the skillet. Place the cover on the skillet and cook the onions, stirring occasionally, until they are browned—about 15 minutes. Add the mushrooms and eggplant, then increase the heat to high, and sauté the vegetables until all are browned and the mushrooms and eggplant are soft—six to eight minutes.

Return the lamb to the skillet; add the pasta, the thyme, and a generous grinding of pepper. Sauté the mixture until the pasta is heated through—about three minutes. Spoon the mixture into a serving dish and top it with the cheese.

Serve immediately.

SUGGESTED ACCOMPANIMENT: *curly endive salad.*

Lamb Paprika

Serves 4
Working time: about 25 minutes
Total time: about 6 hours and 25 minutes
(includes marinating)

Calories **245**
Protein **30g.**
Cholesterol **85mg.**
Total fat **11g.**
Saturated fat **5g.**
Sodium **350mg.**

1 lb. lean lamb (from the leg or loin), trimmed of fat and cut into thin strips
1 tbsp. paprika
freshly ground black pepper
½ tsp. salt
¾ lb. kale, washed, stemmed, and chopped
2 tsp. caraway seeds
1 tbsp. polyunsaturated margarine
1 garlic clove, crushed
3 shallots, thinly sliced
2 bay leaves
3 tomatoes, peeled and chopped
3 tbsp. medium-dry sherry
2 tbsp. sour cream

Put the lamb into a bowl with the paprika, some pepper, and half of the salt, and stir until the meat is evenly coated. Cover the bowl and leave it in a cool place to marinate for at least six hours, or overnight. Stir the meat once during this period.

Pour enough water into a large saucepan to fill it about 1 inch deep. Place a vegetable steamer in the pan and bring the water to a boil. Put the kale into the steamer, and sprinkle it with the remaining ¼ teaspoon of salt and the caraway seeds. Cover and cook until the kale is just tender and bright green—three to four minutes.

Meanwhile, sauté the lamb. Melt the margarine in a large frying pan. Stir in the garlic, shallots, and bay leaves, and cook them over medium heat until the shallots are soft—one to two minutes. Increase the heat to high and sauté the lamb, stirring occasionally, until it has changed color all over—two to three minutes. Stir in the tomatoes and sherry. Bring the mixture to a boil and cook it for two minutes.

Spoon the kale into a hot serving dish, cover it, and keep it warm. Transfer the lamb and its sauce to another hot dish and serve immediately, topped with sour cream and accompanied by the kale.

SUGGESTED ACCOMPANIMENT: *Melba toast.*

Stir-Fried Vegetables with Shredded Lamb

Serves 4
Working (and total) time: about 40 minutes

Calories **255**
Protein **21g.**
Cholesterol **50mg.**
Total fat **13g.**
Saturated fat **3g.**
Sodium **265mg.**

¾ lb. lean lamb (from the loin), cut into thin strips
¼ cup sake or dry sherry
2 tbsp. low-sodium soy sauce
1 tsp. cornstarch
2 tbsp. safflower oil
1 tbsp. finely chopped fresh ginger
1 onion, peeled and sliced
8 frozen or canned baby corn, halved lengthwise if large
1 sweet red pepper, seeded, deribbed, and thinly sliced
½ medium cucumber, halved lengthwise, seeded, and sliced
1 cup small snow peas, stems and strings removed

Mix together the sake or sherry, soy sauce, and cornstarch in a small bowl, and set the mixture aside.

Heat the oil in a wok or a large, heavy-bottomed sauté pan until it is hot but not smoking. Add the ginger and onion, and stir for one minute over high heat, then add the baby corn and continue to stir-fry for one minute more. Add the strips of lamb a few at a time, stirring constantly, until they are completely sealed and lightly colored; then add the pepper and cucumber strips, and stir-fry for one minute more.

Finally, add the snow peas and stir for one minute. Pour the sake or sherry mixture over the meat and vegetables in the wok, and bring it to a boil, stirring until the liquid thickens. Serve immediately.

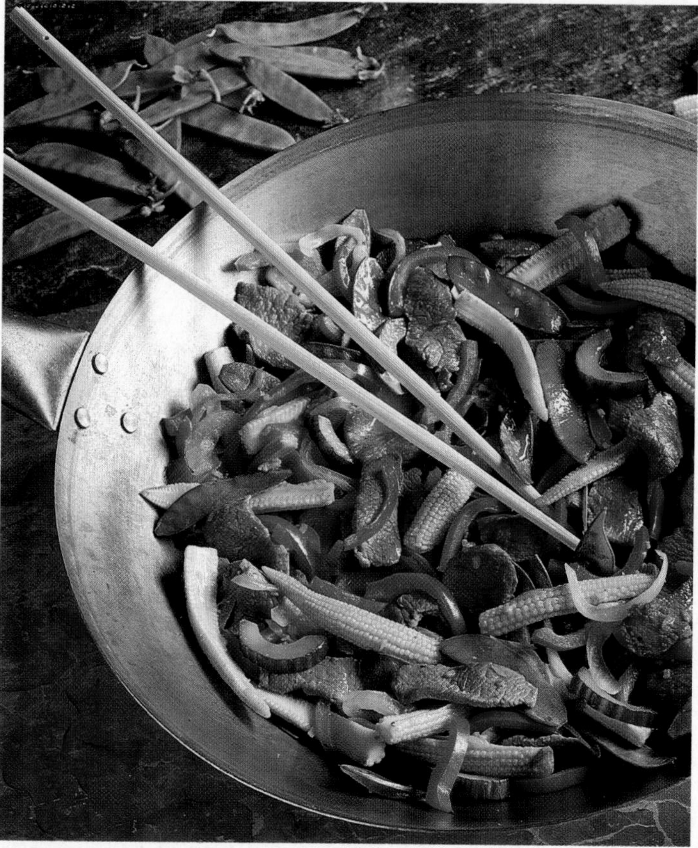

SUGGESTED ACCOMPANIMENT: *rice or noodles.*

Loin and Liver in Bean Sauce

Serves 4
Working time: about 20 minutes
Total time: about 30 minutes

Calories **235**
Protein **22g.**
Cholesterol **265mg.**
Total fat **13g.**
Saturated fat **3g.**
Sodium **425mg.**

6 oz. lean lamb (from the loin), trimmed of fat and cut into thin strips
6 oz. lamb's liver, cut into thin strips
2 tsp. light low-sodium soy sauce
2 tsp. Chinese rice wine or dry sherry
1 tsp. sesame oil
1½ tsp. cornstarch
1 large bunch scallions
one ¾-inch piece fresh ginger
1 garlic clove
2 tsp. safflower oil
½ medium hot red pepper or 1 small hot red pepper, seeded and thinly sliced (cautionary note, page 83)
nori (glossary, page 138), shredded, for garnish

Bean sauce

3 tbsp. bean paste
½ tsp. sugar
1 tsp. dark low-sodium soy sauce
2 tsp. Chinese rice wine or dry sherry

Put the strips of loin and liver into separate bowls. Blend together the light soy sauce, rice wine or sherry, sesame oil, and cornstarch, and divide this marinade between the two bowls. Stir well to coat the meat and liver thoroughly. Allow to marinate for 15 minutes.

To make the bean sauce, mix together the bean paste, sugar, soy sauce, and wine or sherry. Set the sauce aside.

Cut the scallions into 2½-inch lengths. Cut the white sections in half lengthwise; keep the white and green parts separate. Bruise the ginger and garlic with the side of a heavy knife.

Heat a wok over medium heat and add the safflower oil. Drop in the ginger and garlic, and let them sizzle until they turn light brown. Using the tip of a spatula, rub the garlic and ginger all around the wok, then remove and discard them.

Increase the heat to high. Stir-fry the loin, followed

by the liver, the white parts of the scallions, and the bean sauce, by constantly tossing and stirring each ingredient for about 15 seconds before adding the next. If the food seems about to stick and burn, lift the wok off the heat for a few seconds. Add the chili and stir-fry for another 10 seconds, then stir in the green parts of the scallions. Serve the mixture immediately, garnished with shredded nori.

SUGGESTED ACCOMPANIMENT: *egg noodles.*

EDITOR'S NOTE: *Bean paste is made from fermented soybeans and is available at all Chinese groceries.*

Warm Herb Salad

Serves 4
Working time: about 30 minutes
Total time: about 3 hours and 30 minutes
(includes marinating)

Calories **260**
Protein **31g.**
Cholesterol **90mg.**
Total fat **14g.**
Saturated fat **6g.**
Sodium **380mg.**

4 lamb slices (about 4 oz. each), cut from the sirloin end of the leg, trimmed of fat, and flattened to about ¼ inch thick (box, right)
½ cup dry white wine
1 tbsp. chopped fresh tarragon
4 tsp. chopped fresh dill
4 tsp. chopped fresh chervil
1 tbsp. safflower oil
¾ tsp. salt
freshly ground black pepper
½ medium cucumber, cut into bâtonnets
2-3 heads escarole, washed and dried, trimmed and shredded
4 tbsp. sour cream
1 tbsp. plain low-fat yogurt
¼ tsp. sugar

Cut each slice of meat into five strips. Place the meat in a shallow dish with the wine, the tarragon, and 3 teaspoons each of the dill and chervil. Allow the meat to marinate for three to four hours in a cool place, turning it halfway through this period.

Remove the meat from the marinade and dry it well on paper towels; reserve the marinade. Heat the oil in a wide, heavy-bottomed frying pan until it is hot but not smoking. Brown the meat for 30 seconds on each side, then remove it from the pan and season it with ½ teaspoon of the salt and some black pepper. Keep it warm while you prepare the salad.

Skim off any fat from the pan juices, then add the cucumber sticks and cook them over medium heat until they begin to soften—about one and a half minutes. Transfer the cucumber to a large bowl and add the endive.

To make the dressing, strain the reserved marinade into the frying pan and boil it over high heat until only 3 tablespoons of liquid remain. Remove it from the heat, stir in the sour cream, and cook over low heat for one minute. Remove the pan from the heat, and stir in the yogurt, the sugar, and the remaining teaspoon of dill and chervil and ¼ teaspoon of salt. Pour the warm dressing over the escarole and cucumber, toss the salad, and arrange it on four serving plates. Place the strips of lamb on top and serve immediately.

SUGGESTED ACCOMPANIMENT: *whole-grain rolls.*

Flattening Cutlets

POUNDING THE MEAT. Trim off all visible fat and membrane from the meat. Place the meat between two sheets of plastic wrap. Using a meat mallet or the flat of a heavy knife or cleaver, pound the meat to the thickness called for in the recipe.

Lamb Stroganoff

Serves 4
Working (and total) time: about 25 minutes

Calories **230**
Protein **29g.**
Cholesterol **80mg.**
Total fat **12g.**
Saturated fat **5g.**
Sodium **175mg.**

1 lb. lean lamb (from the loin), trimmed of fat and cut into thin strips
1 tbsp. olive oil
1 onion, finely chopped
½ lb. mushrooms, thinly sliced
½ cup sour cream
1 tsp. Dijon mustard
¼ tsp. salt
freshly ground black pepper
1 tbsp. chopped fresh parsley
1 tbsp. finely cut chives

Heat the oil in a large frying pan over medium heat. Add the onion, and cook it until it is soft but not brown—six to eight minutes. Transfer the onion to a plate. Add half of the lamb strips to the frying pan and cook them over high heat until they are lightly browned—one to two minutes—then transfer them to the plate with the onion. Brown the remaining lamb strips, then return the first batch of lamb and the onion to the pan. Add the mushrooms and cook over medium heat until the mushrooms soften—four to five minutes. Stir the sour cream and mustard into the mixture, and heat it through for three to four minutes. Season with the salt and some black pepper.

Transfer the stroganoff to a serving dish. Sprinkle it with the parsley and chives, and serve immediately.

SUGGESTED ACCOMPANIMENT: *mashed-potato nests filled with puréed peas.*

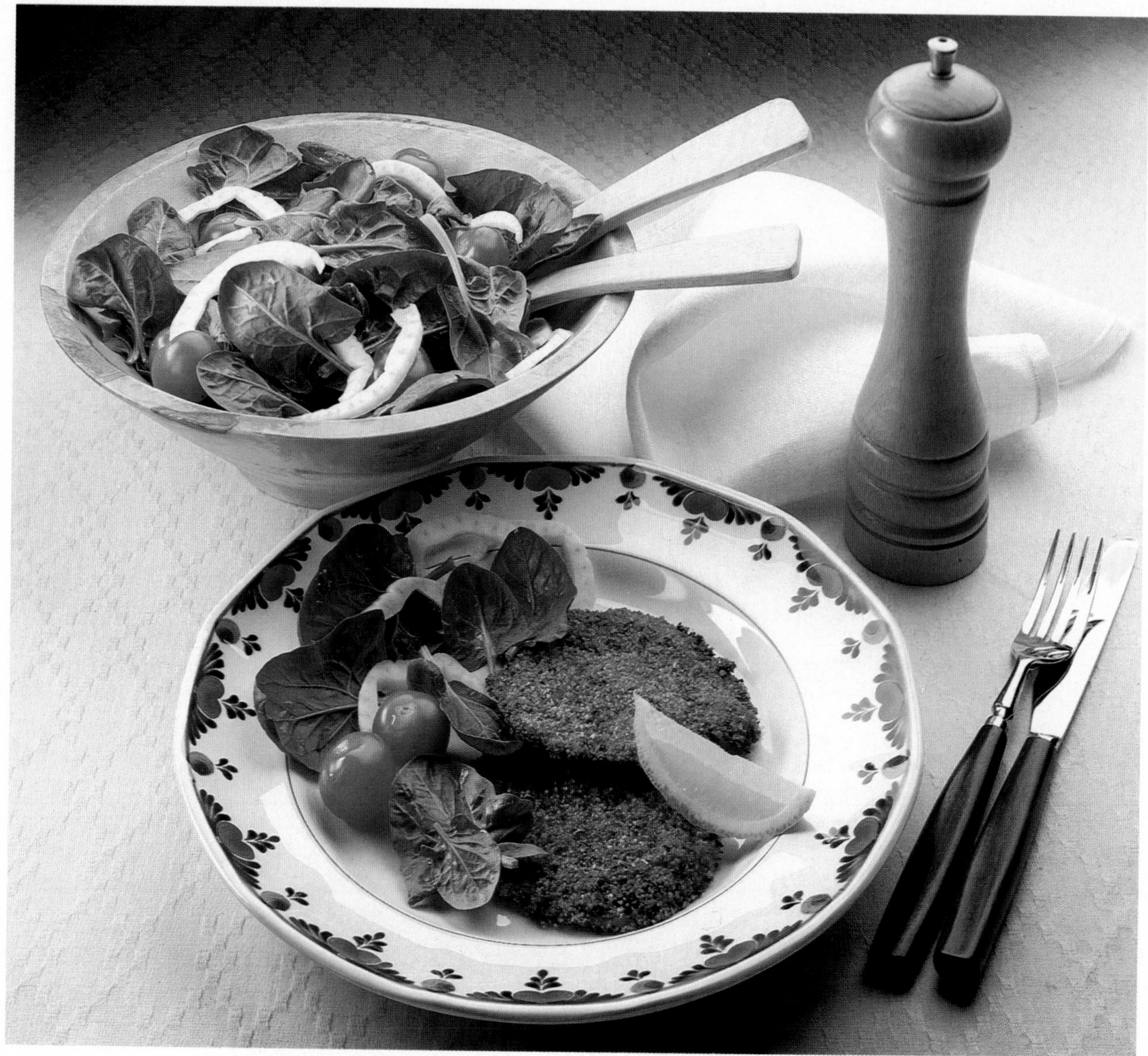

Cutlets with Mustard and Tarragon

Serves 4
Working (and total) time: 20 minutes

Calories **255**
Protein **30g.**
Cholesterol **75mg.**
Total fat **12g.**
Saturated fat **5g.**
Sodium **140mg.**

4 lamb slices (about 4 oz. each), cut from the sirloin end of the leg, trimmed of fat, flattened to about ⅛ inch thick (box, page 24)
½ cup dry whole-wheat breadcrumbs
1 tbsp. chopped fresh tarragon, or 1 tsp. dried tarragon
2 tbsp. chopped fresh parsley
½ lemon, grated zest only
freshly ground black pepper
2 tbsp. Dijon mustard
1 tbsp. virgin olive oil
4 lemon wedges for garnish

Mix together the breadcrumbs, tarragon, parsley, lemon zest, and some pepper. Sprinkle the breadcrumb mixture onto a large sheet of wax paper. Cut the lamb slices in half. Using a brush, lightly coat one side of each lamb slice with the mustard. Set a slice, mustard side down, on the crumb mixture, then turn the meat to coat the other side with crumbs. Repeat with the remaining slices.

Heat half of the olive oil in a large, heavy-bottomed frying pan over medium-high heat, and sauté four of the cutlets until they are golden brown—one and a half to two minutes on each side. Set them aside in a warm place while you cook the remaining cutlets in the rest of the oil. Garnish each portion with a lemon wedge and serve immediately.

SUGGESTED ACCOMPANIMENT: *a salad made with spinach, fennel, and cherry tomatoes.*

Lamb and Barley Salad

Serves 4
Working time: about 20 minutes
Total time: about 2 hours (includes chilling)

Calories **265**
Protein **21g.**
Cholesterol **50mg.**
Total fat **10g.**
Saturated fat **4g.**
Sodium **275mg.**

¾ lb. lean lamb (from the leg or loin), trimmed of fat and cut into ½-inch cubes
½ cup pearl barley
1½ tbsp. finely chopped fresh oregano, or ½ tbsp. dried oregano
1½ tbsp. olive oil
¼ tsp. salt
freshly ground black pepper
3 tbsp. red wine vinegar
1 ripe tomato, seeded and chopped
1 celery stalk, chopped
½ cup chopped red onion
several leaves of Boston lettuce, washed and dried, for garnish

Put the barley, half of the oregano, and 3 cups of water into a saucepan. Bring the water to a boil, then lower the heat to maintain a steady simmer. Cover the pan and cook the barley until it is tender—about 50 minutes. Drain the barley, transfer it to a bowl, and stir in ½ tablespoon of the oil.

Heat the remaining tablespoon of oil in a heavy-bottomed skillet set over high heat. Add the lamb cubes, and sprinkle them with the salt and some pepper. Sauté the lamb, stirring frequently, until it is lightly browned—about two minutes. Pour in the vinegar and cook the mixture for 30 seconds longer.

Transfer the contents of the skillet to the bowl with the barley. Add the tomato, celery, onion, the remaining oregano, and a generous grinding of pepper. Toss the salad well and chill it for at least one hour.

Just before serving, arrange the lettuce leaves on a plate or platter, and mound the salad on top.

SUGGESTED ACCOMPANIMENT: *melon slices.*

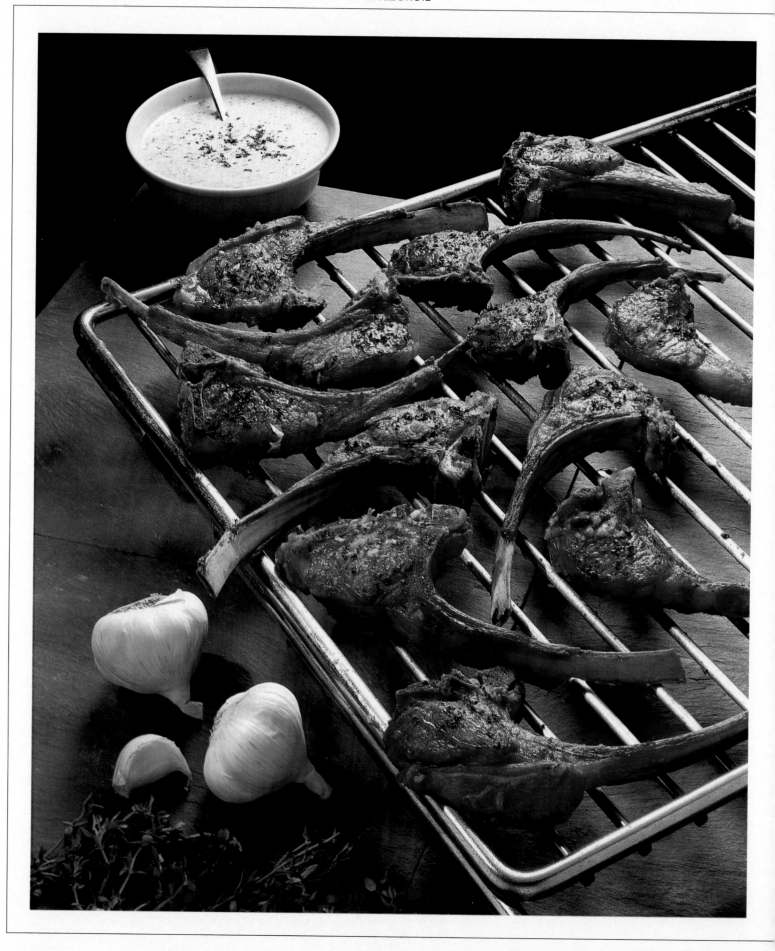

Marinated Chops with Caper and Parsley Sauce

Serves 6
Working time: about 30 minutes
Total time: about 2 hours and 30 minutes
(includes marinating)

Calories **255**
Protein **27g.**
Cholesterol **85mg.**
Total fat **15g.**
Saturated fat **3g.**
Sodium **170mg.**

12 rib chops (about 3 oz. each), trimmed of fat
1 tsp. virgin olive oil
1 garlic clove, finely chopped
1 tbsp. chopped fresh parsley
1 tsp. chopped fresh marjoram, or ¼ tsp. dried marjoram
1 tsp. chopped fresh thyme, or ¼ tsp. dried thyme leaves
¼ tsp. salt
freshly ground black pepper

Caper and parsley sauce

1 tsp. cornstarch
⅓ cup skim milk
¼ cup sour cream
4 pickled onions, finely chopped
2 tbsp. chopped fresh parsley
1 tbsp. finely chopped capers
freshly ground black pepper

Using a sharp knife, scrape the ends of the rib bones free of any flesh or skin. Place the chops in a large, shallow dish. Combine the olive oil, garlic, parsley, marjoram, thyme, salt, and some freshly ground black pepper, and brush this mixture over both sides of the chops. Cover the dish and let the chops marinate in the refrigerator for two to four hours.

Preheat the broiler while you make the sauce. Mix the cornstarch with 1 tablespoon of the milk. Scald the remaining milk in a small saucepan, add the cornstarch paste, and cook over low heat, stirring, until the milk thickens—two to three minutes. Stir in the sour cream, pickled onions, parsley, capers, and some pepper. Heat the sauce through, remove it from the heat, and keep it warm while you cook the chops.

Cook the chops for three to four minutes on each side for rare to medium meat. Serve them with the caper and parsley sauce.

SUGGESTED ACCOMPANIMENT: *braised leeks.*

Chops with Anise Sauce

Serves 4
Working time: about 25 minutes
Total time: about 2 hours and 30 minutes
(includes marinating)

Calories **260**
Protein **29g.**
Cholesterol **75mg.**
Total fat **13g.**
Saturated fat **6g.**
Sodium **280mg.**

8 rib chops (about 3 oz. each), trimmed of fat
2 limes, finely grated zest and juice
¼ cup plain low-fat yogurt
2 tbsp. anise-flavored liqueur
1 tbsp. chopped fresh thyme, or 1 tsp. dried thyme leaves
2 garlic cloves, peeled and crushed
1 tsp. dark brown sugar
freshly ground black pepper
1 tsp. cornstarch
½ tsp. salt
lime wedges for garnish
thyme sprigs for garnish (optional)

Put the lime zest and juice into a shallow dish with the yogurt, anise-flavored liqueur, thyme, garlic, sugar, and some pepper. Whisk the mixture together with a fork, then place the lamb chops in the dish and turn them to coat them evenly. Cover the dish and let the chops marinate in the refrigerator for at least two hours, or preferably overnight.

Preheat the broiler. Lift the chops out of the marinade, reserving the marinade, and broil them for three to four minutes on each side for rare to medium meat.

While the chops are cooking, put the cornstarch into a saucepan, blend in the marinade, and then add the salt. Bring the sauce to a boil and simmer for three minutes, stirring constantly. Arrange the chops on a warm serving dish, and garnish them with the lime wedges and thyme sprigs, if you are using them. Serve the sauce separately.

SUGGESTED ACCOMPANIMENT: *steamed baby carrots.*

Sichuan Peppercorn Lamb

Serves 4
Working time: about 30 minutes
Total time: about 45 minutes

Calories **290**
Protein **32g.**
Cholesterol **80mg.**
Total fat **14g.**
Saturated fat **5g.**
Sodium **135mg.**

4 loin chops (about 5 oz. each), trimmed of fat (technique, page 135)
2 tsp. Sichuan peppercorns
1 tbsp. low-sodium soy sauce
1 tbsp. dry sherry
2 cups green beans, ends removed, cut in half
½ tbsp. safflower oil
1 tbsp. finely chopped scallions
1 large carrot, peeled and julienned
1 sweet red pepper, seeded, deribbed, and julienned
green ends of scallions, sliced diagonally, for garnish

Heat a heavy-bottomed pan over medium heat and toast the peppercorns by stirring them until their aroma increases—about 30 seconds. Grind them to a fine powder with a mortar and pestle, then mix 1 teaspoon of ground peppercorns together with the soy sauce and sherry in a shallow dish. Place the chops in the dish, turn them to coat them, and let them marinate for 20 minutes; turn the chops once during this time.

Parboil the green beans for three minutes. Drain and rinse them under cold running water. Drain again and set them aside. Preheat the broiler.

Remove the chops from the dish and discard the marinade. Dust the chops with the remaining crushed peppercorns, and pin the flap of lean meat to the eye of each chop with a toothpick. Cook the chops for four to six minutes on each side for rare to medium meat.

While the chops are cooking, stir-fry the vegetables. In a wok or a heavy-bottomed frying pan, heat the oil until it is hot but not smoking. Add the chopped scallions and cook them for 30 seconds, stirring constantly, then add the carrot, pepper, and beans. Stir-fry all the vegetables for two minutes, then serve them immediately alongside the chops. Garnish the chops with the scallion slices.

SUGGESTED ACCOMPANIMENT: *egg noodles.*

Noisettes with Julienned Vegetables

Serves 4
Working time: about 45 minutes
Total time: about 1 hour

Calories **265**
Protein **38g.**
Cholesterol **100mg.**
Total fat **10g.**
Saturated fat **5g.**
Sodium **260mg.**

one 2¼-lb. rack of lamb, boned and trimmed of fat (page 136, Steps 1 to 4)
¼ tsp. salt
freshly ground black pepper
1 tsp. finely chopped fresh oregano, or ¼ tsp. dried oregano
2 large carrots, trimmed and julienned
3 celery stalks, trimmed and julienned
1 parsnip, peeled and julienned
2 leeks, trimmed, washed, and julienned
1 tbsp. chopped fresh parsley

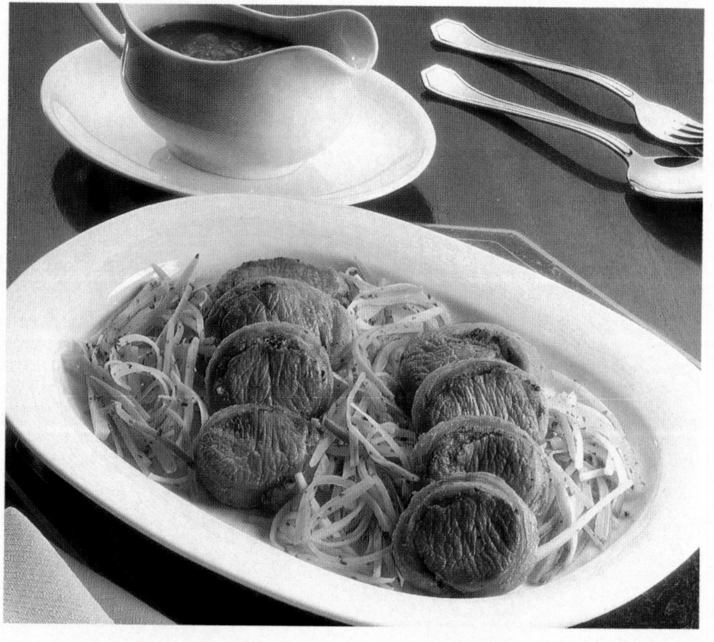

Season the boned side of the meat with the salt, some pepper, and the oregano. Following the technique shown in Step 5 on page 136, roll the lamb into a sausage shape, with the eye of the meat in the center, and tie the roll at eight equally spaced intervals. Cut the roll into slices midway between ties. Place the noisettes on the broiler rack and set aside.

Preheat the broiler. Pour enough water into a saucepan to fill it 1 inch deep. Set a vegetable steamer in the pan and bring the water to a boil. Put the carrots, celery, and parsnip into the steamer, cover the pan tightly, and steam the vegetables for five minutes; add the leeks and continue to steam until the vegetables are tender but still crisp—about three minutes more. Meanwhile, cook the noisettes for three to five minutes on each side for rare to medium meat. When the vegetables are cooked, toss them in the parsley.

Arrange the noisettes on a warm serving dish and surround them with the julienned vegetables.

SUGGESTED ACCOMPANIMENTS: *cranberry sauce; puréed potatoes.*

Noisettes in a Fig Sauce

Serves 4
Working and total time: about 35 minutes

Calories **205**
Protein **27g.**
Cholesterol **80mg.**
Total fat **7g.**
Saturated fat **3g.**
Sodium **270mg.**

8 loin chops (about 3½ oz. each) trimmed of fat, boned, and tied into noisettes
6 dried figs, finely chopped
2 tbsp. balsamic vinegar, or 1½ tbsp. red wine vinegar mixed with ½ tsp. honey
2 tbsp. Madeira
2 tsp. Worcestershire sauce
1 cup unsalted chicken stock (recipe, page 137)
½ tsp. salt
freshly ground black pepper
4 fresh figs, sliced

Preheat the broiler while you make the sauce. Put the dried figs, vinegar, Madeira, and Worcestershire sauce into a small saucepan, and simmer until the liquid reduces to a thick syrup—four to five minutes. Add the chicken stock and bring the mixture to a boil; lower the heat and simmer, uncovered, for two minutes. Remove the saucepan from the heat and press the mixture through a sieve to make a smooth sauce. Return the sauce to the pan, and keep it warm, uncovered, over low heat while you cook the noisettes.

Season the noisettes with the salt and some pepper, and broil the chops for two to four minutes on each side for rare to medium meat. Serve immediately with the sauce and sliced figs.

SUGGESTED ACCOMPANIMENT: *steamed broccoli.*

Noisettes with Glazed Potatoes and Gooseberry Purée

Serves 6
Working time: about 45 minutes
Total time: about 1 hour

Calories **280**
Protein **31g.**
Cholesterol **75mg.**
Total fat **11g.**
Saturated fat **5g.**
Sodium **195mg.**

two 1¼-lb. racks of lamb, trimmed of fat, boned, tied, and cut into 12 noisettes (technique, page 136)
2 tsp. virgin olive oil
freshly ground black pepper
½ tbsp. unsalted butter
2 shallots, peeled and finely chopped
½ cup unsalted chicken stock (recipe, page 137)
⅛ tsp. salt
24 tiny new potatoes, scrubbed
fresh chervil for garnish

Minted gooseberry purée

4 cups fresh gooseberries, ends removed, or frozen gooseberries, thawed
2 sprigs fresh mint
1 tsp. light brown sugar
6 leaves fresh mint
¼ tsp. salt

Brush the noisettes with the olive oil and rub them all over with some pepper. Arrange them on a broiler pan and set them aside.

To make the purée, place the gooseberries in a heavy-bottomed, nonreactive saucepan, together with the sprigs of mint, the sugar, and 1 tablespoon of water. Cover and cook over low heat until the gooseberries are soft—15 to 30 minutes. Remove the mint sprigs, and purée the gooseberries in a blender with the fresh mint leaves and the salt. Pass the purée through a fine sieve; set it aside and keep it warm.

Meanwhile, melt the butter in a heavy-bottomed saucepan over low heat and cook the shallots, covered, until they are soft—about five minutes. Add the stock and salt, bring it to a boil, then add the potatoes and cook them, partly covered, until they are tender—20 to 25 minutes.

Preheat the broiler.

Remove the lid from the pan, and boil the stock rapidly until no liquid remains and the potatoes are glossy—about three minutes. Shake the pan regularly during this process to prevent the potatoes and shallots from burning. Keep them warm.

Cook the noisettes for three to four minutes on each side for rare to medium meat. Arrange them on a warm serving platter with the glazed potatoes and garnish with chervil. Serve the purée separately.

SUGGESTED ACCOMPANIMENT: *green beans or peas.*

Boning a Butterfly Chop

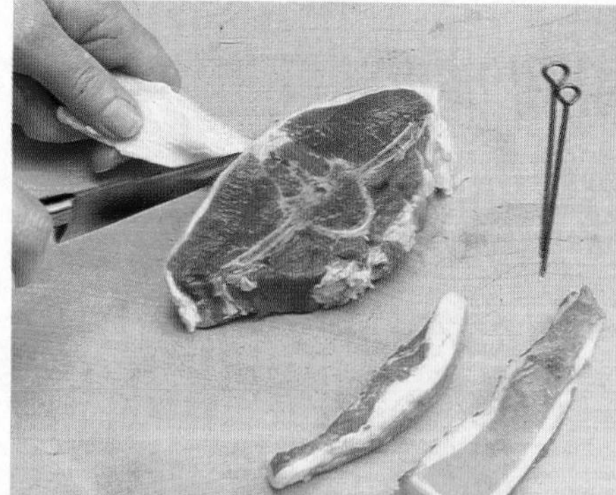

1 *TRIMMING THE FAT. Using a knife, cut off the fatty flaps. Peel the skin and fat from the back of the chop, leaving the connective tissue and fat above the bone intact.*

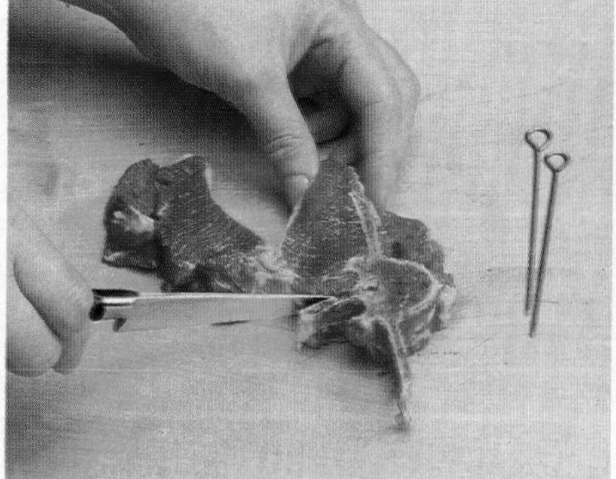

2 *REMOVING THE BONE. Insert the knife point into the base of the chop and carefully run it around the contours of the bone to free the meat. Do not cut through the connective tissue.*

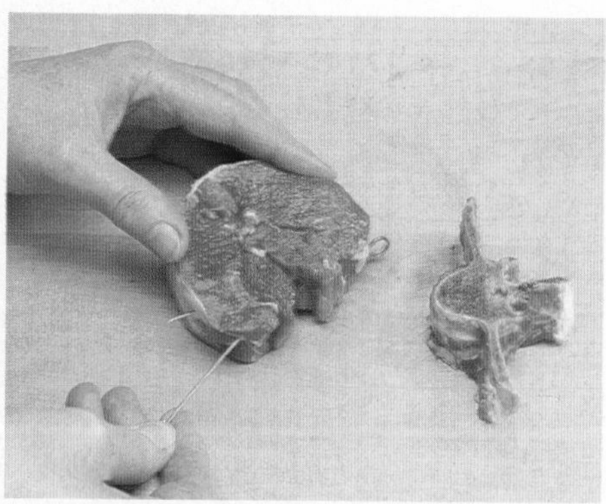

3 *SECURING THE CHOP. Bring the sides of the chop together to form a neat circular shape. Secure the chop with two skewers.*

Butterfly Chops with Peppercorn Sauce

Serves 4
Working time: about 40 minutes
Total time: about 1 hour

Calories **215**
Protein **32g.**
Cholesterol **75mg.**
Total fat **14g.**
Saturated fat **7g.**
Sodium **270mg.**

4 double loin butterfly chops (about 6 oz. each), trimmed, boned, and secured with skewers (opposite, below)
4 slices white bread
1 garlic clove, peeled
1 shallot, finely chopped
6 oz. mushrooms, wiped and finely chopped
1 tsp. grated lemon zest
1 tsp. chopped fresh thyme, or ¼ tsp. dried thyme leaves
1 tbsp. chopped fresh parsley
1½ tsp. fresh green peppercorns or green peppercorns in brine, rinsed and patted dry
½ cup unsalted chicken or veal stock (recipes, page 137)
⅛ tsp. salt
2 tbsp. fresh white or brown breadcrumbs
½ oz. Lancashire cheese, or other white crumbly cheese such as Fontinella or Caerphilly, grated (about 3 tbsp.)
2 tbsp. sour cream

Preheat the oven to 350° F. Cut out four circles from the bread, each slightly larger in diameter than the butterfly chops. Bake them in the oven until they are golden brown—20 to 25 minutes—then rub one side of each crouton with the garlic clove and keep them warm. Preheat the broiler.

While the croutons are baking, brush a heavy, nonstick frying pan with oil, place it over high heat, and stir-fry the chopped shallot for two minutes. Add the mushrooms and cook them over medium heat for four minutes, then increase the heat and cook them rapidly for a minute or two to reduce excess moisture. Remove the pan from the heat, stir in the lemon zest, thyme, and parsley, and set the mixture aside.

Cook the butterfly chops for four to six minutes on each side for rare to medium meat. Meanwhile, heat a small, shallow pan and dry-fry the peppercorns for 30 seconds. Pour in the stock and boil it rapidly until it has reduced by half—about four minutes. Remove the chops from the broiler and set them aside. Skim the fat from the juices in the broiler pan, then pour the juices into the reduced stock. Season the sauce with the salt, and set it over low heat to keep warm.

Spoon the mushroom mixture neatly onto the chops. Mix the breadcrumbs with the cheese, then sprinkle them over the mushrooms. Broil the chops until the cheese turns golden brown. Remove the skewers. Set each chop on top of a crouton.

Remove the sauce from the heat and stir in the sour cream. Serve the sauce with the chops.

SUGGESTED ACCOMPANIMENT: *steamed asparagus.*

Sweet and Spicy Grilled Lamb

Serves 4
Working time: about 1 hour
Total time: about 2 hours (includes marinating)

Calories **310**
Protein **23g.**
Cholesterol **68mg.**
Total fat **8g.**
Saturated fat **3g.**
Sodium **205mg.**

one 2½-lb. lamb loin roast, trimmed of fat and boned (technique, page 134)
freshly ground black pepper
¼ tsp. ground allspice
¼ tsp. ground cloves
2 tbsp. fresh lemon juice
2 tbsp. light brown sugar

Cherry ketchup

1½ cups sweet cherries, stemmed and pitted
¼ cup light brown sugar
¼ tsp. salt
6 tbsp. cider vinegar
one 3-inch strip lemon zest
½ tsp. ground ginger
2 cinnamon sticks
⅛ tsp. cayenne pepper

To make the ketchup, combine the cherries, brown sugar, salt, vinegar, lemon zest, ginger, cinnamon sticks, and cayenne pepper in a heavy-bottomed saucepan. Bring the mixture to a simmer and cook it until it has thickened—about 15 minutes. Discard the cinnamon sticks, and pour the mixture into a food processor or a blender. Purée the mixture, then strain it into a small bowl. Refrigerate the ketchup.

To prepare the marinade, mix a generous grinding of pepper with the allspice, cloves, lemon juice, and brown sugar in a small bowl. Set the loin in a shallow dish and pour the marinade over it, rubbing the spices into the meat. Allow the loin to marinate at room temperature for one hour, turning it every 15 minutes.

If you plan to grill the meat, prepare the coals about 30 minutes before cooking time; to broil, preheat the broiler for about 10 minutes.

Remove the loin from the marinade and cook it for five to seven minutes on each side, brushing it occasionally with any marinade remaining in the dish. Let the lamb rest for five minutes before slicing it. Pass the ketchup separately.

SUGGESTED ACCOMPANIMENT: *steamed cauliflower.*

Steaks with Grated Zucchini and a Tomato Coulis

Serves 4
Working time: about 25 minutes
Total time: about 45 minutes

Calories **280**
Protein **31g.**
Cholesterol **75mg.**
Total fat **13g.**
Saturated fat **5g.**
Sodium **395mg.**

4 boneless lamb steaks (about 4½ oz. each), cut from the sirloin end of the leg and trimmed of fat, or butterfly steaks, boned (technique, page 32)
3 medium zucchini
1 tsp. salt
1 tbsp. olive oil
2 tbsp. chopped fresh marjoram, or 2 tsp. dried marjoram
freshly ground black pepper
ribbon-thin lengthwise slices of zucchini for garnish (optional)

Tomato coulis

1 tsp. virgin olive oil
2 garlic cloves, finely chopped
4 medium ripe tomatoes, peeled, seeded, and finely chopped, or 14 oz. canned tomatoes, chopped
1 tbsp. chopped fresh oregano, or 1 tsp. dried oregano
1 tsp. chopped fresh marjoram, or ¼ tsp. dried marjoram
freshly ground black pepper
⅓ cup medium-dry white wine

Trim the zucchini and coarsely grate them, then transfer them to a sieve set over a bowl. Stir in ½ teaspoon of the salt and let the zucchini stand for 30 minutes.

Meanwhile, brush the steaks with the oil, rub them with half of the marjoram, and sprinkle them with some black pepper. Using toothpicks or skewers, pin the steaks into neat rounds and set them aside.

To make the tomato coulis, heat the oil in a heavy-bottomed saucepan. Cook the garlic for one minute over medium-high heat, then add the tomatoes, oregano, and marjoram, and season with some pepper. Cook until the tomatoes are reduced to a purée—about 10 minutes. Add the wine, heat the coulis through, and keep it warm.

Preheat the broiler. Season the steaks with the remaining salt and broil them for five to six minutes on each side for rare to medium meat.

While the steaks are cooking, squeeze the zucchini dry with your hands and stir-fry them in a nonstick saucepan with the remaining marjoram over medium-low heat until they soften—about three minutes.

When the steaks are cooked, remove the toothpicks or skewers. Spread the zucchini mixture evenly on top of each steak. Pour a little of the tomato coulis onto each of four warmed plates and arrange the prepared steaks on top. Garnish with the strips of zucchini, if you wish, and serve immediately.

SUGGESTED ACCOMPANIMENT: *whole-wheat bread.*

Grilled Lamb with Chutney Glaze and Mint

Serves 10
Working time: about 30 minutes
Total time: about 1 hour and 15 minutes

Calories **200**
Protein **23g.**
Cholesterol **75mg.**
Total fat **8g.**
Saturated fat **3g.**
Sodium **135mg.**

one 5-lb. leg of lamb, trimmed of fat and boned
1 tbsp. safflower oil
¼ tsp. salt
freshly ground black pepper
4 tbsp. chopped fresh mint, or 4 tsp. dried mint
several fresh mint sprigs for garnish

Chutney glaze

1 cup unsalted brown stock or unsalted chicken stock (recipes, page 137)
¼ cup mango chutney
½ tbsp. dry mustard
1 tbsp. cider vinegar
½ tbsp. cornstarch, mixed with 1 tbsp. water

Spread the boned leg of lamb flat on a work surface with the cut side of the meat facing up. Cut out the membranes and tendons, and discard them. Slice horizontally into—but not completely through—the thick section of flesh at one side of the leg and open out the resulting flap. Then slice and open out the opposite side in a similar manner. The meat should be no more than 2 inches thick.

If you plan to grill the lamb, prepare the coals about 30 minutes before cooking time; to broil, preheat the broiler for 10 minutes.

To make the chutney glaze, combine the stock and the chutney in a small saucepan, and bring the mixture to a simmer over medium heat. Stir the mustard and the vinegar into the cornstarch paste, and then whisk this mixture into the simmering stock and chutney. Cook the glaze, stirring continuously, until it thickens—about one minute.

With your fingers, rub both sides of the lamb with the oil. Cook the lamb, turning it every five minutes, until it is well browned on both sides—about 20 minutes in all. Sprinkle the salt and some pepper on the lamb, and brush it with some of the chutney glaze. Continue cooking the lamb, turning and basting it frequently with the glaze, for 10 minutes more.

Transfer the lamb to a cutting board and sprinkle it with the chopped mint. Allow the meat to stand for 10 minutes before carving it. Serve the lamb in slices, accompanied by the remaining chutney glaze and garnished with mint sprigs.

SUGGESTED ACCOMPANIMENT: *a salad of bulgur and tomatoes.*

Marinated Lamb with Spiced Apple Butter

Serves 12
Working time: about 30 minutes
Total time: about 1 hour and 30 minutes

Calories **175**
Protein **19g.**
Cholesterol **62mg.**
Total fat **7g.**
Saturated fat **2g.**
Sodium **140mg.**

one 5-lb. leg of lamb, trimmed of fat and boned
½ cup apple butter
¼ cup cider vinegar
1 onion, finely chopped
2 garlic cloves, finely chopped
1 tbsp. finely chopped fresh sage, or 1½ tsp. dried sage
½ tsp. salt
freshly ground black pepper
1 tbsp. safflower oil

Spread the boned leg of lamb flat on a work surface with the cut side of the meat facing up. Cut out the membranes and tendons, and discard them. Slice horizontally into—but not completely through—the thick section of flesh at one side of the leg and open out the resulting flap. Then slice and open out the opposite side in a similar manner. The meat should be no more than 2 inches thick.

Mix the apple butter, vinegar, onion, garlic, sage, salt, some pepper, and the oil in a large bowl. Put the butterflied lamb into the bowl and slather it all over with the spiced apple butter. Leave the lamb in the bowl to marinate at room temperature for one hour, turning it after 30 minutes.

If you plan to grill the lamb, prepare the coals about 30 minutes before grilling time; to broil, preheat the broiler for 10 minutes. Remove the lamb from the marinade, holding it over the bowl to allow any excess marinade to drip off. Reserve the marinade.

Cook the lamb for 10 minutes on each side for rare to medium meat. Baste the lamb from time to time with the reserved marinade.

Let the lamb rest for 10 minutes before carving it.

SUGGESTED ACCOMPANIMENTS: *steamed zucchini; baked sweet potatoes.*

Flambéed Kabobs

Serves 6
Working time: about 50 minutes
Total time: about 3 hours and 50 minutes
(includes marinating)

Calories **255**
Protein **30g.**
Cholesterol **75mg.**
Total fat **11g.**
Saturated fat **4g.**
Sodium **100mg.**

one 1½-lb. lamb loin, trimmed of fat and cut into 24 cubes
1 large zucchini, cut into ½-inch slices
½ sweet green pepper, seeded and cut into 2½-by-1-inch strips
½ sweet red pepper, seeded and cut into 2½-by-1-inch strips
1 large onion, cut into 12 wedges
2 oranges, zest and pith removed, halved and cut into ½-inch slices
1 ripe but firm mango, peeled and cut into 6 pieces
1 tbsp. olive oil
4 tbsp. brandy

Orange and honey marinade

1 orange, finely grated zest and strained juice
3 tbsp. honey
1 onion, finely grated
4 garlic cloves, crushed
1 tbsp. tomato paste
1 tbsp. olive oil
1 tbsp. paprika
½ tsp. salt
¼ tsp. cayenne pepper

To make the marinade, put the orange zest and juice, honey, onion, garlic, tomato paste, oil, paprika, salt, and cayenne into a large mixing bowl, and stir them well together. Add the lamb and stir until it is thoroughly coated with the marinade. Cover the bowl and allow the lamb to marinate at room temperature for three to four hours, turning it from time to time.

When you are ready to assemble the kabobs, blanch the zucchini and peppers in boiling water for two to three minutes to soften them slightly. Transfer the vegetables to a colander and refresh them under cold running water. Drain well.

Preheat the broiler.

Thread the marinated lamb and pieces of zucchini, pepper, onion, orange, and mango alternately on six kabob skewers. Place the skewers on the broiler rack and sprinkle them with the olive oil. Broil the kabobs for 10 to 15 minutes, carefully turning the skewers three or four times to ensure even cooking. At the end of this time, the lamb should be cooked yet still slightly pink in the center.

When the kabobs are ready, place them on a warmed dish. Put the brandy into a small, shallow sauté pan and warm it over low heat for about 10 seconds. Standing well back, ignite the brandy in the pan with a match and pour it, flaming, over the kabobs. Arrange the kabobs on a serving platter.

SUGGESTED ACCOMPANIMENTS: *saffron rice; cucumber and chili pepper salad.*

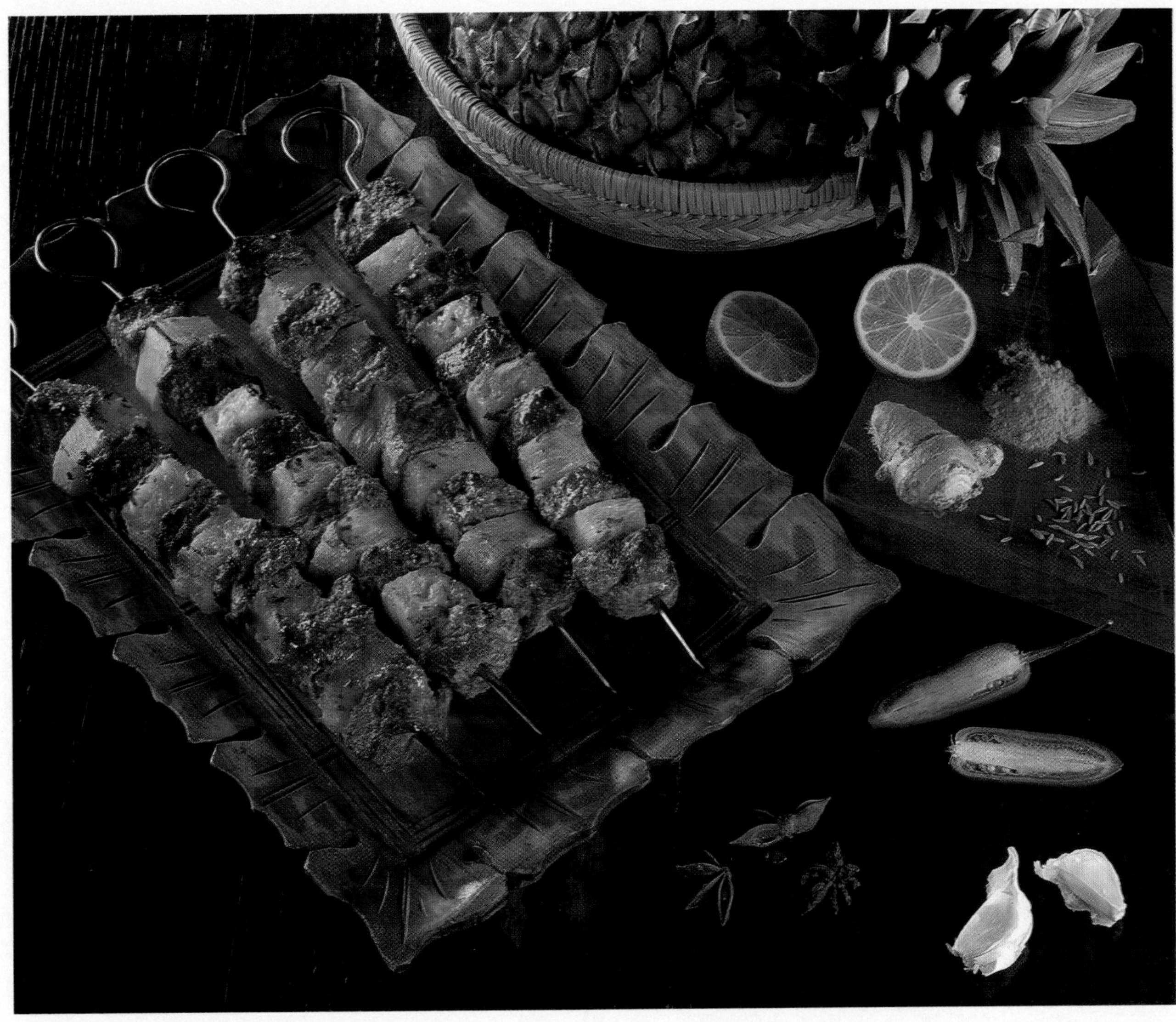

Lamb Tikka

IN THIS VERSION OF THE TRADITIONAL INDIAN *TIKKA*, CHUNKS OF PINEAPPLE CREATE A REFRESHING CONTRAST TO THE HIGHLY SPICED CUBED MEAT.

Serves 4
Working time: about 30 minutes
Total time: about 6 hours (includes marinating)

Calories **255**
Protein **32g.**
Cholesterol **75mg.**
Total fat **9g.**
Saturated fat **4g.**
Sodium **100mg.**

1 lb. lean lamb (from the loin or sirloin end of leg), trimmed of fat and cut into 1½-inch cubes
one 1-inch piece fresh ginger, peeled and coarsely chopped
2 garlic cloves, coarsely chopped
2 green chili peppers, seeded and coarsely chopped (cautionary note, page 83)
2 tsp. cumin seeds
1 tsp. turmeric
½ tsp. ground fenugreek
12 fresh mint leaves
½ cup plain low-fat yogurt
1 tbsp. fresh lime juice
2 star-anise pods
20 1-inch chunks fresh pineapple

Put the cubes of lamb into a bowl. In a blender or a food processor, purée the ginger, garlic, chilies, cumin, turmeric, fenugreek, and mint leaves. Add the yogurt and the lime juice, and blend to mix. Pour the mixture over the meat, add the star anise, and mix well to thoroughly coat the meat. Cover the bowl with plastic wrap and allow the lamb to marinate in a cool place for four to six hours, stirring occasionally.

Preheat the broiler. Thread the cubes of meat and pineapple alternately onto four kabob skewers; reserve the marinade. Place the kabobs on a broiler rack, and broil until the lamb is cooked but still slightly pink in the center—10 to 15 minutes. Turn the skewers frequently and baste the meat with the reserved marinade while broiling.

SUGGESTED ACCOMPANIMENTS: *brown rice; cucumber, mint, and onion salad.*

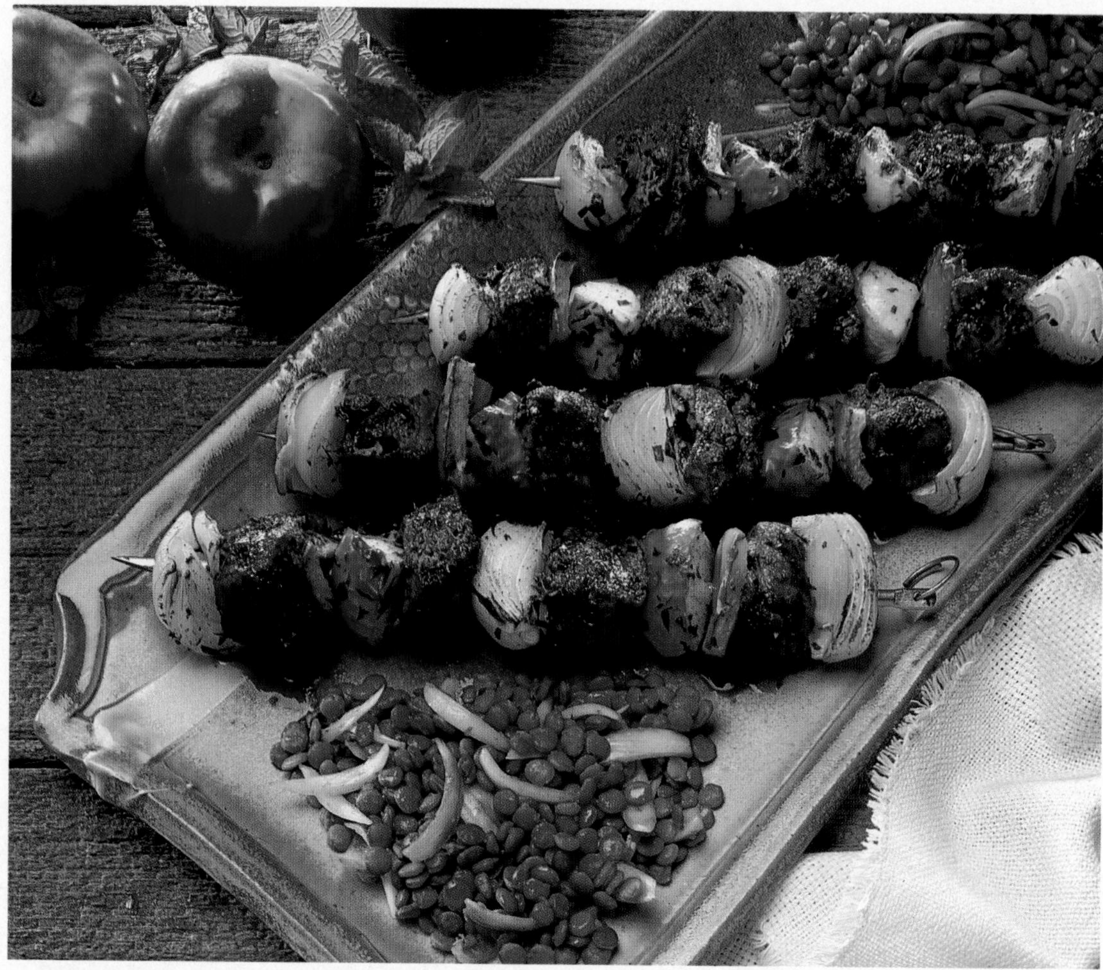

Lamb Kabobs with Olive-Mint Sauce

Serves 4
Working time: about 25 minutes
Total time: about 40 minutes

Calories **240**
Protein **24g.**
Cholesterol **75mg.**
Total fat **12g.**
Saturated fat **3g.**
Sodium **295mg.**

1¼ lb. lean lamb (from the sirloin), trimmed of fat and cut into 16 cubes
½ cup chopped fresh mint
6 oil-cured black olives, pitted and finely chopped
1 tbsp. olive oil
½ tsp. ground allspice
freshly ground black pepper
2 onions, each one cut into 6 wedges
½ green pepper, seeded, deribbed, and cut into 8 pieces
½ red apple, cored and cut into 8 pieces
1 cup unsalted brown stock or unsalted chicken stock (recipes, page 137)
⅛ tsp. salt

To grill the lamb, light the coals 30 minutes ahead of time; to broil, preheat the broiler for 10 minutes.

Put the lamb cubes into a bowl along with 3 tablespoons of the mint, half of the olives, ½ tablespoon of the oil, ¼ teaspoon of the allspice, and a generous grinding of pepper. Stir the lamb cubes to coat them with the marinade and set the bowl aside at room temperature while you prepare the other ingredients.

Gently toss together the onions, green pepper, apple, 3 tablespoons of the remaining mint, the remaining ½ tablespoon of olive oil, the remaining ¼ teaspoon of ground allspice, and some pepper in another bowl, and set it aside.

Pour the stock into a small saucepan over medium heat, then stir in the remaining olives, the remaining 2 tablespoons of mint, and the salt. Cook the sauce until only about ⅓ cup remains—about 10 minutes. Remove the pan from the heat and set it aside.

Thread the lamb cubes and the vegetable and apple chunks onto four skewers.

Grill or broil the kabobs for three to four minutes per side for medium meat. Transfer them to a platter. Reheat the sauce, pour it over the kabobs, and serve them immediately.

SUGGESTED ACCOMPANIMENT: *lentil and onion salad.*

Lamb Sausages on Skewers

Serves 4
Working time: about 30 minutes
Total time: about 1 hour

Calories **245**
Protein **26g.**
Cholesterol **77mg.**
Total fat **11g.**
Saturated fat **4g.**
Sodium **320mg.**

1¼ lb. lean lamb (from the leg or loin), trimmed of fat and chopped (technique, page 43)
1 large ripe tomato, seeded and chopped
¼ tsp. salt
freshly ground black pepper
1 tsp. sugar
1 tbsp. red wine vinegar
3 tbsp. chopped fresh parsley
1 tbsp. chopped fresh oregano, or 1 tsp. dried oregano
1 egg white
1 tbsp. olive oil
⅓ cup dry breadcrumbs
2 scallions, trimmed and thinly sliced
½ tsp. capers, rinsed
½ cup plain low-fat yogurt

Put the tomato, ⅛ teaspoon of the salt, some pepper, the sugar, and the vinegar into a heavy-bottomed skillet set over medium heat. Cook the mixture, stirring frequently, until only about ¼ cup remains—approximately 20 minutes. Transfer the mixture to a bowl and refrigerate it until it has cooled.

In a large bowl, combine the chopped lamb with 2 tablespoons of the parsley, the oregano, egg white, ½ tablespoon of the oil, the breadcrumbs, half of the scallions, the remaining ⅛ teaspoon of salt, and some pepper. Stir the cooled tomato mixture into the lamb mixture and refrigerate the bowl until the contents are thoroughly chilled—about 30 minutes.

If you plan to grill the sausages, prepare the coals about 30 minutes before cooking time; to broil, preheat the broiler for 10 minutes.

Divide the sausage mixture into four parts and form each one into a cylinder about 4 inches long. Thread each cylinder onto a skewer, keeping the meat pressed firmly in place.

Pour the remaining ½ tablespoon of oil onto a large, flat plate. Lightly coat the sausages by rolling them in the oil. Grill or broil the sausages, turning the skewers every now and then, until the meat is lightly browned —8 to 10 minutes.

Meanwhile, finely chop the remaining tablespoon of parsley, the remaining scallions, and the capers. Transfer the chopped parsley mixture to a small bowl, and whisk in the yogurt and some pepper. Serve the sausages immediately, passing the sauce separately.

SUGGESTED ACCOMPANIMENT: *couscous tossed with cinnamon and grated carrots.*

Lamb Kofta with Onion Sauce

COMMON IN INDIAN AND MIDDLE EASTERN COOKING, KOFTA CONSISTS OF CHOPPED MEAT AND SEASONINGS ROLLED INTO SAUSAGE SHAPES OR BALLS.

Serves 4
Working time: about 30 minutes
Total time: about 40 minutes

Calories **260**
Protein **27g.**
Cholesterol **80mg.**
Total fat **14g.**
Saturated fat **5g.**
Sodium **195mg.**

1 lb. lean lamb (from the leg or loin), trimmed of fat and chopped (technique, opposite)
1 onion (about ¼ lb.), finely chopped
12 pitted olives, finely chopped
2 tbsp. chopped cilantro
1 tbsp. Worcestershire sauce
¼ tsp. salt
freshly ground black pepper
1 oz. caul (optional)

Onion sauce

1 tbsp. polyunsaturated margarine
1 red onion, finely chopped
1 tsp. cumin seeds
2 tbsp. raspberry vinegar or cider vinegar
1 tbsp. cornstarch
1¼ cups unsalted brown stock (recipe, page 137)
⅛ tsp. salt
freshly ground black pepper

First, make the onion sauce. Melt the margarine in a sauté pan. Add the onion and cumin seeds, and cook them over medium heat until the onion is soft—about four minutes. Add the vinegar and continue cooking until the liquid reduces to a thick syrup. Mix the cornstarch with 2 tablespoons of the stock to form a paste. Add the remaining stock to the pan and bring it to a boil. Add the cornstarch paste and stir until the sauce thickens—two to three minutes. Season the sauce with the salt and some pepper; keep it warm while you prepare the meat.

To make the kofta, combine the lamb, onion, olives, cilantro, Worcestershire sauce, salt, and some pepper, and mix thoroughly by hand. Shape the meat into 20 sausages, each about 1½ inches long. If you like, wrap eight of the sausages with pieces of caul. Carefully thread the sausages onto four long metal skewers, alternating the caul-wrapped ones with the plain.

Preheat the broiler and cook the kofta for 10 minutes, turning them once. Serve them hot with the onion sauce.

SUGGESTED ACCOMPANIMENT: *crisp mixed lettuce salad.*

EDITOR'S NOTE: *Caul, the weblike fatty membrane that lines a pig's intestines, gives the meat a distinctive flavor and helps moisten lean chopped meat during broiling.*

Lamb and Mushroom Burgers

Serves 4
Working time: about 30 minutes
Total time: about 1 hour and 5 minutes

Calories **350**
Protein **36g.**
Cholesterol **80mg.**
Total fat **10g.**
Saturated fat **5g.**
Sodium **450mg.**

1 lb. lean lamb (from the leg or loin), trimmed of fat and chopped (technique, below)
3 tbsp. fresh whole-wheat breadcrumbs
2 tbsp. fresh orange juice
¼ tsp. finely grated lemon zest
1 tbsp. chopped fresh parsley
2 tsp. finely cut chives
⅛ tsp. dried marjoram
⅛ tsp. salt
freshly ground black pepper
¼ lb. mushrooms, wiped and finely chopped
4 hamburger buns, preferably whole-wheat, split
carrot ribbons for garnish
finely chopped celery for garnish
shredded cabbage for garnish
parsley for garnish

Mustard sauce

1 tbsp. grainy mustard
¼ cup sour cream
1 tbsp. finely cut fresh chives
freshly ground black pepper

Put the lamb, breadcrumbs, orange juice, lemon zest, parsley, chives, marjoram, salt, and some pepper into a bowl, and mix them thoroughly by hand. Set the bowl aside. Heat a heavy-bottomed, nonstick frying pan, brush it with oil, add the mushrooms, and sauté them over high heat for three minutes, stirring them constantly. Allow the mushrooms to cool, then add them to the meat mixture. Shape the mixture into four burgers, each about 4 inches in diameter. Cover and refrigerate them for 30 minutes.

Meanwhile, make the mustard sauce. Mix together the mustard, sour cream, and chives with a generous grinding of pepper. Set the sauce aside.

Preheat the broiler and cook the burgers for about four minutes on each side for medium meat. While they are cooking, toast the buns on the cut sides. Place each burger on the bottom half of a bun, garnish with the carrot, celery, cabbage, parsley, and some mustard sauce, and top with the other half of the bun.

SUGGESTED ACCOMPANIMENT: *roasted potatoes.*

Chopping by Hand

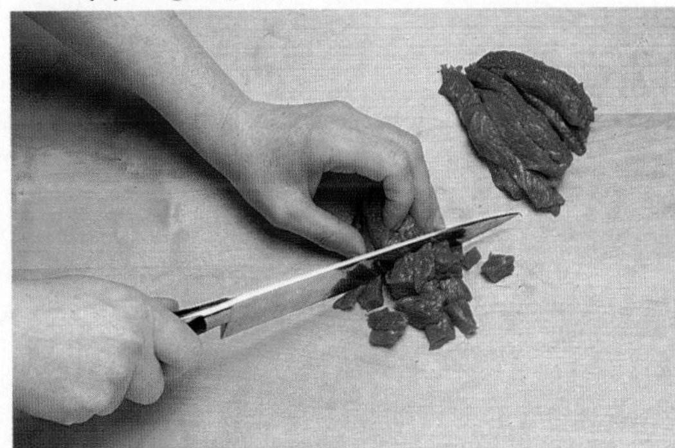

1 CUBING THE MEAT. Trim off all traces of fat and membrane from the meat and cut it into uniform slices. Place the lamb slices on top of one another and cut through to make evenly sized strips. Cut the strips of lean meat into fairly small cubes (above).

2 CHOPPING THE MEAT. Spread the cubed meat out evenly on a cutting board and chop it with a matched pair of sharp, heavy knifes. With a loose-wristed action, work the knives alternately and rhythmically, as if beating a drum (above). From time to time, use one of the knife blades to flip and turn the chopped mass back into the center: This helps achieve a consistent texture. Continue chopping until the meat is as coarse or fine as the recipe dictates.

Leg of Lamb with Pomegranate Sauce

Serves 8
Working time: about 30 minutes
Total time: about 1 hour and 30 minutes

Calories **250**
Protein **30g.**
Cholesterol **90mg.**
Total fat **8g.**
Saturated fat **4g.**
Sodium **130mg.**

one 4½-lb. leg of lamb, trimmed of fat
1 tbsp. fresh thyme
1 pomegranate
1 lime, finely grated zest and juice
1½ tbsp. red-currant jelly
finely grated lime zest for garnish
watercress for garnish

Pomegranate sauce

3 pomegranates
¼ cup red-currant jelly
1 tbsp. sugar
2 limes, juice and zest cut into thin strips
1½ tbsp. cornstarch
⅓ cup rosé wine

Preheat the oven to 400° F. Make four or five incisions into the flesh of the lamb, and fill them with the thyme. Place the lamb in a roasting pan.

Cut open the pomegranate and scoop out the seeds. Reserve one-third of the seeds for garnish. Using a wooden spoon, press all the juice from the remaining seeds through a fine sieve into a bowl. Stir the lime zest and juice into the pomegranate juice, then pour half of the combined juices over the lamb, coating the entire surface of the meat.

Place the leg of lamb in the oven and roast it, basting frequently, for one hour to one hour and 15 minutes for rare to medium meat. Halfway through the cooking time, pour the remaining lime and pomegranate juices over the lamb.

Remove the lamb from the oven, transfer it to a warm platter, and allow it to stand for about 20 minutes. Meanwhile, make the pomegranate sauce. Cut open the pomegranates and scoop out the seeds into a fine sieve set over a nonreactive saucepan. Press the juice from the pomegranate seeds through the sieve. Stir in the red-currant jelly, sugar, and lime juice, then heat the mixture over low heat until the jelly and sugar have dissolved. Cook for 10 minutes. Blend the cornstarch with the rosé wine and stir it into the sauce. Bring it to a boil and continue to cook, stirring, until the mixture thickens and clears—two to three minutes. Add the strips of lime zest, lower the heat, and simmer for five minutes more, stirring frequently. Transfer the sauce to a warm sauceboat.

Just before carving, bring the 1½ tablespoons of red-currant jelly to a boil and brush it over the meat. Sprinkle the meat with the reserved pomegranate seeds and finely grated lime zest; garnish with the watercress. Serve the sauce separately.

SUGGESTED ACCOMPANIMENTS: *new potatoes; tossed salad with watercress.*

Roast Leg with Herbs and Garlic

Serves 8
Working time: about 30 minutes
Total time: about 3 hours (includes marinating)

Calories **260**
Protein **8g.**
Cholesterol **100mg.**
Total fat **12g.**
Saturated fat **5g.**
Sodium **195mg.**

one 5-lb. leg of lamb, trimmed of fat
3 garlic cloves
1 tsp. salt
2 tbsp. chopped mixed fresh herbs (thyme, sage, rosemary, oregano), or 2 tsp. mixed dried herbs
1 tbsp. finely chopped fresh parsley
1 tbsp. virgin olive oil

Using a small, pointed knife, make 10 to 12 evenly spaced deep incisions into the flesh of the lamb.

Crush together the garlic and salt with a mortar and pestle to make a paste. Add the mixed herbs and the parsley. Using your fingers or a small teaspoon, fill each cut in the lamb with the herb and garlic paste. Rub the olive oil all over the leg, then place the lamb in a roasting pan and set it aside in a cool place to marinate for one hour. Preheat the oven to 425° F.

Roast the leg for 15 minutes, then lower the temperature to 375° F. and continue roasting for 50 minutes to one hour for rare to medium meat, basting the leg frequently with the juices. Transfer the leg to a serving dish, cover it loosely with foil, and let it stand in a warm place for 20 minutes before carving.

SUGGESTED ACCOMPANIMENT: *white beans and green beans tossed in parsley.*

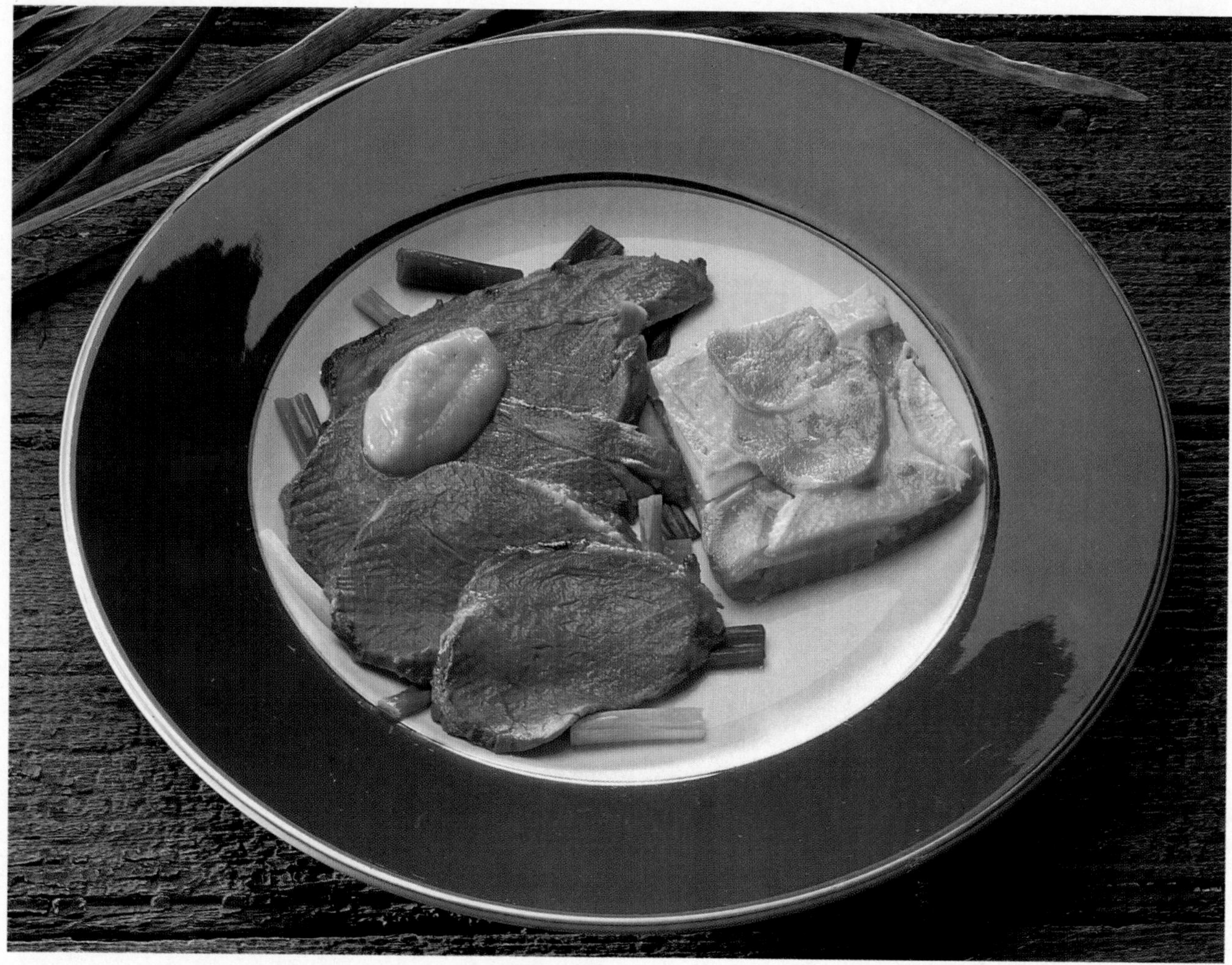

Roast Leg of Lamb with Pear Mustard

Serves 10
Working time: about 1 hour
Total time: about 2 hours and 15 minutes

Calories **225**
Protein **24g.**
Cholesterol **75mg.**
Total fat **9g.**
Saturated fat **3g.**
Sodium **430mg.**

one 5-lb. leg of lamb, trimmed of fat, the pelvic and thigh bones removed, the shank bone left in place
½ tbsp. Dijon mustard
1 tbsp. safflower oil
¼ tsp. salt
3 bunches scallions, trimmed and cut into 1-inch lengths

Pear mustard

½ tbsp. safflower oil
1½ lb. pears (preferably Comice), peeled, cored, and coarsely chopped
1 cup unsalted brown stock or unsalted chicken stock (recipes, page 137)
1½ tbsp. fresh lemon juice
1 shallot, finely chopped, or 1 scallion, white part only, finely chopped
1 garlic clove, finely chopped
1¼ tsp. salt
freshly ground black pepper
1½ tbsp. Dijon mustard

To make the pear mustard, heat the oil in a heavy-bottomed saucepan set over medium-high heat. Add the pears and cook them, stirring frequently, until the juice is syrupy and lightly browned—15 to 20 minutes. Add the stock, lemon juice, shallot or scallion, garlic, salt, some pepper, and the mustard. Lower the heat to medium and simmer the mixture, stirring occasionally, until only about 1½ cups remain—15 to 20 minutes. Transfer the pear mustard to a food processor or a blender, and purée it.

Preheat the oven to 325° F.

While the pear mustard is cooking, prepare the leg of lamb for roasting. Rub the ½ tablespoon of mustard over the exposed inner surface of the leg. Fold the meat over to enclose the mustard, then tie the leg securely with butcher's twine.

Heat the tablespoon of oil in a large, ovenproof skillet set over high heat. When the oil is hot, add the leg of lamb and brown it evenly on all sides—about 10 minutes. Sprinkle the lamb with the salt and transfer the skillet to the oven. Roast the lamb for 20 minutes, then coat it with about one-third of the pear mustard and roast it for 20 minutes more. Brush the lamb with about half of the remaining pear mustard. Increase the oven temperature to 500° F. and cook the lamb until the pear mustard is lightly browned in places—15 to 20 minutes. Remove the leg of lamb from the oven and let it rest for 20 minutes.

Blanch the scallion pieces in boiling water for one minute, then drain them and divide them among 10 warmed dinner plates. Slice the lamb and arrange the pieces on the scallions; dab a little of the remaining pear mustard on top before serving.

SUGGESTED ACCOMPANIMENT: *a gratin of sliced turnips and sweet potatoes.*

Leg of Lamb Roasted with Ginger

Serves 10
Working time: about 25 minutes
Total time: about 4 hours and 30 minutes (includes marinating)

Calories **185**
Protein **24g.**
Cholesterol **75mg.**
Total fat **7g.**
Saturated fat **3g.**
Sodium **170mg.**

one 5-lb. leg of lamb, trimmed of fat
3 tbsp. finely chopped fresh ginger
3 garlic cloves, finely chopped
2 tsp. low-sodium soy sauce
¼ tsp. dark sesame oil
1 tsp. rice vinegar or distilled white vinegar
⅓ cup mirin (glossary, page 138) or sweet sherry
ground white pepper

Dipping sauce

1 tbsp. low-sodium soy sauce
2 tbsp. mirin or sweet sherry
1 tsp. sesame seeds
2 tsp. rice vinegar or distilled white vinegar
1 scallion, trimmed and thinly sliced
1 small carrot, trimmed, peeled, and thinly sliced
2 tbsp. chopped fresh ginger
½ cup unsalted brown stock or unsalted chicken stock (recipes, page 137)

With a knife, lightly score the surface of the lamb in a crosshatch pattern. Transfer the lamb to a shallow baking dish. Mix the ginger, garlic, soy sauce, sesame oil, vinegar, mirin or sherry, and some white pepper in a bowl. Pour the marinade over the lamb and refrigerate it for at least three hours, or as long as overnight. From time to time, baste the lamb with the marinade.

Toward the end of the marinating time, preheat the oven to 450° F. Transfer the lamb to a roasting pan, reserving the marinade, and roast the lamb for 15 minutes. Lower the oven temperature to 325° F. and continue roasting the lamb, basting it occasionally with the reserved marinade, until a meat thermometer inserted in the center registers 140° F.—about 50 minutes more. Let the leg of lamb rest for 20 minutes before you carve it.

While the lamb is resting, combine the dipping-sauce ingredients. Serve the dipping sauce at room temperature with the lamb slices.

SUGGESTED ACCOMPANIMENT: *a cold salad of Asian noodles.*

Garlic-Studded Lamb Shanks with Roasted Onions

Serves 4
Working time: about 20 minutes
Total time: about 2 hours

Calories **285**
Protein **31g.**
Cholesterol **86mg.**
Total fat **9g.**
Saturated fat **3g.**
Sodium **290mg.**

4 lamb shanks (about ¾ lb. each), trimmed of fat
6 garlic cloves, each cut lengthwise into 4 slices
½ tbsp. olive oil
1 tbsp. finely chopped fresh rosemary, or ½ tbsp. dried rosemary
freshly ground black pepper
¼ tsp. salt
4 onions, unpeeled
6 carrots, cut into bâtonnets and blanched for 1 minute in boiling water

Preheat the oven to 350° F.

With the point of a knife, make an incision in the flesh of a shank; press a garlic slice deep into the opening. Repeat the process to insert six garlic slices into each shank. Rub the shanks with the oil, then sprinkle them with the rosemary and some freshly ground black pepper. Put the shanks into a heavy-bottomed roasting pan and bake them until they are very tender—one and a half to two hours.

After the lamb shanks have been baking for 45 minutes, sprinkle them with the salt. Wrap the onions individually in aluminum foil and set them in the oven next to the roasting pan.

When the shanks are done, transfer them to a serving platter. Discard the fat that has collected in the roasting pan, leaving any caramelized juices in the pan. Set the pan on the stovetop over medium heat. Add the blanched carrot sticks and cook them, stirring occasionally, for two minutes. Pour ¼ cup of water into the pan and bring the liquid to a simmer, scraping up the caramelized juices with a wooden spoon.

Transfer the carrots and the sauce to the platter. Unwrap the onions, cut off ½ inch from their tops, and set them on the platter just before serving.

SUGGESTED ACCOMPANIMENTS: *escarole; Italian bread.*

Leg of Lamb Stuffed with Vegetables

Serves 10
Working time: about 40 minutes
Total time: about 2 hours

Calories **240**
Protein **25g.**
Cholesterol **77mg.**
Total fat **11g.**
Saturated fat **4g.**
Sodium **235mg.**

one 5-lb. leg of lamb, trimmed of fat and boned
2 tbsp. safflower oil
1 large carrot, julienned
1 large zucchini, julienned
1 large yellow squash, julienned
½ cup dry sherry
⅓ cup freshly grated Parmesan cheese (about 1 oz.)
½ tsp. salt
freshly ground black pepper
1 tbsp. fresh thyme, or 2 tsp. dried thyme leaves
1 cup unsalted brown stock or unsalted chicken stock (recipes, page 137)
2 tbsp. finely chopped shallot or onion
1½ tbsp. cornstarch, mixed with 2 tbsp. water

To prepare the stuffing, heat 1 tablespoon of the oil in a large, ovenproof skillet over medium heat. Add the carrot julienne and sauté it, stirring often, for two minutes. Stir in the zucchini and yellow squash, and cook the vegetables until the carrot is barely tender—about two minutes more. Remove the skillet from the heat and pour in 2 tablespoons of the sherry. Add the Parmesan cheese and toss the stuffing to mix it well.

Preheat the oven to 325° F. Spread out the boned leg of lamb on a work surface, and season it with ¼ teaspoon of the salt, some pepper, and half of the thyme. Spread the stuffing over the leg of lamb and roll it up as you would a jelly roll. Tie the leg of lamb with butcher's twine to secure it.

Wipe out the skillet and heat the remaining tablespoon of oil in it over high heat. Add the lamb roll and brown it on all sides—two to three minutes altogether. Put the skillet into the oven and roast the lamb until it is tender—about one hour. Transfer the roast to a platter and set it aside.

Discard the fat and set the skillet on the stovetop over low heat. Add the stock, the remaining thyme, the chopped shallot or onion, and the remaining sherry to the skillet, then scrape the bottom with a wooden spoon to dissolve the caramelized roasting juices. Increase the heat to medium high and boil the liquid until about one-third of it remains—7 to 10 minutes. Reduce the heat to low and whisk in the cornstarch mixture. Cook the sauce, stirring continuously, until it has thickened—about one minute. Season the sauce with the remaining ¼ teaspoon of salt and some freshly ground black pepper.

Cut the roast into slices. Pour the sauce into a gravy boat and pass it separately.

SUGGESTED ACCOMPANIMENTS: *broccoli; mashed potatoes.*

Roast Shoulder with Rosemary

Serves 12
Working time: about 40 minutes
Total time: about 3 hours (includes marinating)

Calories **310**
Protein **20g.**
Cholesterol **75mg.**
Total fat **12g.**
Saturated fat **5g.**
Sodium **130mg.**

one 5-lb. shoulder of lamb, trimmed of fat
1 tbsp. virgin olive oil
2 tsp. mixed dried herbs
½ tsp. salt
4 long sprigs rosemary
1½ tsp. all-purpose flour
2½ cups unsalted chicken or brown stock (recipes, page 137)
freshly ground black pepper

Make four diagonal incisions with a sharp knife across the shoulder, almost down to the bone. Rub the virgin olive oil, mixed dried herbs, and salt all over the lamb, then insert the rosemary sprigs in the diagonal cuts. Place the lamb shoulder in a roasting pan and set it aside in a cool place to marinate for one hour. Preheat the oven to 425° F.

Roast the shoulder for 15 minutes, then lower the oven temperature to 375° F. and continue to roast for 45 minutes to one hour for rare to medium meat, basting frequently with the juices in the pan. Transfer the shoulder to a serving dish, cover it loosely with aluminum foil, and set it aside in a warm place while you make the gravy.

To make the gravy, tip the roasting pan slightly so that the juices run to one corner, then skim off any fat. Sprinkle the flour over the juices left in the pan and stir with a wooden spoon until the mixture is well blended. Gradually stir in the stock. Place the pan over medium heat and bring the gravy to a boil, stirring all the time until it thickens; season with some freshly ground black pepper. Reduce the heat to low and simmer for six to eight minutes, stirring occasionally. Strain the gravy through a sieve into a hot gravy boat and serve with the shoulder.

SUGGESTED ACCOMPANIMENTS: *steamed rutabaga and parsnips; green salad.*

Shoulder Stuffed with Wild Rice and Spinach

Serves 12
Working time: about 1 hour
Total time: about 4 hours

Calories **225**
Protein **22g.**
Cholesterol **75mg.**
Total fat **13g.**
Saturated fat **5g.**
Sodium **140mg.**

one 3-lb. shoulder of lamb, boned and trimmed of fat
⅓ cup wild rice
2 tsp. virgin olive oil
4 shallots, coarsely chopped
1 medium celeriac, or 2 medium parsnips, grated
6 oz. fresh spinach, washed, stems removed
½ tsp. finely grated nutmeg
¾ tsp. salt
freshly ground black pepper
1¼ cups unsalted chicken stock (recipe, page 137)
1 tsp. cornstarch

To make the stuffing, wash the wild rice and put it into a large saucepan in twice its depth of water. Bring the water to a boil, cover the pan, and simmer until the husks have split and the rice is soft—50 minutes to one hour. Drain the rice and allow it to cool. Heat the oil in a frying pan, add the shallots, and cook them over very low heat until they are soft but not brown. Add the celeriac or parsnips, and continue cooking until they begin to look translucent—about three minutes—then add the spinach and cook until it wilts—about one minute. Blend this mixture very briefly in a food processor to make a coarse-textured purée; do not overprocess. Mix the purée with the wild rice, and season with the nutmeg, ½ teaspoon of the salt, and some black pepper.

Preheat the oven to 450° F. Stuff and tie the shoulder into a melon shape *(technique, page 52).* Put the lamb into a roasting pan, and season the outside with the remaining ¼ teaspoon of salt and some pepper. Place the lamb in the oven until it is well browned—10 to 15 minutes—then lower the oven temperature to 400° F., and cook for one and a quarter to one and a half hours for medium-rare to medium meat. Transfer the lamb to a cutting board and allow it to rest in a warm place for 15 minutes.

Meanwhile, make the gravy. Skim off any fat from the surface of the roasting juices and transfer the pan to the stove. Add the stock and boil it over high heat, stirring to loosen any browned bits from the bottom of the pan. Mix the cornstarch with 1 tablespoon of water and add it to the pan, stirring constantly until the gravy thickens—two to three minutes. Season with some pepper. Cut off the string and carve the lamb into wedges. Serve the gravy separately.

SUGGESTED ACCOMPANIMENT: *zucchini and mushrooms.*

Stuffing and Tying a Boned Shoulder

1 STUFFING THE MEAT. Lay a boned shoulder of lamb, inner side uppermost, on the work surface. Open up the cavity left by the shoulder blade and fill it with stuffing. Fold two opposite sides of the shoulder over to cover the stuffing.

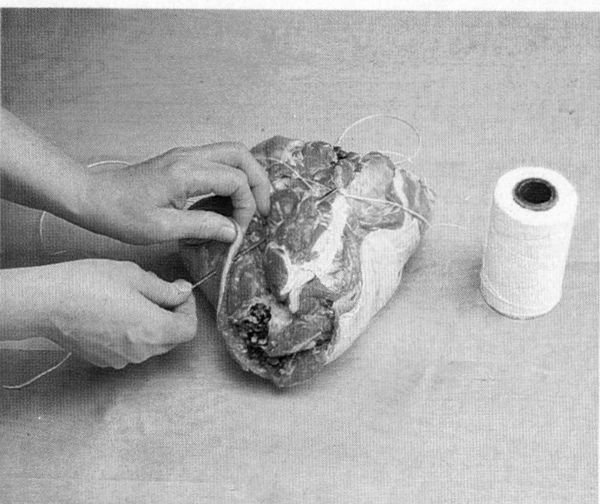

2 ENCLOSING THE STUFFING. Push a threaded trussing needle through the ends of the two flaps that were folded over in Step 1. Take the string out of the needle and tie the string, pulling the flaps tightly together. Fold over the other two sides of the shoulder to enclose the stuffing; stitch them and tie them together.

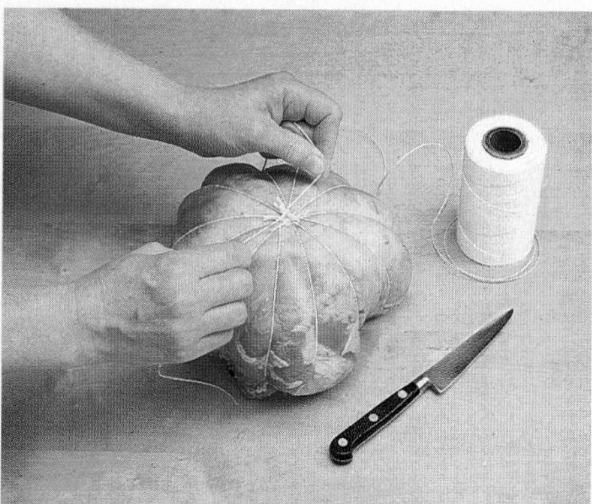

3 FORMING A MELON SHAPE. Cut six pieces of string, each about 24 inches long. Tie one length around the meat, pulling the string taut, then tie a second length across the first to section the meat into quarters. Continue tying the shoulder until it is divided into 12 segments and resembles a melon in shape.

Roast Saddle of Lamb with Plum Sauce

Serves 12
Working time: about 1 hour
Total time: about 2 hours and 40 minutes

Calories **335**
Protein **28g.**
Cholesterol **75mg.**
Total fat **14g.**
Saturated fat **6g.**
Sodium **180mg.**

one 10-lb. saddle of lamb
1 tbsp. virgin olive oil
2 tbsp. sugar
¾ tsp. salt
freshly ground black pepper
4-6 large plums (about 1½ lb.), halved and pitted
2½ cups red wine
one 1-inch piece cinnamon stick
½ cup unsalted chicken stock (recipe, page 137)

Fruit garnish

3 sweet apples
¼ cup sugar
2 tbsp. fresh lemon juice
6 large plums, halved, pitted, and sliced

Preheat the oven to 425° F.

Spread the saddle of lamb out flat on a cutting board and trim off the fatty strip—or apron—of flesh along each side; leave just enough flesh to slightly overlap when tucked underneath the saddle. Carefully remove excess fat from the meat.

Rub the olive oil all over the meat, then sprinkle it with the sugar, and season with ½ teaspoon of the salt and some black pepper. Tuck the side flaps neatly under the saddle and place it in a large roasting pan.

Roast the saddle for 20 minutes, then lower the oven temperature to 350° F. and place the halved plums in the roasting pan, tucking them closely around the lamb. Pour half of the wine over the lamb and add the piece of cinnamon. Continue roasting for about one hour and 20 minutes to one hour and 30 minutes for rare to medium meat. Baste the meat frequently while it roasts; each time you baste, add some more wine until it is all used up.

Ten minutes before the lamb is cooked, begin to prepare the garnish. Peel and core the apples, and cut them into ¼-inch-thick rings. Put the sugar into a wide, shallow, nonreactive saucepan with the lemon juice and ½ cup of cold water. Heat on low until the sugar dissolves. Cook the apple rings in the sugar syrup until they are soft but still firm—three to five minutes. Using a slotted spoon, transfer the apple rings from the saucepan to a plate. Cover the apples and keep them warm. Add the sliced plums to the syrup and cook them until they begin to soften—about one minute. Transfer the plums to the plate with the apples. Reduce the syrup by boiling rapidly until it thickens slightly—two to three minutes. Set the fruit garnish aside.

When the lamb is cooked, carefully transfer it to a large, hot serving platter. Cover it with foil and allow it to stand for about 20 minutes.

Meanwhile, make the plum sauce. Place a fine sieve over a nonreactive saucepan and pour the juices from the roasting pan into it. Using a wooden spoon, press the halved plums through the sieve into the saucepan. Stir the chicken stock into the plum mixture, and season it with the remaining ¼ teaspoon of salt and some black pepper. Heat the sauce through, then pour it into a hot gravy boat.

Garnish the lamb with the plum slices and apple rings, and brush the fruit with the reduced syrup. Serve with the plum sauce.

SUGGESTED ACCOMPANIMENTS: *new potatoes; green beans.*

Rack of Lamb with a Spiced Parsley Crust

Serves 6
Working time: about 30 minutes
Total time: about 4 hours and 45 minutes
(includes marinating)

Calories **260**
Protein **30g.**
Cholesterol **75mg.**
Total fat **8g.**
Saturated fat **4g.**
Sodium **200mg.**

two 1½-lb. racks of lamb, each with 6 chops, chine bones removed, bone tips shortened by 2 inches, trimmed of fat, and prepared for roasting (technique, page 135)
1 small onion, finely chopped
2 garlic cloves, crushed
2 tbsp. chopped parsley
¼ tsp. ground cumin
¼ tsp. ground paprika
½ tsp. salt
freshly ground black pepper
1 tsp. saffron threads, soaked in 1 tsp. of boiling water for 1 hour
½ cup white wine
1 tsp. cornstarch

Scrape clean the last 2 inches of the rib bones. Thoroughly mix together the onion, garlic, parsley, cumin, paprika, ¼ teaspoon of the salt, and some pepper. Stir in the saffron and its soaking water. Spread this mixture over the outer fleshy side of the racks and allow them to marinate in a cool place, loosely covered, for four to six hours.

Preheat the oven to 425° F. Place the meat on a rack in a roasting pan, marinated side upward. Roast for 25 minutes, then add the wine and ½ cup of water to the roasting pan, and return the meat to the oven until the crusts are beginning to turn dark around the edges—about 20 minutes. (The meat will still be slightly pink in the center; cover the racks with aluminum foil and roast them for 15 minutes more if you like your lamb more thoroughly cooked.)

When the meat is cooked, transfer it to a warmed plate. Skim off the fat from the cooking liquid and boil the liquid to reduce it slightly. Mix the cornstarch with 1 tablespoon of water and stir it into the pan. Continue cooking over medium heat until the gravy thickens—two to three minutes. Season with the remaining ¼ teaspoon of salt and some black pepper. Slice the racks into chops and serve with the gravy.

SUGGESTED ACCOMPANIMENTS: *new potatoes; green beans.*

Guard of Honor

Serves 7
Working time: about 35 minutes
Total time: about 1 hour and 35 minutes

Calories **220**
Protein **28g.**
Cholesterol **75mg.**
Total fat **9g.**
Saturated fat **3g.**
Sodium **125mg.**

two 1¾-lb. racks of lamb, each with 7 chops, chine bones removed, bone tips shortened by 2 inches, trimmed of fat, and prepared for roasting (technique, page 135)

1 garlic clove, peeled and cut in half

freshly ground black pepper

1 tbsp. tahini

1 tbsp. Dijon mustard

1 tbsp. honey

1 tbsp. mustard seeds

1½ tbsp. sesame seeds

1 tbsp. finely chopped fresh tarragon, or 1 tsp. dried tarragon

Red-wine gravy

½ cup red wine

½ cup unsalted chicken or brown stock (recipes, page 137) or water

1 sprig fresh tarragon, or ¼ tsp. dried tarragon

½ tsp. honey

¼ tsp. salt

Scrape clean the last 2 inches of the rib bones. Rub the garlic clove all over the flesh and bones, and season the meat generously with black pepper.

Mix together the tahini, mustard, honey, mustard seeds, and sesame seeds. Combine 2 teaspoons of this paste with the chopped tarragon, and spread the mixture over the concave inside of the racks.

Preheat the oven to 450° F. Assemble the guard by interlocking the exposed rib-bone tips. Using kitchen twine, tie the racks as shown on page 56. To prevent charring during cooking, cover the exposed bone tips with a single layer of aluminum foil, pressing the foil around the bones.

Spread the remaining tahini-mustard paste over the outside surface of the assembled guard. Place the meat in a roasting pan.

Roast the lamb for 50 minutes to one hour and 10 minutes for rare to medium meat. Transfer the guard to a warm platter, cut away the strings, and let it rest in a warm place.

To make the gravy, skim off the fat from the liquid in the roasting pan and transfer the pan to the stove. Add the wine and boil it over high heat, stirring to scrape off any browned bits from the bottom of the pan. Add the stock, tarragon, honey, and salt, and boil to reduce the liquid by about one-half. Strain the gravy into a gravy boat. Carve the meat at the table.

SUGGESTED ACCOMPANIMENTS: *steamed zucchini and carrots; new potatoes.*

EDITOR'S NOTE: *For this recipe, ask your butcher for matching racks—ideally from the same animal.*

Forming a Guard of Honor

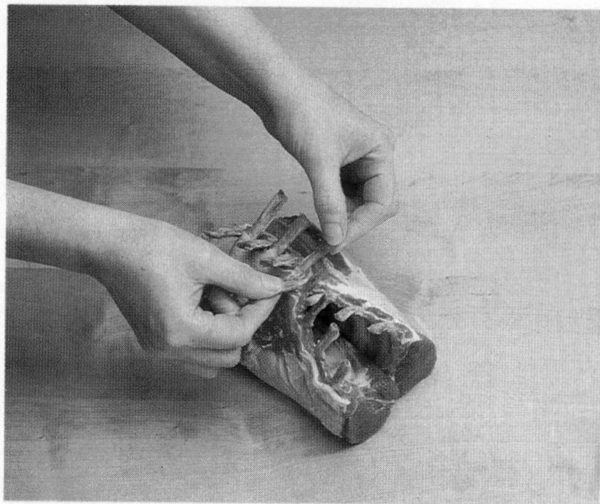

1 *INTERLOCKING THE BONE TIPS. Stand up two racks (prepared according to the instructions on page 135), concave sides facing each other. Press them together so that the tips of the bones are interlaced.*

2 *TYING THE RACKS TOGETHER. Cut three lengths of string, each about 18 inches long. Tie each length around the racks. Cut another length of string—approximately 30 inches—and weave it in and out of the crossed ribs from one end to the other. Bring the ends of the string back along the outside of the crossed ribs and tie them in a knot.*

Crown Roast Garnished with Glazed Onions

Serves 7
Working time: about 1 hour
Total time: about 2 hours

Calories **290**
Protein **29g.**
Cholesterol **75mg.**
Total fat **14g.**
Saturated fat **6g.**
Sodium **265mg.**

two 1¾-lb. racks of lamb, each with 7 chops, chine bones removed, bone tips shortened by 2 inches, trimmed of fat, and prepared for roasting (technique, page 135)
¼ tsp. salt
freshly ground black pepper
½ tbsp. virgin olive oil
1 tbsp. sugar
18 pearl onions, peeled
6 tbsp. unsalted chicken stock (recipe, page 137)

Asparagus stuffing

1 lb. asparagus, washed, trimmed, and peeled
1 tbsp. virgin olive oil
1 onion, finely chopped
1 garlic clove, crushed
¾ cup fresh white breadcrumbs
2 tbsp. chopped parsley
1 tsp. finely grated lemon zest
1 egg white
¼ tsp. salt
freshly ground black pepper

Assemble the racks of lamb for a crown roast following the technique shown opposite. To prevent charring during cooking, cover the exposed bone tips with a single layer of aluminum foil, pressing the foil around the bones. Season the crown with the salt and some black pepper; place it in a roasting pan. Preheat the oven to 425° F.

To make the stuffing, cut off the asparagus tips and set them aside. Cut the stalks into thin slices and blanch them in boiling water for one minute. Using a slotted spoon, transfer the slices to a colander to drain well, then set them aside. Add the tips to the water and cook them until they are tender—two to three minutes. Pour them into a colander and refresh them under cold running water. Drain the tips well and set them aside for the garnish.

Heat the oil for the stuffing in a heavy-bottomed frying pan over medium heat. Add the chopped onion, reduce the heat to low, and cook it until it is soft but not brown—six to eight minutes. Add the garlic and asparagus stalks, and continue cooking for three minutes. Remove the pan from the heat, and stir in the breadcrumbs, parsley, lemon zest, and egg white. Season the stuffing with the salt and some black pepper, and squeeze it gently together.

Fill the center of the crown with the asparagus stuffing. Roast the crown for 10 minutes, then lower the oven temperature to 350° F. and continue roasting for 50 to 60 minutes for rare to medium meat.

Fifteen minutes before the crown roast is ready, prepare the garnish. Heat the oil in a frying pan over medium heat and sprinkle in the sugar. Heat until the sugar turns a golden caramel. Add the onions and shake the pan gently until they are evenly coated with the caramel. Reduce the heat to low, add the stock, and cover the pan. Cook until the onions are tender—about 12 minutes—then add the reserved asparagus tips. Cook until the asparagus is heated through—two to three minutes more.

Place the crown on a warm serving dish, and garnish it with the glazed onions and asparagus tips.

SUGGESTED ACCOMPANIMENTS: *julienned carrots; boiled potatoes tossed in parsley.*

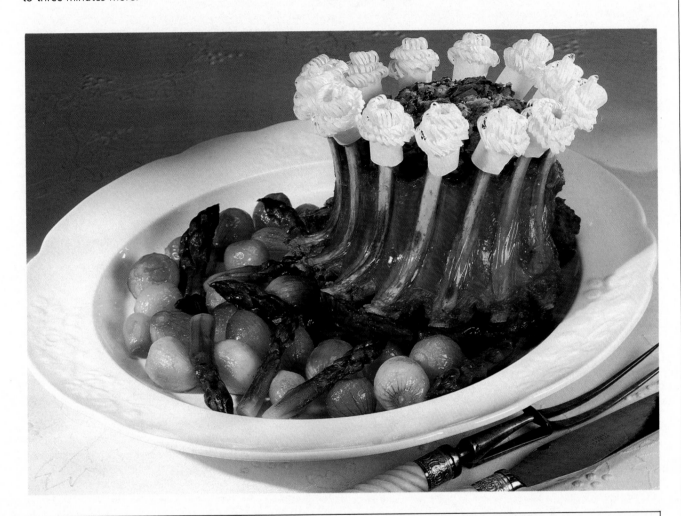

Shaping a Crown Roast

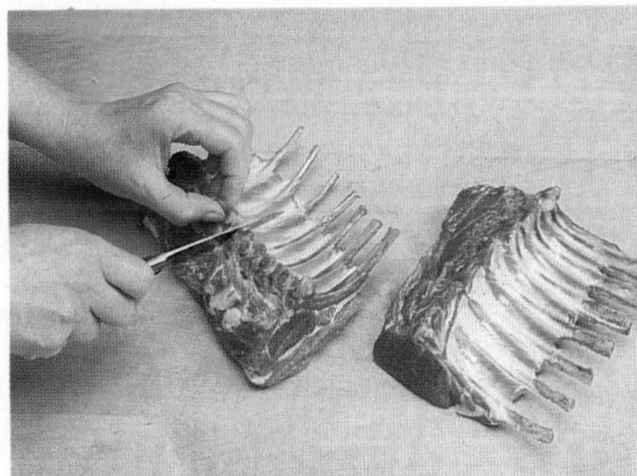

1 *FREEING THE RIB BONES. Place two racks (prepared according to the instructions on page 135) concave side up on a work surface. With a knife, make ¼-inch-deep cuts between the thick end of the rib bones of each rack.*

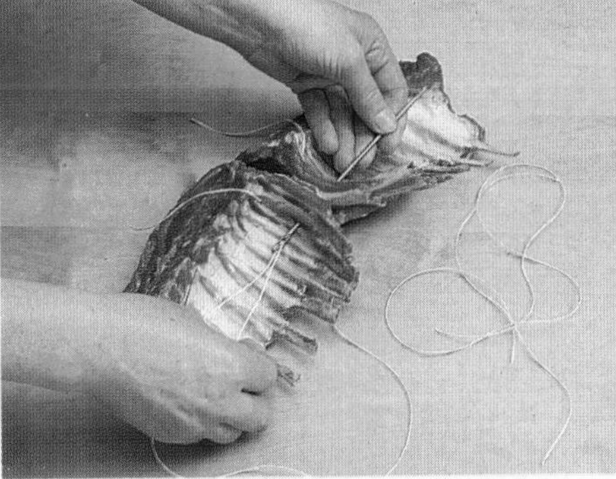

2 *JOINING THE TWO RACKS. Lay the racks end to end. Cut two lengths of string, each about 12 inches long. Using a large trussing needle, sew the end rib bones of the two racks together, then knot the string.*

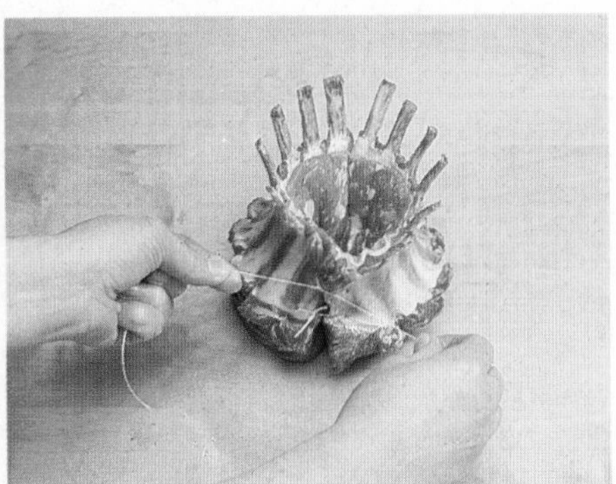

3 *COMPLETING THE CROWN. Curve the racks, concave side out, into semicircles. Cut two or more lengths of string, and sew and tie the two free rack ends together to form a circle.*

Chilled Chops Coated with Mint Aspic

TO MAKE A CLEAR ASPIC, THE BOWLS, CHEESECLOTH, AND COOKING UTENSILS MUST BE SCRUPULOUSLY CLEAN. HERE, EVERYTHING IS SCALDED TO ENSURE THAT THE LIQUID DOES NOT BECOME CLOUDED BY IMPURITIES.

Serves 6
Working time: about 1 hour and 15 minutes
Total time: about 4 hours and 30 minutes
(includes cooling and setting)

Calories **255**
Protein **35g.**
Cholesterol **75mg.**
Total fat **12g.**
Saturated fat **6g.**
Sodium **230mg.**

two 1½-lb. racks of lamb, each with 6 chops, chine bones removed, bone tips shortened by 2 inches

½ tsp. salt

shredded lettuce for garnish

12 scallions, cut into brushes, for garnish

Mint aspic

1 qt. unsalted chicken stock (recipe, page 137)

3 eggs, whites and shells only

6 envelopes powdered gelatin

2 tbsp. red wine vinegar

¼ cup chopped fresh mint

Preheat the oven to 425° F.

Assemble the racks for roasting, as shown on page 135, and sprinkle them with the salt. Place the racks in a roasting pan and roast them for 10 minutes, then lower the temperature to 350° F. and continue roasting for about 40 minutes more for rare to medium meat. Transfer the lamb to a large plate and allow it to cool for one hour, then refrigerate it until it is chilled—about one hour.

Meanwhile, prepare the aspic. Put a large piece of cheesecloth, a wire balloon whisk, and a large metal sieve into a saucepan. Fill the saucepan with cold water, and bring it to a boil to scald the contents and the saucepan. Pour the boiling water into a large mixing bowl, to scald that also, then discard the water. Wring out the cheesecloth. Line the sieve with the cheesecloth and place it over the mixing bowl.

Put the stock into the saucepan, and add the egg whites, egg shells, gelatin, and vinegar. Place the saucepan over medium heat and bring the mixture to a boil, stirring with the balloon whisk until a thick foam forms on the surface. Stop stirring and allow the liquid to boil until the foam rises to the top of the saucepan. At once, remove the saucepan from the heat and allow the foam to settle back down in the saucepan. Repeat this process twice, without stirring, then remove the saucepan from the heat and allow it to stand for 10 minutes. Very carefully pour the liquid into the cheesecloth-lined sieve, without allowing the foam to break up. When the liquid has completely drained through the cheesecloth, discard the foam. Allow the aspic to cool for approximately one hour, then stir in the chopped mint.

Cut down between the ribs to divide each rack of

lamb into six chops. Carefully cut away all the excess fat to leave just the lean eye of the meat attached to the bone. Place the lamb chops on a wire rack set over a large, clean tray.

Stir the aspic over ice, or refrigerate it, until it begins to thicken. Spoon aspic over each chop to coat it evenly. Refrigerate the chops until the aspic has set—10 to 15 minutes—then coat them once again. Refrigerate them until the aspic is firmly set—about 20 minutes. Serve the chops on a bed of shredded lettuce, garnished with the scallion brushes.

EDITOR'S NOTE: *To make scallion brushes, trim off the bulb and scallion top to leave a 3-inch length of firm stalk. Make three or four 1-inch-long cuts into the ends of each scallion. Place the scallions in ice water until the ends curl—about one hour. The chops may be prepared up to 24 hours in advance and kept in a covered container in the refrigerator.*

Chops Stuffed with Walnuts and Parsley

Serves 4
Working time: about 20 minutes
Total time: about 40 minutes

Calories **280**
Protein **23g.**
Cholesterol **65mg.**
Total fat **14g.**
Saturated fat **5g.**
Sodium **215mg.**

4 loin chops (about 4 oz. each), trimmed of fat
2 tsp. safflower oil
1 onion, chopped
½ cup unsalted chicken stock (recipe, page 137)
3 tbsp. currants
5 tbsp. fresh breadcrumbs
2 tsp. chopped fresh parsley
2 tbsp. finely chopped walnuts
1 tsp. chopped fresh thyme, or ¼ tsp. dried thyme leaves
¼ tsp. salt
freshly ground black pepper

First, prepare the stuffing. Heat 1 teaspoon of the oil in a nonstick frying pan over medium heat. Add the onion and cook it until it is translucent—two to three minutes. Add the stock and currants, and bring the liquid to a simmer. Remove the pan from the heat and cover it. Let the mixture stand until the currants have plumped up—about five minutes. Stir in the breadcrumbs, parsley, walnuts, thyme, ⅛ teaspoon of the salt, and some pepper, and set the stuffing aside.

Preheat the oven to 400° F. Arrange the chops in front of you with the loin on the right and the apron farthest from you. Insert a small, sharp knife horizontally into each chop in turn on the right side, near the end of the bone that divides the tenderloin from the loin. Extend the cut leftward toward the loin, but make sure the knife does not emerge on the far side of the loin. Rotate the knife to create a pocket within the flesh of the loin. Using a spoon or your fingers, fill the pockets with the stuffing. Fold the long, thin apron of the chop to cover the opening of the pocket, and secure the apron to the loin with a toothpick.

Heat the remaining teaspoon of oil in a shallow, ovenproof casserole over medium-high heat. Place the stuffed chops in the oil and cook them on one side until they are lightly browned—one to two minutes. Turn the chops over, and season them with the remaining ⅛ teaspoon of salt and some more pepper. Put the casserole into the oven and bake the chops for 10 to 12 minutes. Remove the casserole from the oven and let the chops rest for five minutes. Remove the toothpicks before serving.

SUGGESTED ACCOMPANIMENT: *ratatouille.*

Lamb with Hazelnut Sauce

Serves 6
Working (and total) time: about 30 minutes

Calories **175**
Protein **23g.**
Cholesterol **65mg.**
Total fat **14g.**
Saturated fat **5g.**
Sodium **200mg.**

two 1¼-lb. racks of lamb, boned, the fatty flap of meat that extends from the loin removed
2 cups unsalted brown or chicken stock (recipes, page 137)
½ cup dry white wine
½ tsp. salt
freshly ground black pepper
2 medium turnips, peeled and finely diced
⅓ cup hazelnuts, toasted and chopped

Preheat the oven to 450° F.

To make the sauce, put the stock and wine into a saucepan, and boil rapidly until only half of the liquid remains—8 to 10 minutes. Season with ¼ teaspoon of the salt and some black pepper. Add the turnips and simmer them until they are just tender—about five minutes—then remove from the heat and set aside.

While the sauce is cooking, brush a heavy-bottomed frying pan with a little oil. Set the pan over high heat, then quickly sear the meat in the hot pan and transfer it to a roasting pan. Season the meat with the remaining ¼ teaspoon of salt and some black pepper. Roast the lamb for 5 to 10 minutes for rare to medium meat.

Just before the meat is ready, return the sauce to the heat, stir in the chopped hazelnuts, and heat the sauce through. Carve the lamb and arrange slices on six plates. Spoon the sauce over the meat and serve.

SUGGESTED ACCOMPANIMENT: *fettucine.*

EDITOR'S NOTE: *To toast hazelnuts, put them on a baking sheet in a preheated 350° F. oven for 10 minutes.*

Loin with Juniper-Berry Sauce

Serves 8
Working time: about 20 minutes
Total time: about 30 minutes

Calories **250**
Protein **25g.**
Cholesterol **90mg.**
Total fat **12g.**
Saturated fat **5g.**
Sodium **70mg.**

two 2¼-lb. loins of lamb, boned and trimmed of fat (technique, page 134), tenderloin reserved for another dish
1 qt. unsalted brown or chicken stock (recipes, page 137)
1¼ cups dry Madeira
4 tsp. red-currant jelly
4 tsp. juniper berries, coarsely crushed with a mortar and pestle
1 tsp. virgin olive oil

Preheat the oven to 425° F.

Put the stock, Madeira, and red-currant jelly into a heavy-bottomed saucepan, and boil them over high heat until the liquid is reduced to about 2 cups. Add 2 teaspoons of the juniper berries and continue boiling until the stock has reduced to about 1 cup, then remove the pan from the heat and set the sauce aside.

Meanwhile, brush the loins of lamb with the olive oil, sprinkle them with the remaining juniper berries, and place in a roasting pan. Roast the meat on the middle shelf of the oven for 12 minutes. Turn off the heat and leave the lamb in the pan on the floor of the oven for 10 minutes.

Transfer the lamb to a hot serving dish, cover the dish, and keep it warm. Skim off any fat from the juices in the pan and pour the remaining juices into the juniper-berry sauce. Reheat the sauce, pour some of it around the lamb to moisten it, and pour the rest into a gravy boat. Serve immediately.

SUGGESTED ACCOMPANIMENTS: *steamed red cabbage; mashed potatoes.*

Loin Stuffed with Wild Mushrooms

Serves 4
Working time: about 1 hour
Total time: about 1 hour and 45 minutes

Calories **235**
Protein **24g.**
Cholesterol **69mg.**
Total fat **11g.**
Saturated fat **4g.**
Sodium **225mg.**

one 2½-lb. lamb loin roast, trimmed of fat and boned (technique, page 134)
1 oz. dried wild mushrooms (chanterelle, porcini, or shiitake), soaked in 1 cup very hot water for 20 minutes
1 tbsp. olive oil
3 scallions, the white parts finely chopped, the green tops cut into 1-inch pieces
1 tbsp. finely chopped celery
2 garlic cloves, finely chopped
2 tsp. fresh thyme, or ¾ tsp. dried thyme leaves
¼ lb. fresh mushrooms, wiped clean and chopped
1 cup unsalted brown stock (recipe, page 137)
1 tbsp. fresh lemon juice
¼ tsp. salt
freshly ground black pepper

Remove the dried mushrooms from their soaking liquid, and cut off any woody or sandy stems. Finely chop the mushrooms and set them aside. Carefully pour the soaking liquid through a cheesecloth-lined sieve set over a bowl to strain out any grit. Set the bowl aside.

Heat ½ tablespoon of the oil in a heavy-bottomed saucepan over medium heat. Add the white parts of the scallions, the celery, garlic, and half of the thyme. Cook the mixture, stirring occasionally, for three minutes. Add all the mushrooms to the pan, along with ¼ cup of the stock, the lemon juice, ⅛ teaspoon of the salt, and a generous grinding of pepper. Cover the pan, reduce the heat to low, and cook the mushrooms, stirring them every now and then, until all the liquid has been absorbed—20 to 25 minutes. Transfer the mushroom stuffing to a bowl; refrigerate the stuffing until it has reached room temperature.

Preheat the oven to 425° F. To butterfly the loin and prepare it for stuffing, cut the meat in half horizontally, leaving the halves hinged at one side. Open out the meat and spread the stuffing down the center of it. Fold the halves back together and tie the loin roast securely. Place the roast in a heavy-bottomed roasting pan and brush it with the remaining ½ tablespoon of olive oil. Roast the loin for approximately 25 minutes, or until a thermometer inserted in the meat registers 150° F. for medium.

Remove the pan from the oven and set the roast aside on a cutting board while you prepare the sauce. Discard the fat from the pan, leaving behind any caramelized juices. Place the pan over medium heat. Pour the strained mushroom liquid and the remaining ¾ cup of stock into the pan, stirring well with a wooden spoon to dissolve the caramelized juices in the bottom. Stir in the remaining ⅛ teaspoon of salt, the remaining thyme, the scallion tops, and some pepper. Boil the liquid until about ½ cup of sauce remains—approximately 10 minutes.

Cut the loin into 12 slices, and arrange them on a platter or on individual plates. Pour the sauce over the slices and serve them immediately.

SUGGESTED ACCOMPANIMENTS: *green peas; French bread.*

Loin on a Bed of Spring Greens

ASK YOUR BUTCHER TO SAW THROUGH THE CHINE BONE OF THE ROASTS SO YOU CAN CARVE THE MEAT.

Serves 8
Working time: about 40 minutes
Total time: about 1 hour and 30 minutes

Calories **225**
Protein **24g.**
Cholesterol **68mg.**
Total fat **11g.**
Saturated fat **3g.**
Sodium **195mg.**

two 2½-lb. lamb loin roasts, trimmed of fat
1 tbsp. olive oil
1 tbsp. grainy mustard
⅛ tsp. salt
freshly ground black pepper
2 garlic cloves, finely chopped
½ cup fresh whole-wheat breadcrumbs
1 tbsp. chopped fresh parsley
1 tsp. chopped fresh thyme, or ¼ tsp. dried thyme leaves
1 tsp. chopped fresh rosemary, or ¼ tsp. dried rosemary, crumbled

Wilted spring-greens salad

1 tbsp. olive oil
2 scallions, trimmed and chopped
1 lb. dandelion greens, mustard greens, or spinach, stemmed, washed, and dried
1 bunch watercress, trimmed, washed, and dried
16 cherry tomatoes, cut in half
1 tbsp. red wine vinegar
⅛ tsp. salt
freshly ground black pepper

Set the lamb roasts in a roasting pan with their bone sides down. In a small bowl, combine 1 teaspoon of the oil, the mustard, salt, some pepper, and half of the garlic. Rub this mixture over the lamb and let it stand at room temperature for one hour.

Preheat the oven to 450° F. Roast the lamb until it has browned—about 15 minutes. In the meantime, mix together the breadcrumbs, parsley, thyme, rosemary, the remaining garlic, and some pepper.

Sprinkle the breadcrumb mixture over the top of the lamb roasts; drizzle the remaining 2 teaspoons of oil over the breadcrumbs. Continue roasting the lamb until the breadcrumbs have browned and the meat is medium rare—about 10 minutes more, or until a meat thermometer inserted in the center registers 140° F. Keep the lamb warm while you make the salad.

For the salad, heat the tablespoon of olive oil in a skillet over medium-high heat. Add the scallions and sauté them for 45 seconds. Add the greens or spinach, along with the watercress, tomatoes, and vinegar. Toss the vegetables in the skillet until the greens are slightly wilted—about 30 seconds. Remove the pan from the heat, and season the salad with the salt and some freshly ground black pepper.

Carve the lamb roasts into 16 pieces and serve them atop the salad.

SUGGESTED ACCOMPANIMENTS: *parslied potatoes; rolls.*

2 *Toasted walnuts, added just before the end of cooking, lend crunch to lamb and vegetables simmered in an anchovy-wine sauce (recipe, page 76).*

Simmering for Flavor

Slow cooking in liquid is the traditional way of tenderizing firmer, more gelatinous cuts of lamb. In time, tough meat yields almost magically, but since the cuts usually selected for moist cooking—shoulder, neck, and breast—are high in fat, many health-conscious cooks avoid moist methods for lamb. This chapter demonstrates that they need not. Lean, tender cuts from the leg or loin, normally associated with dry cooking, respond as well to moist cooking as the fattier cuts. And fattier cuts, scrupulously degreased, can be rescued for the calorie-conscious guest.

Braising and stewing involve the same techniques, but the pieces of meat for braising are usually quite large, whereas meat for stewing is generally cut into small pieces before it is cooked. In either case, the meat is often first seared in a heavy-bottomed pan. The liquid then makes a distinctive contribution of its own: Stock, wine, beer, or tomatoes can all enhance the flavor of the lamb. Accompanying vegetables may be cooked with the meat from the beginning for a rewarding exchange of flavors—as in the lamb *dhansak* on page 68—or added in stages to maintain their individual tastes and textures—as in the *navarin* on page 72. At the end of cooking, the braising liquid serves as a sauce. Poaching, another method of moist cooking, uses more liquid than braising; the poaching liquid may be served as a soup at another meal.

Because lean, prime cuts from the leg or loin have less muscle and connective tissue than conventional stewing lamb, cooking times are shorter. Although a conventional stew may take two to three hours to cook, most of the recipes here require little more than an hour. Whatever the quality of the meat, however, moist cooking is slow cooking, for meat that is boiled becomes tough. Keep the liquid to the gentlest of simmers. A striking exception to this rule is the Mongolian hot pot *(page 86),* in which thin strips of loin, plunged into boiling stock, cook in seconds—too quickly to become stringy.

Even lean lamb will leave a trace of fat on the surface of a stew after simmering for an hour. This should be skimmed off with a spoon or paper towels before serving. And if you prepare a dish in advance and remove the fat when it has cooled and solidified, you degrease even more effectively—so thoroughly that you can afford to use such cuts as shoulder or neck. In the *navarin (page 72),* cubes of shoulder are partly cooked, then refrigerated for at least four hours, and the solid crust of surface fat is lifted off and discarded before the recipe is completed. Most recipes in this chapter can be adapted for traditional stewing lamb by following this chilling and degreasing procedure and extending the cooking time by an hour or so.

Moroccan Spiced Stew

SINCE MEDIEVAL TIMES, SPICED STEWS OF MEAT AND PRUNES HAVE BEEN POPULAR STAPLES OF THE NORTH AFRICAN DIET.

Serves 4
Working time: about 30 minutes
Total time: about 1 hour and 45 minutes

Calories **315**
Protein **36g.**
Cholesterol **80mg.**
Total fat **14g.**
Saturated fat **4g.**
Sodium **175mg.**

1 lb. lean lamb (from the leg), trimmed of fat and cut into 1-inch cubes
½ tsp. safflower oil
16-20 pearl onions, blanched and peeled
2 cups unsalted brown or chicken stock (recipes, page 137)
1 tbsp. honey
1 tsp. ground cinnamon
½ tsp. saffron threads
½ tsp. ground ginger
¼ tsp. ground nutmeg
½ orange, grated zest and juice
12 ready-to-eat pitted prunes
¼ cup blanched almonds
¼ tsp. salt
freshly ground black pepper

Heat the safflower oil in a nonstick frying pan over medium-high heat and sauté the onions until they are golden brown—approximately five minutes. Transfer them to a bowl and set them aside. Add the lamb cubes to the frying pan and cook them until they are browned all over—two to three minutes. Transfer them to a large, heavy-bottomed saucepan or flameproof casserole.

Pour off any fat from the frying pan, then add the stock and bring it to a boil, stirring with a wooden spoon to dislodge any browned bits from the bottom of the pan. Pour the boiling stock over the lamb. Add the honey, cinnamon, saffron, ginger, and nutmeg to the casserole, cover, and simmer for 30 minutes.

Add the onions, orange zest and juice to the lamb, and simmer for 30 minutes more. Finally, add the prunes, almonds, and salt, season with pepper, and simmer, uncovered, for 15 minutes.

SUGGESTED ACCOMPANIMENT: *couscous.*

EDITOR'S NOTE: *The prunes used in this recipe are sold for eating straight from the packet and do not require presoaking or pitting. If you use ordinary dried prunes, soak them in cold water for three hours and pit them before cooking.*

Braised Lamb with Mango

Serves 4
Working time: about 30 minutes
Total time: about 7 hours and 30 minutes
(includes marinating)

Calories **300**
Protein **45g.**
Cholesterol **75mg.**
Total fat **10g.**
Saturated fat **4g.**
Sodium **320mg.**

1 lb. lamb slices, cut from the sirloin end of the leg, trimmed of fat, and cut into 3-inch-long strips
1 cup plain low-fat yogurt
1 tsp. finely chopped fresh ginger
1 tbsp. ground coriander
1 tsp. ground cumin
2 tsp. safflower oil
1 onion, finely sliced
1 garlic clove, crushed
2 tsp. coriander seeds, crushed
1 tbsp. cornstarch
½ cup unsalted chicken stock (recipe, page 137)
1 bay leaf
⅛ tsp. powdered saffron
1 tsp. salt
2 mangoes
4 large cilantro leaves

Mix together the yogurt, ginger, ground coriander, and cumin, then stir in the strips of lamb, coating them in the mixture. Cover the meat and let it marinate in the refrigerator for at least six hours, or overnight.

In a heavy-bottomed, flameproof casserole, heat the oil, and stir in the onion and garlic. Cook them over low heat for one minute, then add the crushed coriander seeds and sauté until the seeds begin to pop. Mix the cornstarch with 1 tablespoon of the lamb marinade. Stir the cornstarch mixture into the rest of the marinade. Transfer the meat and its marinade to the casserole, and continue cooking over low heat for one minute. Add the stock, bay leaf, saffron, and salt. Cover the casserole and simmer the stew over low heat until the meat is tender—about one hour.

Peel the mangoes; cut two thin slices from one of them and reserve these for a garnish. Remove the pits and cut the flesh into ½-inch cubes. Add the mango cubes to the lamb and simmer the casserole over low heat for five minutes more.

Just before serving, coarsely chop the cilantro leaves and sprinkle them over the lamb. Serve it garnished with the reserved slices of mango.

SUGGESTED ACCOMPANIMENTS: *chapati; boiled rice.*

Lamb Dhansak

THE PARSEES, WHO MOVED FROM PERSIA TO SETTLE IN INDIA IN THE EIGHTH CENTURY AD, BROUGHT WITH THEM THE *DHANSAK*, A MILDLY SPICED STEW OF MEAT AND LENTILS.

Serves 4
Working time: about 50 minutes
Total time: about 10 hours (includes soaking)

Calories **285**
Protein **35g.**
Cholesterol **75mg.**
Total fat **8g.**
Saturated fat **4g.**
Sodium **340mg.**

1 lb. lean lamb (from the leg), trimmed of fat and cut into 1-inch cubes
1 large onion, finely chopped
2 tsp. ground coriander
2 tsp. ground cumin
1 tsp. ground cinnamon
1 tsp. ground cardamom
1 tsp. turmeric
1 tsp. black peppercorns
¾ cup plain low-fat yogurt
2 garlic cloves, crushed
2 fresh hot green chilies, finely chopped (cautionary note, page 83)
one 1-inch piece fresh ginger, finely chopped
1 cup mixed lentils, washed, soaked for 8 hours or overnight, drained
1 medium eggplant, trimmed and cut into 1-inch cubes
¼ medium butternut squash, peeled and cut into 1-inch cubes
2 medium tomatoes, finely chopped
5 oz. fresh spinach, thoroughly washed and torn into small pieces
½ tsp. salt
3 tbsp. finely chopped cilantro

Brush a flameproof casserole or heavy-bottomed saucepan with oil. Add the chopped onion and cook it over medium-high heat, stirring constantly, until it is soft—two to three minutes. Stir in the lamb cubes, ground coriander, cumin, cinnamon, cardamom, turmeric, and peppercorns, then add 1 tablespoon of the low-fat yogurt. Cook over high heat, turning the meat until the yogurt is completely absorbed—three to five minutes. Add the rest of the yogurt, 1 tablespoon at a time, stirring constantly after each addition, until all of it is absorbed.

Stir in the garlic, chilies, and ginger, and cook for one minute. Add the lentils, eggplant, squash, tomatoes, and spinach, and pour in just enough water to cover the ingredients. Bring the mixture to a boil, then reduce the heat to low, cover, and simmer until the lamb is tender—about one hour. Check the pan from time to time and add a little more water if the stew becomes dry. About 10 minutes before the end of cooking, add the salt and 2 tablespoons of the cilantro.

Lift out the meat and about half of the vegetable and lentil mixture with a slotted spoon, and set it aside. Using a potato masher, mash the lentil and vegetable mixture left in the pan, then reincorporate the meat and the rest of the lentil and vegetable mixture, and reheat it over low heat. Serve the stew garnished with the remaining tablespoon of cilantro.

SUGGESTED ACCOMPANIMENTS: *nan bread; basmati or other long-grain rice.*

EDITOR'S NOTE: *The mixture of lentils called for in this recipe can be varied; Asian food shops generally stock several varieties of lentils.*

Lamb with Puréed Asparagus and Jerusalem Artichokes

Serves 6
Working time: about 1 hour
Total time: about 2 hours and 30 minutes

Calories **225**
Protein **30g.**
Cholesterol **80mg.**
Total fat **9g.**
Saturated fat **4g.**
Sodium **270mg.**

1½ lb. lean lamb (from the leg or loin), trimmed of fat and cut into 3-inch strips
1 lb. asparagus, trimmed and peeled
1 tsp. salt
½ tbsp. safflower oil
3 shallots, peeled and halved
1 lb. Jerusalem artichokes or potatoes
4 tsp. fresh lemon juice
½ bunch watercress, washed, trimmed, blanched for 30 seconds, and chopped
ground white pepper
3 tbsp. sour cream

Cut off the tips of the asparagus spears and set them aside. Cook the stalks in boiling water to cover, with ½ teaspoon of the salt, until they are soft—approximately 15 minutes. Remove the stalks with a slotted spoon, drain them, and set them aside; strain and reserve the cooking liquid.

While the asparagus is cooking, heat the safflower oil in a frying pan, add the shallots, and cook them over medium heat until they are soft—about five minutes. Transfer the shallots to a flameproof casserole. Increase the heat under the frying pan and lightly brown the lamb strips in two batches, transferring each batch to the casserole. Pour the reserved asparagus cooking liquid over the meat and shallots. The liquid should cover the lamb; if necessary, add extra water. Simmer the casserole until the meat is tender—approximately one hour.

Meanwhile, cook the artichokes or potatoes. Put 1 teaspoon of the lemon juice into a nonreactive saucepan with 1 quart of water. Peel and chop the artichokes or potatoes, dropping them into the water immediately to prevent discoloration. Bring the water to a boil, and cook the artichokes or potatoes until they are tender—20 to 30 minutes. Drain the artichokes or potatoes, and purée them in a blender. Purée and sieve the asparagus stalks. Set the purées aside.

Skim off any fat from the casserole, and remove the meat and shallots. Bring the liquid in the casserole to a boil, add the asparagus tips, and cook them over low heat until they are just tender—about three minutes. Remove the asparagus tips with a slotted spoon and keep them warm.

Stir the asparagus and artichoke purées and the watercress into the cooking liquid to make a sauce. Heat the sauce on low and season it with the remaining lemon juice and salt and some white pepper. Return the meat to the sauce and heat it through. Add the asparagus tips and swirl the sour cream on top.

SUGGESTED ACCOMPANIMENT: *mixed wild and white rice.*

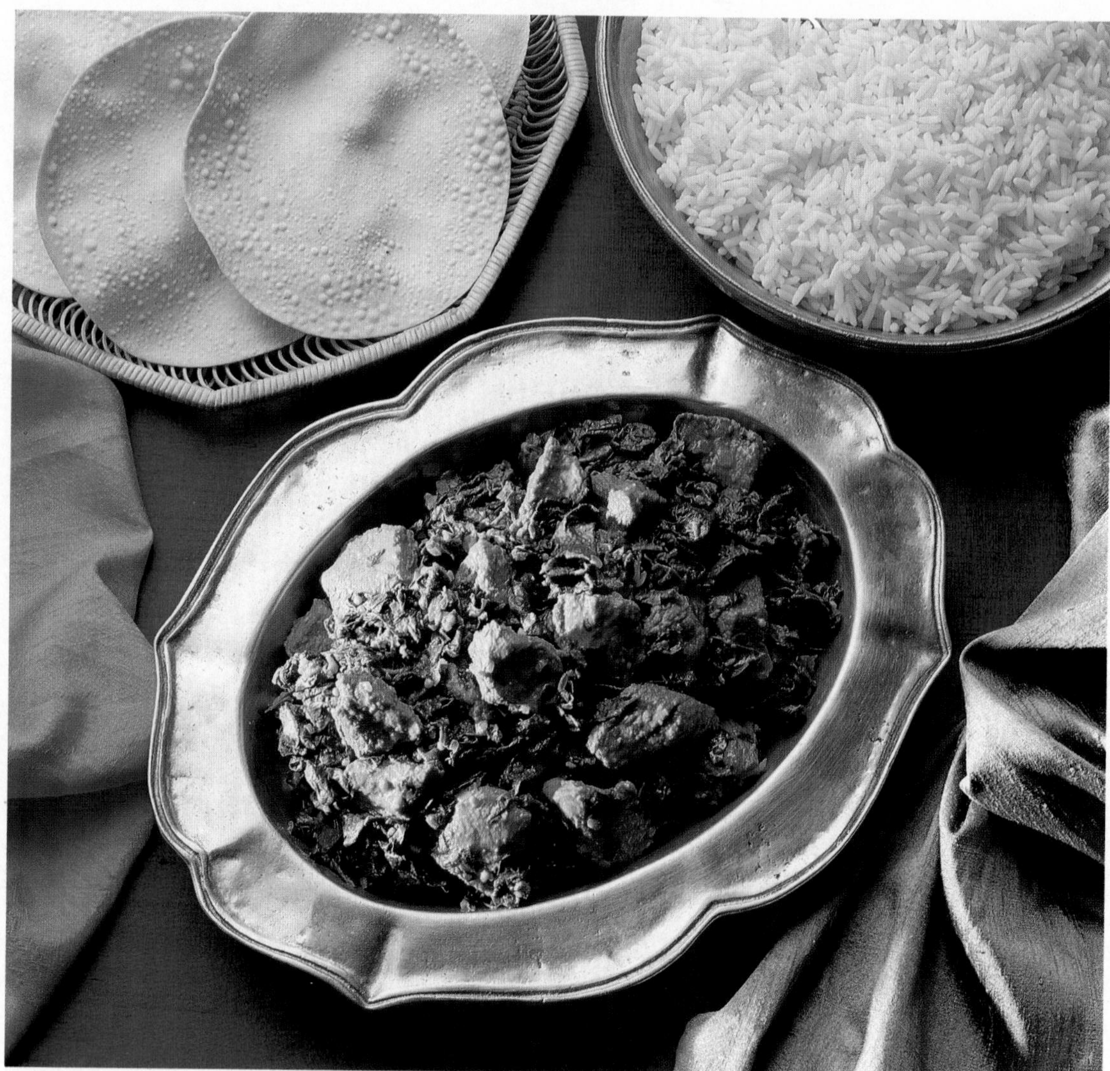

Indian Lamb with Spinach

Serves 6
Working time: about 50 minutes
Total time: about 2 hours

Calories **275**
Protein **37g.**
Cholesterol **75mg.**
Total fat **9g.**
Saturated fat **4g.**
Sodium **400mg.**

1 lb. lean lamb (from the leg), trimmed of fat and cut into 1-inch cubes
1 large onion, finely chopped
4 tsp. ground coriander
1 tbsp. mustard seeds
2 tsp. ground cumin
1 tsp. chili powder
1 tsp. turmeric
¾ cup plain low-fat yogurt
one 1-inch piece fresh ginger, finely chopped
3 garlic cloves, crushed
2 lb. fresh spinach, trimmed, thoroughly washed, and torn into small pieces
¼ tsp. salt

Brush a heavy, nonstick, flameproof casserole or saucepan with oil, add the onion, and cook it over medium-high heat, stirring constantly, until it is soft—two to three minutes. Stir in the lamb, coriander, mustard seeds, cumin, chili powder, and turmeric, and mix all the ingredients thoroughly together. Add 1 tablespoon of the yogurt and cook over high heat, stirring the meat constantly until all of the yogurt is absorbed—three to five minutes. Add the rest of the yogurt, 1 tablespoon at a time, stirring constantly after each addition, until it is completely absorbed.

Stir in the ginger and garlic, add just enough water to cover the meat, and bring to a boil. Cover the casserole, lower the heat, and simmer until the lamb is tender—about one hour.

When the meat is cooked, increase the heat to medium and add the spinach in batches, stirring each batch until it is wilted. When all the spinach is incorporated, cook the stew, uncovered, over high heat to evaporate any excess liquid—about five minutes. Add the salt just before serving.

SUGGESTED ACCOMPANIMENTS: *poppadoms; saffron rice; Indian chutney or relish.*

Lamb and Apple Casserole

Serves 4
Working time: about 30 minutes
Total time: about 2 hours and 25 minutes

Calories **430**
Protein **40g.**
Cholesterol **75mg.**
Total fat **10g.**
Saturated fat **5g.**
Sodium **290mg.**

1 lb. lean loin of lamb, cut into thin slices
3-4 medium potatoes (about 1½ lb.), peeled and very thinly sliced
2 tsp. finely chopped fresh sage, or ½ tsp. dried sage
1 orange, finely grated zest and juice
½ tsp. salt
freshly ground black pepper
3 sweet apples, peeled, cored, and sliced
1 large onion, sliced into very thin rings
½ cup apple cider or beer

Preheat the oven to 350° F. Arrange half of the potato slices in the bottom of a casserole. Sprinkle them with a little of the sage, orange zest, and salt, and plenty of black pepper. Cover the potatoes with half of the apple slices; season this layer in the same way.

Continue to build up the casserole in layers as follows, seasoning each layer with some of the sage, orange zest, salt, and some freshly ground black pepper. Arrange the slices of lamb evenly over the apple slices, and spread the onion rings over the lamb, leaving a small space uncovered in the center of the layer. Cover the onion rings with the remaining apples, and top the casserole with the remaining potatoes, maintaining the small gap in the center of both layers and overlapping the slices of potato on the top layer in neat concentric circles.

Mix the orange juice and cider or beer together, and pour the liquid slowly into the hole in the center of the potato topping. Cover and cook the casserole in the oven for one and a half hours, then remove the lid, and continue cooking until the ingredients feel tender when pierced with a fine skewer and the potato topping is golden brown—30 to 45 minutes. Serve hot, straight from the casserole.

SUGGESTED ACCOMPANIMENT: *steamed broccoli.*

Navarin with Mustard Croutons

THIS CLASSIC FRENCH STEW OF LAMB AND YOUNG VEGETABLES IS COOKED SEVERAL HOURS IN ADVANCE SO THAT ALL EXCESS FAT CAN RISE TO THE SURFACE AND THEN BE EASILY DISCARDED.

Serves 4
Working time: about 45 minutes
Total time: about 7 hours (includes chilling)

Calories **430**
Protein **35g.**
Cholesterol **75mg.**
Total fat **9g.**
Saturated fat **4g.**
Sodium **600mg.**

1 lb. lean stewing lamb, trimmed of fat and cut into ¾-inch cubes
1 tbsp. unbleached all-purpose flour
2½ cups unsalted brown or chicken stock (recipes, page 137)
1 onion, sliced
2 tbsp. tomato paste
2 fresh bay leaves
1 tsp. chopped fresh thyme, or ¼ tsp. dried thyme leaves
¼ tsp. salt
freshly ground black pepper
2 medium turnips, peeled
8 tiny new potatoes, scrubbed
2 medium zucchini
16 cherry tomatoes, peeled, or 4 small tomatoes, peeled and quartered
1 small loaf French bread (about 14 inches long)
2 garlic cloves
4 tsp. grainy mustard

Preheat the oven to 375° F. Toss the meat in the flour. Heat a flameproof casserole over high heat and add the meat, stirring until the cubes are seared on all sides. Stir in the stock, onion, tomato paste, bay leaves, thyme, salt, and some pepper. Bring the mixture to a boil. Cover the casserole, transfer it to the oven, and cook it for 50 minutes.

Cut the turnips into 1-inch pieces, then use a potato peeler to pare down their sharp edges, giving the pieces an attractive rounded shape. Add the turnips and potatoes to the casserole, and return it to the oven for 50 minutes more. Remove the casserole from the oven, allow the stew to cool, then transfer it to a bowl and refrigerate it until a layer of fat forms on the surface—four hours or overnight.

Preheat the oven to 375° F. Lift off and discard the layer of fat, remove the bay leaves, and transfer the lamb stew to a clean casserole. Prepare the zucchini in the same way as the turnips, and stir them into the casserole with the tomatoes. Cut the bread diagonally into ½-inch slices. Halve the cloves of garlic and rub their cut surfaces all over the bread. Spread one side of the bread slices with mustard and arrange them, mustard side up, around the edge of the casserole. Cook the *navarin,* uncovered, until it is heated through and the bread is crisp—about 25 minutes.

Meatballs with Lentils

Serves 6
Working time: about 45 minutes
Total time: about 1 hour and 30 minutes

Calories **280**
Protein **25g.**
Cholesterol **52mg.**
Total fat **8g.**
Saturated fat **3g.**
Sodium **205mg.**

1¼ lb. lean lamb (from the leg or loin), trimmed of fat and ground or very finely chopped (technique, page 43)
¼ cup dry breadcrumbs
2 tbsp. freshly grated Parmesan cheese
1 tbsp. chopped fresh rosemary, or 1 tsp. dried rosemary, crumbled
2 tsp. olive oil
1 turnip, chopped
1 onion, chopped
2 carrots, chopped
2 celery stalks, chopped
½ lb. fresh mushrooms, wiped clean and thinly sliced
4 garlic cloves, finely chopped
½ tsp. hot red-pepper flakes
1 cup lentils, picked over
⅛ tsp. salt
3 cups unsalted chicken stock (recipe, page 137)

Mix together the lamb, breadcrumbs, cheese, and rosemary. With your hands, form the mixture into 12 balls. Heat the oil in a large, nonstick or heavy-bottomed skillet set over high heat. Add the meatballs and brown them all over—four to five minutes. Remove the meatballs from the skillet with a slotted spoon and set them aside.

Add the turnip, onion, carrots, celery, mushrooms, garlic, and red-pepper flakes to the skillet. Reduce the heat to low and sauté the vegetables until they are soft—about eight minutes.

Increase the heat to medium high. Add the lentils, salt, and stock, and bring the liquid to a boil. Add the meatballs, cover the skillet with the lid ajar, and reduce the heat to low. Simmer the meatballs and lentils until the lentils are tender—about 45 minutes.

Serve the meatballs and lentils piping hot.

SUGGESTED ACCOMPANIMENT: *carrot and zucchini salad.*

Loin Chops with Lima Beans

Serves 4
Working time: about 15 minutes
Total time: about 30 minutes

Calories **340**
Protein **32g.**
Cholesterol **77mg.**
Total fat **11g.**
Saturated fat **4g.**
Sodium **255mg.**

4 lamb loin chops (about 5 oz. each), trimmed of fat
freshly ground black pepper
2 tsp. safflower oil
1 paper-thin slice of prosciutto or other dry-cured ham (about 1 oz.), cut into thin strips
1 onion, finely chopped
2 garlic cloves, finely chopped
14 oz. canned unsalted whole tomatoes, seeded and coarsely chopped, with their juice
2 tbsp. chopped fresh basil, or 2 tsp. dried basil
1 tsp. red wine vinegar
2 cups lima beans
⅛ tsp. salt

Season the loin chops with pepper. Heat the oil in a heavy-bottomed skillet set over medium-high heat. Add the chops and sear them on both sides—about one minute per side. Transfer the chops to a plate. Add the ham and onion to the skillet, lower the heat to medium, and cook the mixture, stirring frequently, until the onions have become translucent—approximately four minutes. Add the garlic and cook the mixture for one minute more.

Return the chops to the skillet, and then add the tomatoes and their juice, the basil, vinegar, lima beans, and salt; bring the mixture to a simmer. Partially cover the skillet, reduce the heat to low, and simmer the mixture until the chops are firm yet slightly springy to the touch—about 10 minutes. Serve at once.

SUGGESTED ACCOMPANIMENT: *orzo tossed with chives.*

Port Paupiettes

Serves 8
Working time: about 1 hour
Total time: about 2 hours

Calories **220**
Protein **27g.**
Cholesterol **75mg.**
Total fat **8g.**
Saturated fat **4g.**
Sodium **215mg.**

8 lamb slices (about 3 oz. each), cut from the sirloin end of the leg, trimmed of fat, and flattened (technique, page 24)
½ lb. lean lamb (from the leg or loin), trimmed of fat and ground or very finely chopped (technique, page 43)
4 oz. canned tomatoes, drained and seeded
2 tbsp. chopped fresh tarragon, or 2 tsp. dried tarragon
freshly ground black pepper
¾ tsp. salt
1 tsp. virgin olive oil
½ cup ruby port
1¼ cups unsalted brown stock (recipe, page 137)
6 black peppercorns
6 garlic cloves, unpeeled
1 tsp. arrowroot
2 tbsp. tomato paste

Mix together the ground or chopped lamb with the tomatoes, tarragon, some freshly ground black pepper, and ½ teaspoon of the salt. Distribute this mixture among the flattened slices of lamb and roll up each slice to form a paupiette. Secure each paupiette in several places with string.

Preheat the oven to 325° F. Heat the olive oil in a large, heavy-bottomed frying pan over medium heat until it is hot but not smoking. Sear the paupiettes, turning them until they are evenly browned. Remove the paupiettes from the pan and place them in a shallow casserole.

Increase the heat under the frying pan to high and pour in half of the port. Bring it to a boil and allow it to bubble for a minute, scraping loose any browned bits in the pan. Add the stock to the pan and bring the mixture to a boil. Pour it over the paupiettes. Add the peppercorns and garlic, cover the casserole, and cook in the oven until the lamb is completely tender when pierced with a thin skewer—about one hour.

Transfer the paupiettes to a cutting board, remove the string, and slice each paupiette into five pieces. Arrange the pieces in a heated serving dish and keep them warm while you make the sauce.

Strain the stock through a fine sieve into a saucepan, and discard the garlic and peppercorns. Add the remaining port, and boil the liquid over high heat until it is reduced by one-third and is slightly syrupy—about five minutes. Mix the arrowroot with 1 tablespoon of water and add it to the sauce. Continue boiling until the sauce clears—two to three minutes. Add the remaining ¼ teaspoon of salt, remove the sauce from the heat, and stir in the tomato paste. Serve the paupiettes immediately with the hot sauce.

SUGGESTED ACCOMPANIMENT: *steamed white cabbage with thyme and parsley.*

Old-Fashioned Lamb and Celery Stew

Serves 8
Working time: about 45 minutes
Total time: about 1 hour and 30 minutes

Calories **325**
Protein **33g.**
Cholesterol **90mg.**
Total fat **13g.**
Saturated fat **4g.**
Sodium **225mg.**

2 lb. lean lamb (from the leg or loin), trimmed of fat and cut into 1-inch cubes
2½ cups unsalted chicken stock or unsalted brown stock (recipes, page 137)
8 small onions, peeled
1 lb. mushrooms, wiped and trimmed
8 celery stalks, chopped
2 tbsp. cornstarch
2½ cups red wine
2 sprigs fresh rosemary
8 anchovy fillets, drained, dried on paper towels, and finely chopped
freshly ground black pepper
16 walnut halves, toasted

Heat a large, nonstick frying pan and quickly brown the cubes of meat on all sides. Transfer the meat to a flameproof casserole, add the stock, and simmer, covered, for 30 minutes.

Meanwhile, dry-fry the onions in the nonstick frying pan over medium heat for one minute. Add the mushrooms and chopped celery, and continue cooking, stirring frequently, until the vegetables are golden brown—three to four minutes.

Mix the cornstarch with a little of the red wine and stir this mixture into the casserole. Add the rest of the wine and bring the liquid to a boil, stirring all the time. Add the dry-fried vegetables, together with the rosemary, chopped anchovies, and some freshly ground black pepper, then cover the casserole and simmer the stew until the meat is tender—approximately 45 minutes. Stir in the walnuts five minutes before the end of the cooking time.

There should be just enough liquid left to cover the meat; if there is too much, transfer some of it to a saucepan set over high heat, reduce it, then return it to the casserole. Serve the stew hot.

SUGGESTED ACCOMPANIMENT: *baked potatoes.*

EDITOR'S NOTE: *To toast walnuts, place them on a baking sheet in a 350° F. oven for 10 minutes.*

Braised Steaks with Pumpkin Purée

Serves 4
Working time: about 30 minutes
Total time: about 2 hours and 15 minutes

Calories **370**
Protein **30g.**
Cholesterol **90mg.**
Total fat **13g.**
Saturated fat **5g.**
Sodium **370mg.**

4 boneless lamb steaks (about 4 oz. each), cut from the sirloin end of the leg, trimmed of fat
1 tsp. safflower oil
½ tsp. saffron threads
¼ tsp. salt
1¼ cups unsalted chicken stock (recipe, page 137)
2 lb. pumpkin or butternut squash, peeled and cut into 1½-inch cubes
4 sprigs fresh oregano
½ tsp. salt
ground white pepper
4 tbsp. sour cream, mixed with 1 tbsp. water
¼ cup walnuts, quartered and toasted, for garnish
fresh oregano leaves for garnish

Secure the steaks with short skewers to form neat rounds. Heat the safflower oil in a wide, heavy-bottomed frying pan over high heat and brown the steaks for about five minutes. Transfer the meat to a large, flameproof casserole.

Grind the saffron with the salt in a mortar and pestle. Bring the stock to a boil, dissolve the saffron and salt in the stock, and pour it over the meat in the casserole. Add the pumpkin or squash and the oregano sprigs to the casserole, and simmer, partly covered, over very low heat until the meat is tender—about one and three quarter hours. From time to time, remove any scum or fat that has risen to the surface.

Lift the steaks out of the casserole and remove the skewers; keep the steaks warm while you prepare the sauce. Discard the sprigs of oregano. Purée the pumpkin or squash with a little of the stock in a blender or a food processor, then blend in the remaining stock. Reheat the purée, and season it with the ½ teaspoon of salt and some white pepper. Spoon it onto four warm plates and place a steak in the center of each. Drop small spoonfuls of sour cream into the purée surrounding the meat and draw a pattern using the technique shown on page 118. Garnish with the walnuts and oregano leaves.

SUGGESTED ACCOMPANIMENT: *long-grain rice.*

EDITOR'S NOTE: *To toast walnuts, place them on a baking sheet in a 350° F. oven for 10 minutes.*

Mexican Lamb

IN THIS DISH, LAMB IS PAIRED WITH A VERSION OF THE MEXICAN MOLE POBLANO, A SPICY CONCOCTION FEATURING CHILI PEPPERS AND CHOCOLATE.

Serves 8
Working time: about 45 minutes
Total time: about 1 hour and 45 minutes

Calories **220**
Protein **24g.**
Cholesterol **75mg.**
Total fat **11g.**
Saturated fat **3g.**
Sodium **210mg.**

2½ lb. lean lamb (from the leg or loin), trimmed of fat and cut into ½-inch cubes

2 tbsp. olive oil

5 garlic cloves, finely chopped

1 jalapeño pepper, seeded, deribbed, and finely chopped (cautionary note, page 83)

1 tsp. cumin seeds

1 onion, cut into ½-inch cubes

1 green pepper, seeded, deribbed, and cut into ½-inch pieces

2 large ripe tomatoes, peeled, seeded, and cut into ½-inch pieces

1 cup unsalted brown stock or unsalted chicken stock (recipes, page 137)

½ tsp. salt

¼ tsp. grated nutmeg

1½ tbsp. unsweetened cocoa powder

Heat 1 tablespoon of the olive oil in a large, heavy-bottomed skillet set over high heat. Add half of the lamb cubes and sauté them until they are browned on all sides—five to seven minutes. With a slotted spoon, remove the cubes from the skillet and transfer them to a bowl. Return the skillet to the heat; pour in ½ tablespoon of the remaining oil and brown the rest of the lamb cubes. Set them aside also.

Add the remaining ½ tablespoon of oil to the skillet and return it to the heat. Add the garlic, jalapeño pepper, and cumin seeds, and cook the mixture until the garlic is lightly browned—about one minute. Add the onion, green pepper, tomatoes, stock, salt, and nutmeg, and bring the mixture to a simmer. Return the lamb cubes and their juices to the skillet, then stir in the cocoa powder. Reduce the heat to low and simmer the stew, stirring occasionally, until the meat is very tender and the sauce has thickened—about one hour. Remove the stew from the heat and let it stand for 10 minutes before serving.

SUGGESTED ACCOMPANIMENT: *corn tortillas.*

Lamb Shanks with Chickpeas

Serves 6
Working time: about 30 minutes
Total time: about 3 hours and 20 minutes
(includes soaking)

Calories **240**
Protein **25g.**
Cholesterol **52mg.**
Total fat **6g.**
Saturated fat **2g.**
Sodium **185mg.**

4 lamb shanks (about 3 lb.), trimmed of fat
½ lb. dried chickpeas, picked over
2 cups unsalted brown stock or unsalted chicken stock (recipes, page 137)
¼ tsp. salt
freshly ground black pepper
¾ tsp. ground coriander
1 onion, quartered
3 garlic cloves, thinly sliced
1 tbsp. tomato paste
1½ tsp. fresh thyme, or ½ tsp. dried thyme leaves
1 tbsp. fresh lemon juice

Rinse the chickpeas under cold running water, then put them into a large, heavy-bottomed pot, and pour in enough water to cover them by about 3 inches. Cover the pot, leaving the lid ajar, and slowly bring the liquid to a boil over medium-low heat. Boil the chickpeas for two minutes, then turn off the heat and soak them, covered, for at least one hour.

Place the lamb shanks in a large pot filled with 2 quarts of water. Bring the water to a boil and blanch the lamb for three minutes. Drain the lamb shanks, transfer them to a plate, and set the plate aside.

Drain the chickpeas and return them to the heavy-bottomed pot. Pour in 4 cups of water and the stock, and bring the liquid to a boil over high heat. Add the blanched lamb shanks and the salt, some pepper, and the coriander. Lower the heat to maintain a simmer, and cook the lamb and chickpeas for 45 minutes.

Add the onion, sliced garlic cloves, tomato paste, thyme, and fresh lemon juice to the lamb and chickpeas, and stir to combine them. Simmer the mixture until the lamb is very tender—one hour to one hour and 30 minutes.

With a slotted spoon, remove the lamb shanks from the pot and transfer them to a plate. Let them stand until they are cool enough to handle. Skim the fat from the surface of the chickpea mixture and keep the mixture warm. Remove the meat from the shank bones and cut it into ½-inch pieces; discard the bones. Return the lamb pieces to the pot.

This dish can be served immediately or prepared one day in advance. To reheat, add ½ cup of water to the mixture, bring it to a simmer over low heat, and cook it for 10 minutes.

SUGGESTED ACCOMPANIMENTS: *French bread; green salad.*

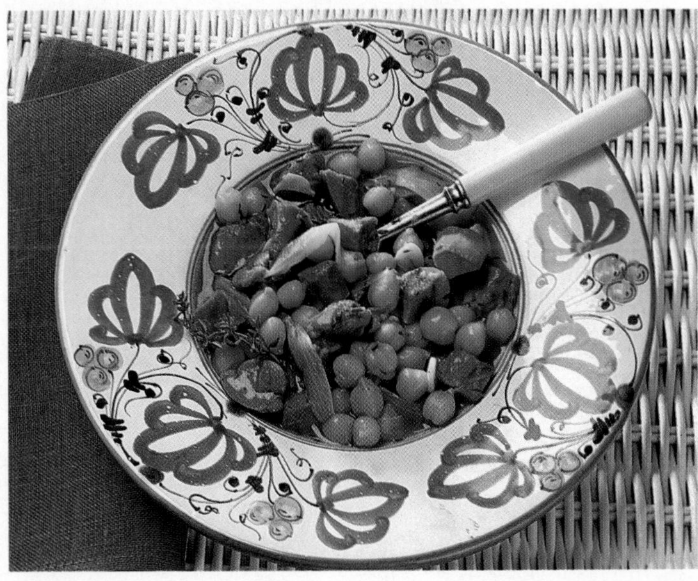

Scandinavian Casserole

SCANDINAVIANS TRADITIONALLY ENRICH THIS DILL-FLAVORED STEW WITH EGGS AND CREAM. IN THIS VERSION, A MIXTURE OF YOGURT AND SOUR CREAM ACHIEVES THE SAME EFFECT WITH LESS CHOLESTEROL AND FEWER CALORIES.

Serves 4
Working time: about 30 minutes
Total time: about 1 hour and 45 minutes

Calories **230**
Protein **30g.**
Cholesterol **75mg.**
Total fat **9g.**
Saturated fat **3g.**
Sodium **380mg.**

1 lb. lean lamb (from the leg or loin), trimmed of fat and cut into 1-inch cubes
¾ tsp. salt
1 small onion, peeled and quartered
2 sprigs fresh dill
1 bay leaf
4 black peppercorns
1 large fennel bulb (about 10 oz.), trimmed, sliced vertically
¼ lb. mushrooms, wiped and trimmed
2 tsp. cornstarch
1 tbsp. skim milk
½ lemon, grated zest and juice
1 tsp. sugar
¼ cup plain low-fat yogurt
¼ cup sour cream
1 tsp. mild German mustard
¼ cup chopped fresh dill
ground white pepper

Place the lamb in a flameproof casserole and cover it with cold water; add ¼ teaspoon of the salt. Bring the water to a boil over medium heat and skim off the scum that rises to the surface. Add the onion, dill, bay leaf, and peppercorns, then cover and simmer for 45 minutes. Add the fennel to the casserole and simmer for 15 minutes more. Stir in the mushrooms and continue simmering until the meat is very tender—about 15 minutes more. Lift the lamb, fennel, and mushrooms out of the casserole with a slotted spoon, and keep them warm while you make the sauce.

Strain the stock through a fine sieve into a 1-quart container. Rinse out the casserole and pour the strained stock back into it. The sauce requires 1¼ cups of stock: If you have more, then boil it rapidly to reduce it to that amount. Blend the cornstarch with the milk and add it to the stock, stirring well. Cook the stock over low heat until it thickens—about three minutes. Stir the lemon zest and juice and the sugar into the thickened stock.

Return the lamb and vegetables to the casserole, and heat them on low, uncovered, for five minutes. Remove the casserole from the heat. Blend the yogurt and sour cream with the mustard, chopped dill, some white pepper, and the remaining salt. Stir the seasoned yogurt into the casserole and serve immediately.

SUGGESTED ACCOMPANIMENTS: *peas and baby carrots.*

Lamb Shanks with Orange and Cinnamon

Serves 4
Working time: about 45 minutes
Total time: about 2 hours and 40 minutes

Calories **285**
Protein **20g.**
Cholesterol **52mg.**
Total fat **10g.**
Saturated fat **2g.**
Sodium **255mg.**

4 lamb shanks (about ¾ lb. each), trimmed of fat
⅓ cup all-purpose flour
freshly ground black pepper
2 tbsp. chopped fresh oregano, or 2 tsp. dried oregano
1½ tbsp. safflower oil
1 onion, chopped
2 garlic cloves, finely chopped
½ cup red wine
¼ cup fresh orange juice
¼ tsp. salt
1 bay leaf
1 cinnamon stick, or ¼ tsp. ground cinnamon
2 cups pearl onions (about 10 oz.), blanched for 2 minutes in boiling water and peeled
1 lb. carrots, cut crosswise into 2-inch-long pieces
1 tbsp. julienned orange zest
¼ cup finely chopped parsley

Put the flour, some pepper, and half of the oregano into a large plastic bag. Add the shanks and shake the bag to coat the meat with the mixture.

Heat the oil in a large, heavy-bottomed skillet over medium-high heat. Sauté the shanks in the skillet, turning them from time to time, until they have browned. Add the chopped onion, reduce the heat to low, and cover the skillet. Cook the lamb and onion for five minutes, stirring occasionally.

Increase the heat to medium high and add the garlic, wine, orange juice, and 3 cups of water. Bring the liquid to a simmer, scraping the bottom of the skillet with a wooden spoon to dissolve any caramelized juices. Add the salt, bay leaf, cinnamon, and the remaining oregano. Lower the heat, cover the skillet, and continue simmering the meat until it is barely tender—one and a half to two hours.

Skim any fat from the surface of the liquid; add the pearl onions, carrots, and orange zest. Simmer, partially covered, until the vegetables are tender—about 30 minutes. Skim off any more fat, stir in the parsley, and serve the lamb with the vegetables and the sauce.

SUGGESTED ACCOMPANIMENT: *rice.*

Braised Leg of Lamb with Mustard Seeds

Serves 8
Working time: about 40 minutes
Total time: about 3 hours

Calories **205**
Protein **20g.**
Cholesterol **56mg.**
Total fat **7g.**
Saturated fat **2g.**
Sodium **155mg.**

one 3-lb. leg of lamb, shank half, trimmed of fat
1 tbsp. olive oil
12 oz. dark beer
1 cup unsalted brown stock (recipe, page 137)
2 onions, quartered
3 garlic cloves
1 tsp. mustard seeds
½ tsp. celery seeds
¼ tsp. salt
freshly ground black pepper
4 bay leaves
3 whole cloves
1 small rutabaga (about 1 lb.), peeled and cut into 1-inch cubes
1 small green cabbage (about 2 lb.), quartered and cored, the leaves separated

Heat the oil in a large, heavy-bottomed casserole set over high heat. When the oil is hot, add the lamb and brown it on all sides—about 10 minutes in all. Pour in the beer and the stock, then add the onions, garlic, mustard seeds, celery seeds, salt, and some pepper. Tie up the bay leaves and cloves in a piece of cheesecloth, and add them to the casserole. Bring the liquid to a boil, then lower the heat to maintain a simmer.

Partly cover the casserole and braise the lamb for about one hour and 15 minutes, turning it two or three times during the cooking. Add the rutabaga cubes and continue braising the lamb until it is tender—approximately 30 minutes more.

While the rutabagas are cooking, pour enough water into a large pot to fill it about 1 inch deep. Set a vegetable steamer in the pot, add the cabbage, and cover the pot. Bring the water to a boil and steam the cabbage until it is tender—about 10 minutes.

Transfer the cabbage to a large platter and cover it loosely with aluminum foil. Remove the lamb from the casserole and set it on a cutting board. With a slotted spoon, transfer the rutabaga and onions to a bowl, and cover them with foil, too.

Remove the bundle of bay leaves and cloves from the casserole, and discard it. Reduce the sauce over high heat until only about 1 cup of it remains—approximately 10 minutes. Carve the leg of lamb and arrange the slices on the cabbage. Surround the lamb with the rutabaga and onions, then pour the sauce over all. Serve at once.

SUGGESTED ACCOMPANIMENT: *whole-wheat bread.*

Lamb Chili Verde

Serves 6
Working time: about 30 minutes
Total time: about 2 hours and 30 minutes (includes soaking)

Calories **360**
Protein **37g.**
Cholesterol **75mg.**
Total fat **12g.**
Saturated fat **5g.**
Sodium **185mg.**

1½ lb. lean lamb (from the leg or loin), trimmed of fat and cut into ½-inch cubes
1 cup dried pinto beans, picked over
1 tbsp. safflower oil
1 onion, finely chopped
¼ tsp. salt
freshly ground black pepper
2 garlic cloves, finely chopped
2 fresh hot green chili peppers, seeded and chopped (cautionary note, right)
4 medium green tomatoes, peeled, seeded, and coarsely chopped
1½ cups unsalted brown stock or unsalted chicken stock (recipes, page 137)
2 tbsp. dark brown sugar
½ tsp. cumin seeds
1 cucumber, peeled, seeded, and coarsely chopped
1 oz. cheddar cheese, grated (about 2 tbsp.)

Rinse the pinto beans under cold running water, then put them into a large, heavy-bottomed saucepan and pour in enough water to cover them by about 3 inches. Discard any beans that float to the surface. Cover the pan, leaving the lid ajar, and slowly bring the liquid to a boil over medium-low heat. Boil the beans for two minutes, then turn off the heat and soak the beans, covered, for at least one hour. (Alternatively, soak the beans in cold water overnight.)

Heat the oil in a large, heavy-bottomed saucepan over medium-high heat. Add the lamb cubes and sauté them until they are browned on all sides—about three minutes. Lower the heat to medium, and add the onion, the salt, and some pepper. Cook the mixture, stirring frequently, until the onion is translucent—about three minutes. Add the garlic and cook the mixture for one minute more. Drain the beans and add them to the pan. Stir in the chili peppers, all but 1 of the tomatoes, the stock, brown sugar, cumin seeds, and 2 cups of water. Bring the mixture to a simmer and cook it, covered, for one hour. Add the chopped cucumber and remaining tomato, and simmer for 15 minutes more, then remove the cover and continue simmering the chili until the beans are tender—approximately 15 minutes more.

Ladle the chili into 6 bowls and top it with the grated cheddar cheese.

SUGGESTED ACCOMPANIMENTS: *corn salad; crusty bread.*

Chilies—A Cautionary Note

Both dried and fresh hot chilies should be handled with care. Their flesh and seeds contain volatile oils that can make skin tingle and cause eyes to burn. Rubber gloves offer protection—but the cook should still be careful not to touch the face, lips, or eyes when working with chilies.

Soaking fresh chilies in cold, salted water for an hour will remove some of their fire. If canned chilies are substituted for fresh ones, they should be rinsed in cold water in order to eliminate as much of the brine used to preserve them as possible.

Red Pepper and Okra Lamb Stew

Serves 4
Working time: about 20 minutes
Total time: about 1 hour

Calories **380**
Protein **35g.**
Cholesterol **90mg.**
Total fat **13g.**
Saturated fat **4g.**
Sodium **125mg.**

1¼ lb. lean lamb (from the leg or loin), trimmed of fat and cut into 1-inch pieces
2 tbsp. unbleached all-purpose flour
2 tbsp. paprika
⅛ tsp. salt
freshly ground black pepper
1 tbsp. safflower oil
1 onion, finely chopped
1½ cups unsalted brown stock or unsalted chicken stock (recipes, page 137)
2 tsp. cider vinegar
1 tsp. Dijon mustard
8 drops hot red-pepper sauce
1 garlic clove, finely chopped
1 sweet red pepper, seeded, deribbed, and cut into 1-inch strips
8 medium okra, trimmed, sliced diagonally into ¾-inch pieces

Combine the flour and paprika in a large bowl. Season the lamb pieces with the salt and some freshly ground black pepper, then toss the lamb in the flour mixture. Remove the meat from the bowl, shaking off any excess flour, and set it aside.

Heat 2 teaspoons of the oil in a flameproof casserole over medium-high heat. Add the lamb and onion, and cook them, stirring continuously, until the onion is translucent and the meat is browned—two to three minutes. Stir in the stock, cider vinegar, Dijon mustard, hot red-pepper sauce, and garlic, and bring the mixture to a simmer. Reduce the heat to low and simmer the stew for 30 minutes.

Heat the remaining teaspoon of safflower oil in a nonstick frying pan set over medium-high heat, and stir-fry the pepper and okra for two minutes. Then transfer the vegetables to the flameproof casserole and simmer the stew until the meat is tender—20 to 30 minutes more.

SUGGESTED ACCOMPANIMENT: *boiled rice.*

Lamb Poached in Buttermilk

Serves 4
Working time: about 15 minutes
Total time: about 1 hour and 15 minutes

Calories **480**
Protein **34g.**
Cholesterol **78mg.**
Total fat **13g.**
Saturated fat **3g.**
Sodium **410mg.**

1¼ lb. lean lamb (from the leg or loin), trimmed of fat and cut into ¾-inch cubes
2 tsp. safflower oil
1 green pepper, seeded, deribbed, and cut into 1-inch squares
1 onion, cut into 1-inch cubes
¼ tsp. salt
ground white pepper
1 large carrot, cut into 1-inch pieces
2 tsp. caraway seeds
cayenne pepper
1½ cups unsalted chicken stock (recipe, page 137)
1 cup buttermilk
1½ tbsp. cornstarch
½ lb. dried egg noodles

Heat the oil in a large saucepan set over medium heat. Add the green pepper and onion, and cook them, stirring frequently, until the onion is translucent—about five minutes. Add the lamb, salt, some white pepper, the carrot pieces, the caraway seeds, a pinch of cayenne pepper, and the stock; bring the liquid to a simmer. Mix the buttermilk and cornstarch in a small bowl, then whisk them into the simmering liquid. Partly cover the saucepan and simmer the lamb until it is tender—about 45 minutes.

Add the noodles to 3 quarts of boiling water with 1½ teaspoons of salt. Start testing the noodles after six minutes and cook them until they are *al dente.* Drain the noodles and transfer them to a serving dish. Top the noodles with the lamb and serve at once.

SUGGESTED ACCOMPANIMENT: *zucchini cooked with shallots.*

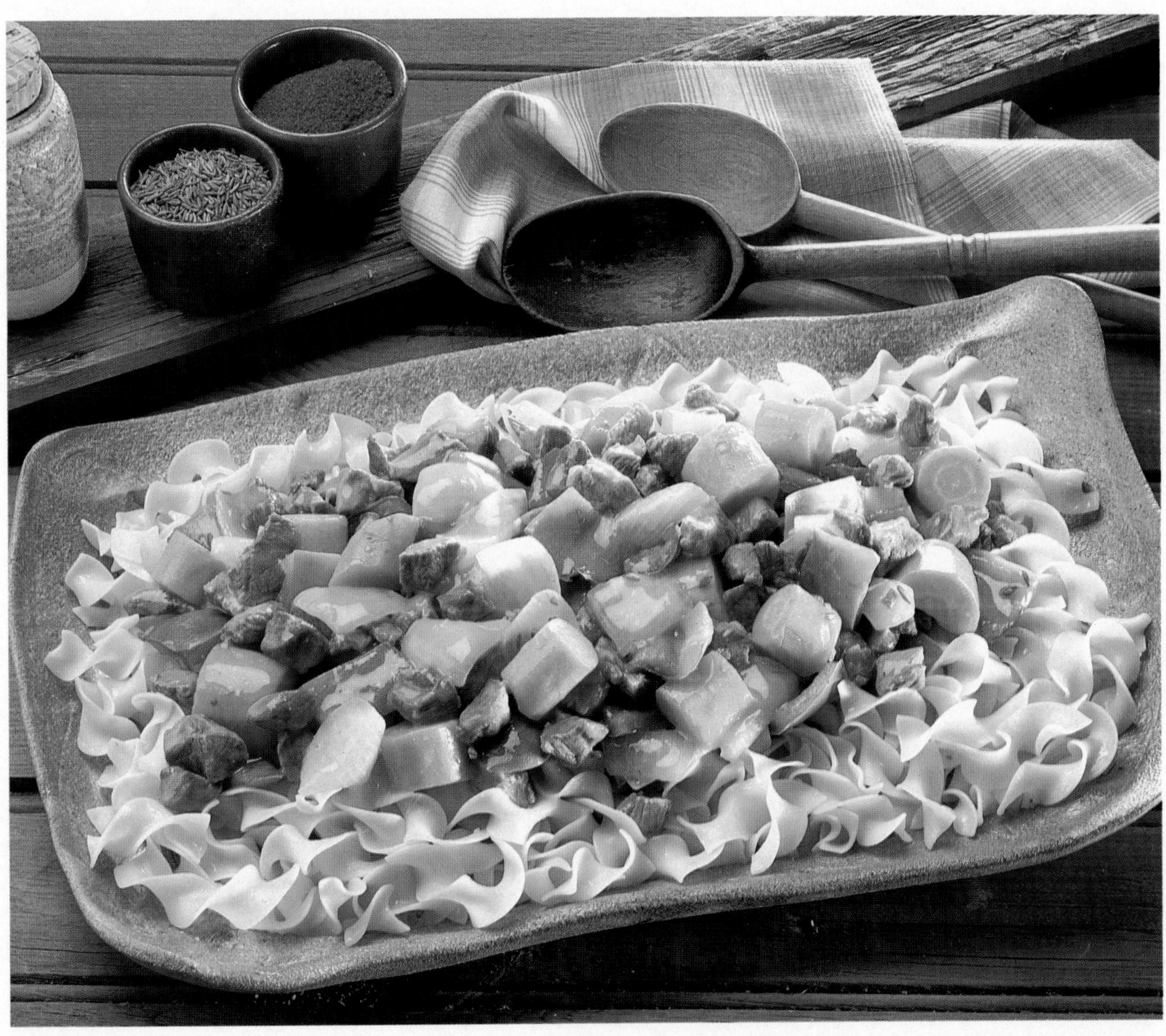

Mongolian Hot Pot

CENTRAL TO THIS ANCIENT ORIENTAL DISH IS THE "FIREPOT" OF BOILING BROTH, WHICH FIRST COOKS THE MEAT AND VEGETABLES AT THE TABLE AND THEN PROVIDES A NOURISHING SOUP.

Serves 4
Working time: about 1 hour
Total time: about 7 hours (includes chilling)

Calories **385**
Protein **38g.**
Cholesterol **75mg.**
Total fat **12g.**
Saturated fat **4g.**
Sodium **100mg.**

1 lb. lean lamb (from the loin), trimmed of fat
10 oz. firm tofu (bean curd), cut into strips about 1½ by ½ inches
½ lb. mushrooms, wiped and trimmed
½ lb. snow peas, stems and strings removed
2 medium sweet red peppers, seeded, deribbed, and cut into thin strips
¼ small head Nappa cabbage, shredded
5 oz. spinach leaves, stems removed, washed
3 scallions, trimmed and finely chopped
2 garlic cloves, peeled and crushed
one ½-inch piece fresh ginger, peeled and finely chopped
2 tbsp. chopped cilantro
¼ lb. rice noodles, broken into short lengths

Chicken and ginger broth

1½ lb. chicken pieces (about 3 inches each), on the bone, skin removed, trimmed of fat
one 2-inch piece fresh ginger, coarsely chopped
3 scallions, cut in half
6 sprigs cilantro
2 tbsp. rice wine or dry sherry

Dipping sauce

6 tbsp. low-sodium soy sauce
1½ tsp. dark brown sugar
3 scallions, trimmed and finely chopped
one ¾-inch piece fresh ginger, finely chopped
2 garlic cloves, peeled and crushed
hot red-pepper sauce

Prepare the broth at least seven hours in advance. Put the chicken into a large saucepan with the ginger, scallions, and cilantro. Pour in 2 quarts of cold water, bring it to a boil, then skim off the scum with a slotted spoon. Lower the heat, cover, and simmer gently for two hours. Remove the cooked chicken and reserve it for use in another recipe. Strain the broth into a bowl, allow it to cool, then chill it in the refrigerator for at least four hours, or overnight, until the fat forms a solid layer on the surface.

About one hour before serving, wrap the lamb in foil and place it in the freezer until it is semifrozen—50 minutes to one hour.

Meanwhile, make the dipping sauce. In a bowl, whisk together the soy sauce, sugar, scallions, ginger, and garlic, and set the mixture aside. Lift off and discard the surface fat on the chilled chicken broth, then heat the broth on low in a saucepan until it liquefies. Stir the rice wine or sherry into the broth. Dilute the dipping sauce with 4 tablespoons of the broth and add several drops of hot red-pepper sauce. Divide the sauce equally among four individual bowls.

Unwrap the lamb and cut it across the grain into paper-thin slices with a very sharp knife. Arrange the lamb, tofu, mushrooms, snow peas, peppers, Nappa cabbage, and spinach on a large platter. Lay chopsticks, a bowl of dipping sauce, and a soup bowl and soup spoon at each place setting.

Stir the scallions, garlic, ginger, and cilantro into the broth, and bring it to a boil. Fill a prepared firepot or metal fondue pot with the boiling broth, and place the pot in the center of the table. As the meal progresses, cook the lamb, tofu, and vegetables in the broth for 30 seconds to one minute. Scoop out each batch of cooked food with a wire mesh spoon and distribute it among the diners' soup bowls, to be dipped into the sauce. When all the lamb, tofu, and vegetables have been consumed, bring any remaining broth to a boil, pour it into the pot, and stir in the noodles. Cook them for two to three minutes to soften them, then ladle the broth and noodles into the soup bowls.

EDITOR'S NOTE: *Firepots, heated by charcoal, are available at Oriental groceries; they come complete with wire mesh spoons for lifting the ingredients out of the hot stock. A metal fondue set makes a perfect substitute.*

3 An herb sauce cloaks pancakes filled with a savory sauté of lamb, onions, and mushrooms (recipe, page 100); the ensemble will heat through in the oven.

Inspired Combinations

The many ways of preparing lamb do not end with simple dry and moist cooking. Lamb can be part of a salad, a stuffing, or a pie. It can be molded in aspic or wrapped in green leaves. This chapter explores a number of imaginative presentations for lamb in dishes devised or adapted for the health-conscious cook.

Lamb and vegetables combine to form a naturally happy marriage. Vegetables suitable for stuffing include such unusual varieties as acorn squash *(page 118)*, as well as the more common potatoes *(page 114)* and onions *(page 115)*. Baked assemblies of lamb and sliced vegetables include not only the familiar moussaka *(page 109)*, but loin chops layered with fennel and zucchini *(page 110)*.

Enclosing lamb in pasta or pastry is the basis for a number of other ideas. One of the most successful wrapping materials is phyllo dough—a low-fat, paper-thin pastry that provides the crispness of a crust with only a fraction of the calories found in shortcrust or chou-puff dough.

As befits a widely popular meat, many of the recipes have an exotic flavor. Marinated in the traditional five-spice seasoning of China, a leg of lamb acquires a distinctively Oriental appeal *(page 120)*. Sautéed with chili peppers and tomatoes, finely chopped lamb and beans fill a Mexican tortilla *(page 101)*. A *salade niçoise* using roast lamb *(page 90)* and a lasagna layered with lamb and sweet peppers *(page 102)* draw on Mediterranean traditions.

Whether stuffed with plum purée into Mongolian dumplings *(page 103)* or rolled up with mushrooms in pancakes *(left)*, ground lamb plays an important part in many of the recipes in this chapter. Ground lamb is not readily found, and when available, it is invariably fatty. In addition, butchers are not always willing to grind lean meat in the small quantities required. Chopping by hand, as shown on page 43, is a straightforward alternative technique. And by purchasing lean lamb, then trimming it of all excess fat and chopping it yourself, you can be assured of high quality.

Salade Niçoise

Serves 6
Working time: about 50 minutes
Total time: about 1 hour and 15 minutes

Calories **330**
Protein **31g.**
Cholesterol **75mg.**
Total fat **14g.**
Saturated fat **6g.**
Sodium **270mg.**

one 2¼-lb. loin of lamb, trimmed of fat
freshly ground black pepper
6-8 small new potatoes (about 1 lb.), scrubbed
½ lb. green beans
½ cucumber
3 tomatoes, cut into thin wedges
1 head Boston lettuce, washed and dried
3 anchovy fillets, rinsed, patted dry with paper towels, and chopped
6 black olives, pitted and halved

Herb vinaigrette

2 garlic cloves, crushed
1 tsp. Dijon mustard
¼ tsp. salt
½ lemon, juice only
2 tbsp. virgin olive oil
1 tbsp. chopped fresh parsley
1 tbsp. chopped fresh basil
½ tbsp. chopped fresh oregano

Preheat the oven to 450° F. Season the loin all over with black pepper, place it on a roasting pan, and cook it for 45 minutes to one hour for rare to medium meat. Allow it to cool at room temperature while you prepare the vegetables.

Boil the potatoes until they are tender—20 to 25 minutes—then drain them and let them cool. Cook the beans in boiling water until they are tender but still crisp—three to four minutes. Drain them and rinse them under cold water.

Peel the cucumber and cut it in half lengthwise. Scoop out the seeds, then slice the cucumber.

To make the herb vinaigrette, mix together the garlic, Dijon mustard, and salt in a small bowl, then whisk in the lemon juice and olive oil. Stir in the parsley, basil, and oregano.

Cut the loin off the bone and cut it into strips about 3 inches long by ½ inch wide. Put the strips of meat into a large bowl, add the vinaigrette, and stir to coat them thoroughly. Add the potatoes, beans, cucumber, and tomatoes, and toss all the ingredients.

Line a salad bowl with the lettuce leaves and transfer the tossed salad into it. Sprinkle the salad with the chopped anchovies and add the olives.

SUGGESTED ACCOMPANIMENT: *herb garlic bread.*

EDITOR'S NOTE: *This recipe is a good way of using lean leftover roast lamb.*

Roast Lamb and Pink Grapefruit Salad

Serves 8
Working time: about 35 minutes
Total time: about 2 hours and 50 minutes (includes cooling)

Calories **265**
Protein **30g.**
Cholesterol **75mg.**
Total fat **14g.**
Saturated fat **6g.**
Sodium **170mg.**

one 4½-lb. leg of lamb, trimmed of fat
2 pink grapefruit
1 tbsp. safflower oil
1 tbsp. Dijon mustard
1 tbsp. dry mustard
1 tbsp. honey
freshly ground black pepper
mixed salad leaves (such as radicchio, oak leaf, and red leaf), watercress, and scallions

Mustard-honey dressing

1 tsp. Dijon mustard
½ tsp. dry mustard
1 tsp. honey
½ tsp. salt
ground white pepper
1 tsp. wine vinegar
1 tbsp. safflower oil
1 tbsp. hazelnut oil

Preheat the oven to 450° F. Finely grate the zest of one grapefruit into a small mixing bowl. Add the safflower oil, the Dijon and dry mustard, and the honey. Mix the ingredients well; then spread the mustard paste all over the leg of lamb. Season the meat with freshly ground black pepper.

Put the lamb into a roasting pan and cook it for 15 minutes; lower the heat to 350° F. and continue to roast the lamb for one hour to one hour and 15 minutes for rare to medium-rare meat. Let the lamb rest at room temperature for at least one hour; if you are serving it much later in the day, chill the leg as soon as it has cooled to room temperature.

Remove the skin and white pith from both grapefruits. Holding each grapefruit over a bowl to catch the juice, carefully remove the segments by cutting between the flesh and the connecting tissue with a sharp knife. Keep the segments separate from the juice.

To make the dressing, whisk the mustards and honey with the salt, some white pepper, and the wine vinegar. Whisk in the oils and 4 tablespoons of the grapefruit juice. Toss the salad leaves in the dressing. Carve the meat and serve the slices alternated with the grapefruit segments, accompanied by the salad leaves.

SUGGESTED ACCOMPANIMENT: *French bread.*

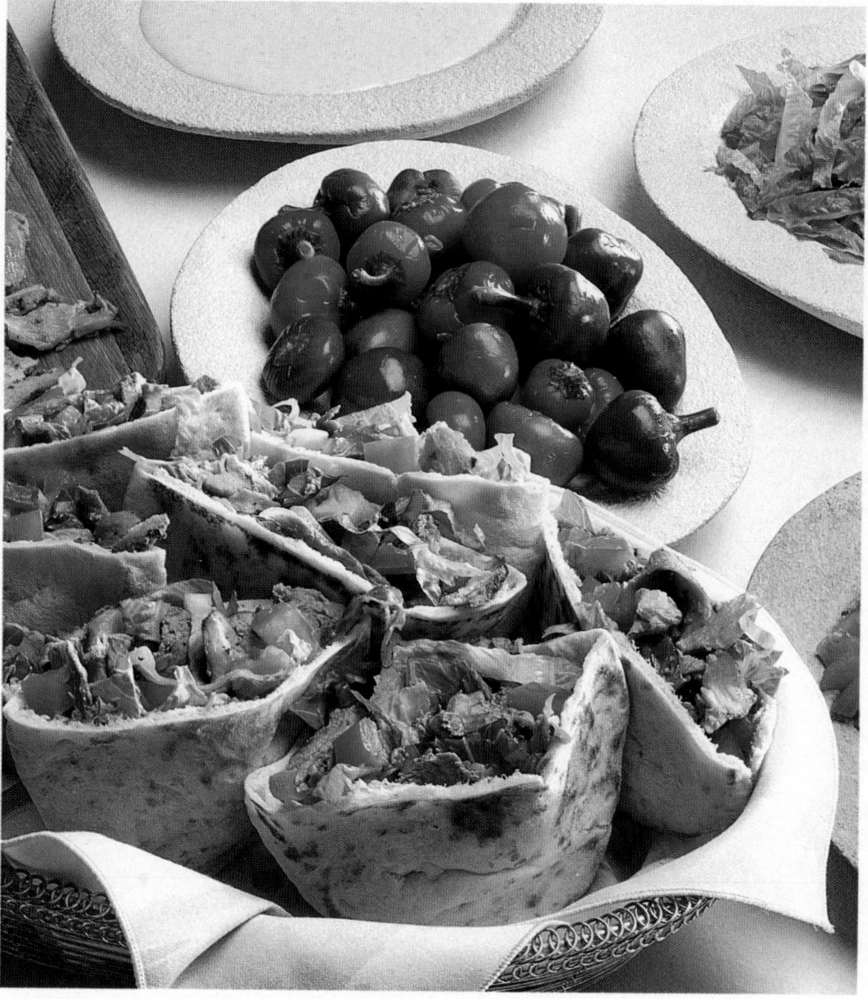

Gyros

TRADITIONAL FARE IN GREEK NEIGHBORHOODS, GYROS ARE MADE UP OF LAYERS OF MEAT AND HERBS. THE ACCOMPANYING TZATZIKI IS A YOGURT SAUCE SEASONED WITH CUCUMBER AND DILL.

Serves 12
Working time: about 45 minutes
Total time: about 2 hours (includes marinating)

Calories **360**
Protein **35g.**
Cholesterol **80mg.**
Total fat **10g.**
Saturated fat **3g.**
Sodium **330mg.**

one 2½-lb. boneless leg of lamb, trimmed of fat
1 lb. beef eye round, trimmed of fat
juice of 1 lemon
3 garlic cloves, finely chopped
3 tbsp. finely chopped fresh oregano, or 1 tbsp. dried oregano
½ tsp. ground coriander
½ tsp. salt
freshly ground black pepper
2 egg whites
½ tbsp. paprika, preferably Hungarian
1 tbsp. safflower oil
12 pita breads, cut in half
1 head of romaine lettuce, washed, dried, and shredded
3 large ripe tomatoes, chopped

Tzatziki

1 cup plain low-fat yogurt
1 cucumber, peeled, halved, and seeded
¼ cup loosely packed fresh dill, finely cut, or 3 tbsp. chopped fresh parsley mixed with 1 tbsp. dried dill
½ tsp. distilled white vinegar
⅛ tsp. salt

Cut the lamb against the grain into thin slices. Place the lamb slices between two sheets of plastic wrap or wax paper, and pound the meat with a mallet or the flat of a heavy knife *(page 24)* to a thickness of about ⅛ inch. Transfer the lamb slices to a bowl.

Cut the beef against the grain into slices about ¼ inch thick. Pound the slices as you did the lamb and transfer them to a second bowl.

In a small bowl, stir together the lemon juice, garlic, oregano, coriander, salt, and some pepper. Divide this mixture between the beef and lamb slices, and toss them in their separate bowls to distribute the seasonings evenly. In another small bowl, lightly beat the egg whites with the paprika.

To assemble the gyros, brush a slice of beef with some of the egg-white mixture and set the slice on a clean work surface. Top the beef with two slices of lamb and brush them with the egg-white mixture, too. Continue stacking and brushing the beef and lamb slices, ending with a slice of beef. Press down on the stack to compact it, forcing out any excess liquid. Insert a long metal skewer through the stack, slightly off center. Lay the stack on its side and thread a second skewer through the meat from the other end. Let the meat stand at room temperature for one to two hours before you grill it.

Purée the tzatziki ingredients in a food processor or a blender. Transfer the sauce to a bowl and chill it.

About 30 minutes before cooking time, light the coals in an outdoor grill. When the coals are hot, bank them against the sides of the grill. Place a foil drip pan in the center of the grate and set the rack in place. Brush the meat with the oil and lay it on the center of the rack. Grill the meat, turning it often to ensure that it cooks evenly—about 30 minutes for medium meat, or until an instant-reading meat thermometer inserted in the center registers 150° F.

Remove the meat from the grill and let it stand for 10 minutes before removing the skewers. With a very sharp knife, cut the meat lengthwise into thin slices. Fill the pita pockets with the meat, lettuce, tomato, and tzatziki sauce. Serve immediately.

SUGGESTED ACCOMPANIMENT: *pickled hot peppers.*

Mediterranean Lamb Salad

Serves 4
Working time: about 35 minutes
Total time: about 2 hours and 15 minutes

Calories **280**
Protein **32g.**
Cholesterol **96mg.**
Total fat **13g.**
Saturated fat **5g.**
Sodium **350mg.**

4 lamb shanks (about 3 lb.), trimmed of fat
¼ tsp. salt
freshly ground black pepper
1 tbsp. olive oil
1 large onion (about ½ lb.), thinly sliced
2 garlic cloves, finely chopped
2 tsp. fresh thyme, or ½ tsp. dried thyme leaves
¾ tsp. dry mustard
⅓ cup cider vinegar
1 head of escarole (about 1 lb.), trimmed, washed, dried, and cut crosswise into 1-inch-wide strips
1 large ripe tomato, cored and cut into thin wedges
1½ oz. feta cheese

Preheat the oven to 350° F. Sprinkle the lamb shanks with the salt and a generous grinding of pepper. Place the shanks in a heavy-bottomed roasting pan and bake them until they are tender—one hour and 30 minutes to two hours—turning them once after one hour and adding ¼ cup of water to the pan if the juices begin to burn. Remove the lamb from the oven and set it aside to cool; do not wash the roasting pan.

When the meat is cool enough to handle, pull it off the bones and tear it into shreds with your fingers. Transfer the meat to a bowl, cover it loosely with aluminum foil, and keep it warm.

Spoon off any fat that has accumulated in the roasting pan and set the pan over medium-low heat. Stir in the oil, onion, garlic, thyme, mustard, and a generous grinding of pepper. Cook the mixture, scraping up the caramelized juices with a wooden spoon, until the onion becomes translucent—10 to 15 minutes. Pour in the vinegar and continue cooking the mixture, stirring constantly, for one minute. Add the escarole and the tomato wedges, and keep stirring the salad until the escarole begins to wilt—approximately one minute. Stir in the shredded lamb and toss well.

Transfer the salad to a serving bowl. Crumble the cheese on top and serve the salad while it is still warm.

SUGGESTED ACCOMPANIMENT: *Italian bread.*

Aspic Mold with Summer Vegetables

TO MAKE A CLEAR VEGETABLE ASPIC, THE BOWLS AND COOKING UTENSILS MUST BE SCRUPULOUSLY CLEAN. HERE, EVERYTHING IS SCALDED TO ENSURE THAT THE LIQUID DOES NOT BECOME CLOUDED BY IMPURITIES.

Serves 6
Working time: about 2 hours
Total time: about 15 hours and 30 minutes
(includes chilling and setting)

Calories **320**
Protein **33g.**
Cholesterol **75mg.**
Total fat **12g.**
Saturated fat **3g.**
Sodium **270mg.**

2 lb. lean lamb on the bone, cut from the sirloin end of the leg
1½ tsp. salt
1 leek, white part only, sliced and washed
1 small onion, sliced
1 carrot, sliced
1 parsnip, sliced
1 bay leaf
2 sprigs parsley
8 black peppercorns
6 young carrots, trimmed, or 3 medium carrots, trimmed and split lengthwise
3½ oz. young green beans, ends removed
6 tbsp. (6 envelopes) powdered gelatin
4 eggs, whites and shells only
¼ cup Madeira
1 tbsp. fresh chervil leaves
1 tbsp. capers, rinsed
curly endive or lettuce for garnish

Place the lamb in a large, nonreactive saucepan and cover it with cold water. Bring the water to a boil, then lower the heat and simmer the lamb for three minutes. Transfer the lamb to a colander standing in the sink, drain off the water, and rinse the lamb with boiling water. Rinse the saucepan.

Return the lamb to the saucepan, and add the salt, leek, onion, carrot, parsnip, bay leaf, parsley, and black peppercorns. Pour in just enough cold water to cover the lamb and the vegetables. Bring the liquid to a boil over medium heat, skimming off any scum that rises to the surface. Partially cover the saucepan, reduce the heat to low, and simmer the lamb until a thin skewer inserted in the center of the meat easily penetrates to the bone—two to two and a half hours. Remove the saucepan from the heat. Allow the lamb to cool in the liquid to room temperature—one and a half to two hours—then chill it for at least six hours, or overnight.

Remove and discard the layer of fat from the surface of the chilled stock, together with any pieces of fat adhering to the lamb. Strain the stock into a clean bowl; discard the vegetables.

Cook the small whole carrots in a little of the skimmed stock until they are tender—about 10 minutes—then remove them with a slotted spoon. Cook the beans in the same stock for about five minutes; remove them with a slotted spoon and set them aside. Return the stock to the bowl.

Put a large piece of cheesecloth, a wire balloon whisk, and a large metal sieve into a saucepan. Fill the saucepan with cold water and bring it to a boil to scald the contents and the saucepan. Pour the boiling water into a mixing bowl, to scald that also, then discard the water. Wring out the cheesecloth. Line the sieve with the cheesecloth and place it over the mixing bowl.

Measure the stock; you should have about 2 quarts. If not, make up the quantity with chicken stock or water. Pour the stock into the scalded saucepan, then add the gelatin, egg whites, egg shells, and Madeira. Set the saucepan over medium heat and bring the mixture to a boil, stirring with the balloon whisk until a thick foam forms on the surface. Stop stirring and allow the liquid to boil until the foam rises to the top of the saucepan. Immediately remove the saucepan from the heat and allow the foam to settle back down in the saucepan. Repeat this process twice, without stirring, then remove the saucepan from the heat and allow it to stand for 10 minutes. Carefully pour the liquid into the cheesecloth-lined sieve, without allowing the foam to break up. When the liquid has completely drained through the cheesecloth, discard the foam. Allow the strained aspic jelly to stand until it is cool but not set—about one hour.

Meanwhile, prepare the lamb. Cut the meat from the bone, following muscle divisions where possible. Remove any remaining fat and tendons. Slice each piece of meat across the grain into thin medallions, about ½ inch thick and 2 inches long.

Pour a thin layer of the cold aspic into the bottom of a 6-cup rectangular loaf pan. Refrigerate until the aspic sets—about five minutes. Remove the pan from the refrigerator. Dip the chervil leaves in the liquid aspic, then arrange them decoratively over the set aspic. Refrigerate the pan for two to three minutes to set the leaves in position, then pour in just enough aspic to cover them. Refrigerate for five minutes more.

Select one-third of the most attractive, even-size medallions of lamb and arrange them neatly over the set aspic in the mold. Pour in just enough aspic to cover the lamb, then refrigerate the pan for 10 minutes.

Arrange the carrots and the capers over the lamb. Cover them with a little more aspic and refrigerate the pan for 10 minutes to set. Continue building up the mold with two more layers: half of the remaining slices of lamb topped with the beans. Cover each layer with a little of the aspic and chill it for 10 minutes before proceeding. Finally, arrange the remaining lamb over the set beans and cover the lamb with a final layer of aspic. Refrigerate the mold until it is very firmly set—at least four hours.

To unmold the aspic, loosen the top edges carefully with a thin-bladed knife and invert the mold onto a flat serving dish. Soak a dishtowel in very hot water, wring it out, and wrap it around the outside of the mold. Repeat the soaking and wrapping until you can lift the pan off after freeing the mold with a gentle shake. Garnish with a few endive or lettuce leaves.

SUGGESTED ACCOMPANIMENTS: *potato salad; green salad.*

EDITOR'S NOTE: *Any remaining aspic can be allowed to set, and then chopped for garnish around the mold. Aspic may be made up to two or three days in advance and kept in the refrigerator until needed. Once set, it can be quickly melted by placing the bowl over a saucepan of hot water.*

Phyllo-Wrapped Chops with Quince

Serves 8
Working time: about 1 hour and 15 minutes
Total time: about 2 hours

Calories **240**
Protein **14g.**
Cholesterol **60mg.**
Total fat **11g.**
Saturated fat **5g.**
Sodium **185mg.**

8 rib chops (about 3 oz. each), trimmed of fat
freshly ground black pepper
7 oz. fresh chestnuts, shelled and peeled
1¼ cups unsalted brown or chicken stock (recipes, page 137)
1 cinnamon stick
¾ tsp. salt
10 oz. fresh quinces or firm apples
1 tbsp. sugar
1 tsp. fresh lemon juice
2 tbsp. quince preserves or apple jelly
1 tbsp. honey
1 tsp. ground cinnamon
2 tbsp. unsalted butter
1 tbsp. virgin olive oil
16 sheets phyllo pastry, each 12 by 7 inches

Sprinkle the chops generously with black pepper, and leave them at room temperature while you prepare the chestnuts and quinces or apples.

Put the chestnuts into a saucepan with the stock and half the cinnamon stick. Cover the pan, bring the stock to a boil, and boil until the chestnuts are tender—20 to 30 minutes—adding water if necessary. Remove the cooked chestnuts, discard the cinnamon, and rapidly boil the remaining stock until only about 4 tablespoons of liquid remain. Press the chestnuts through a sieve or grind them into fine crumbs in a food processor, then stir in enough of the reduced stock to make a thick purée. Season the purée with ¼ teaspoon of the salt and set it aside to cool.

Peel, quarter, and core the quinces or apples, retaining the trimmings. Cut the flesh lengthwise into ¼-inch-thick slices. Put the fruit and trimmings into a nonreactive saucepan, together with the sugar, fresh lemon juice, and remaining half stick of cinnamon. Cover with water and simmer over low heat until the quinces or apples are completely tender—10 to 30 minutes for the quinces, two to three minutes if you are using apples. Lift out the pieces of cooked fruit and put them on a plate; discard the trimmings and cooking liquid. Finely dice any pieces of fruit in the quince preserves, then warm the preserves or jelly, if you are using it, over low heat, and spoon it over the slices of cooked fruit. Set the glazed fruit aside.

Preheat the broiler and brush the broiler pan lightly with olive oil. Arrange the chops in the pan and spread half of the honey over their upper surfaces. Broil them until the honey begins to caramelize—about one minute—then turn the chops, spread the remaining honey over the uncooked sides, and broil them for one minute more. Allow the chops to cool for 10 minutes.

Preheat the oven to 375° F. and lightly oil a baking sheet. Season the chops on both sides with the remaining salt and some more black pepper. Spread the chestnut purée on top of the chops and cover them with the slices of quince or apple. Sprinkle the prepared chops with the ground cinnamon.

Melt the butter with the olive oil. Take a sheet of phyllo pastry and lay it out flat on a work surface with a short side nearest you. Brush it with a little of the butter mixture, then place another sheet of phyllo pastry on top. Cover the remaining sheets of phyllo with a damp cloth or plastic wrap to prevent them from becoming brittle.

Position one of the prepared chops on the doubled sheet of pastry, angling it so that the rib bone protrudes 1 inch beyond the lower left-hand corner. Fold the lower right-hand corner of the pastry over the chop, then fold over the right-hand side of the pastry, partially covering the chop. Carefully roll the chop up in the pastry to enclose it completely. Trim off any excess pastry to ensure that the seams are underneath. Pinch the pastry tightly around the protruding bone.

Wrap up the remaining chops in the same way and place them seam side down on a greased baking sheet. Brush the pastry with the remaining oil and butter mixture, and bake the packages until they are golden brown—12 to 15 minutes. Allow them to rest at room temperature for five minutes before serving.

SUGGESTED ACCOMPANIMENT: *green beans.*

EDITOR'S NOTE: *To shell and peel chestnuts, slit the shells down the rounded side and parboil them for one to two minutes. Remove the shell and peel while the chestnuts are still hot.*

Lamb and Zucchini Pie

Serves 6
Working time: about 1 hour
Total time: about 2 hours and 25 minutes

Calories **240**
Protein **21g.**
Cholesterol **75mg.**
Total fat **12g.**
Saturated fat **4g.**
Sodium **220mg.**

1 lb. lean lamb (from the sirloin end of the leg), trimmed of fat and cut into ¼-inch dice
1 tbsp. virgin olive oil
1 large onion, finely chopped
2 garlic cloves, crushed
3 medium carrots, peeled and cut into ¼-inch dice
2 medium zucchini, cut into ¼-inch dice
¼ cup unbleached all-purpose flour
1 cup unsalted brown or chicken stock (recipes, page 137)
1 tsp. mixed dried herbs
½ tsp. salt
freshly ground black pepper
5 sheets phyllo pastry, about 18 by 12 inches
2 tbsp. polyunsaturated margarine, melted

Heat the oil in a large, heavy-bottomed sauté pan over medium heat. Add the onion, garlic, and carrots. Reduce the heat to low, and cook until the vegetables are soft but not brown—10 to 15 minutes. Increase the heat to high, then add the diced lamb. Cook, stirring with a wooden spoon to keep the pieces of meat separated, until the lamb changes color—one to two minutes. Add the zucchini, then stir in the flour, stock, mixed herbs, salt, and some pepper. Bring to a boil, stirring. Reduce the heat to low, cover the pan, and simmer until the zucchini are soft—8 to 10 minutes. Remove the pan from the heat and allow the lamb mixture to cool for about 45 minutes.

Preheat the oven to 425° F. Pour the lamb mixture into an 8-inch pie plate.

Cut four of the phyllo sheets in half widthwise. Brush the edge of the pie plate with a little cold water, then cover the meat mixture with a half phyllo sheet, brush the phyllo with a little of the melted margarine, then cover it with another half sheet of phyllo. Repeat with the remaining six half sheets. Using scissors, cut the pastry to fit the dish exactly.

Fold the remaining sheet of phyllo into quarters, trim the edges, then cut it lengthwise into two strips and cut these into diamond shapes. Brush the top of the pie with the melted margarine, then decorate it with the phyllo diamonds, brushing them individually with margarine so that they stay in place. Make a small hole in the center of the pie to allow the steam to escape during cooking.

Place the pie on a baking sheet and cook it in the oven until the pastry is golden—35 to 40 minutes.

SUGGESTED ACCOMPANIMENTS: *green salad; steamed new potatoes tossed in parsley.*

Spinach and Lamb Strudel

Serves 4
Working time: about 30 minutes
Total time: about 1 hour and 15 minutes

Calories **200**
Protein **23g.**
Cholesterol **70mg.**
Total fat **7g.**
Saturated fat **3g.**
Sodium **235mg.**

10 oz. lean lamb (from the leg or loin), trimmed of fat and finely chopped
½ lb. fresh spinach, washed and stemmed
½ lb. mushrooms, finely chopped
1 onion, finely chopped
⅓ cup fine whole-wheat breadcrumbs
2 garlic cloves, crushed
¼ tsp. salt
freshly ground black pepper
2 sheets phyllo pastry, about 18 by 12 inches
½ tsp. safflower oil
1 tsp. sesame seeds
cherry tomatoes for garnish

Preheat the oven to 375° F.

Set aside four spinach leaves for garnish, then plunge the rest into a saucepan of boiling water, bring the water back to a boil, and cook for one minute. Drain the spinach in a colander and rinse under cold water, then squeeze it dry and chop it finely.

Brush a nonstick frying pan with oil, heat it over high heat, then sear the lamb quickly. Remove the pan from the heat, and stir in the spinach, mushrooms, onion, breadcrumbs, garlic, salt, and some pepper. Mix all the ingredients thoroughly together.

Lay one sheet of the phyllo pastry on a work surface and cover it with the second sheet. Spoon the lamb filling along one short side of the pastry, keeping it 1 inch away from the edge. Shape the filling into a firm sausage with your fingers. Roll up the pastry and transfer it to a baking sheet, seam side down. Squeeze the ends together lightly to keep the filling from falling out. Brush the strudel with the safflower oil and sprinkle it with the sesame seeds. Bake it until the pastry is golden—about 40 minutes. Allow it to cool for five minutes before cutting it into eight slices.

Serve garnished with the reserved spinach leaves and cherry tomatoes.

SUGGESTED ACCOMPANIMENT: *tomato and basil salad.*

Phyllo-Wrapped Lamb Medallions

A MEDALLION IS A SMALL OVAL OR ROUND SLICE OF MEAT.

Serves 4
Working time: about 25 minutes
Total time: about 45 minutes

Calories **325**
Protein **28g.**
Cholesterol **78mg.**
Total fat **12g.**
Saturated fat **4g.**
Sodium **320mg.**

one 2½-lb. lamb loin roast, trimmed of fat and boned (technique, page 134)
1 ripe pear
2 tsp. safflower oil
¼ tsp. salt
freshly ground black pepper
2 tsp. finely chopped fresh ginger
½ cup port or Madeira
1 tsp. red wine vinegar
½ cup unsalted brown stock or unsalted chicken stock (recipes, page 137)
4 sheets phyllo pastry, about 18 by 12 inches
1 egg white, lightly beaten
4 sprigs parsley, for garnish (optional)

Peel the pear. (If you like, julienne some of the skin for a garnish and set it aside.) Halve and core the pear, then thinly slice one half, and set the slices aside. Chop the remaining half and set it aside, too.

Slice the lamb into four pieces. Place the pieces between two sheets of plastic wrap or wax paper; with a meat mallet or the flat of a heavy knife, pound the pieces as shown on page 24 to a thickness of about ½ inch. Heat the oil in a large, nonstick skillet over medium-high heat. Add the lamb medallions and sear them for one minute on each side. Remove the medallions from the skillet, and season them with ⅛ teaspoon of the salt and some pepper; set the medallions aside.

Add the ginger, wine, vinegar, and chopped pear to the skillet. Lower the heat and simmer the liquid until it is reduced by half—about seven minutes. Add the stock, the remaining salt, and some pepper, and return the liquid to a simmer. Transfer the sauce to a food processor or a blender, and purée it. Keep the sauce warm while you prepare the phyllo packages.

Preheat the oven to 425° F.

Fold one of the phyllo sheets in half. Pat a lamb medallion dry with a paper towel and position the medallion in the center of the folded phyllo sheet. Arrange one-fourth of the pear slices on top, then fold the phyllo over the meat and fruit. Brush the seams with some of the beaten egg white. Put the phyllo package seam side down on a baking sheet. Brush the top with more egg white. Wrap the remaining lamb medallions and pear slices the same way.

Bake the packages for eight minutes for medium-rare lamb. Divide the sauce among individual plates and set a phyllo package on each plate. Garnish each serving, if you like, with a sprig of parsley and some julienned pear skin.

SUGGESTED ACCOMPANIMENTS: *Brussels sprouts; rice.*

Ground Lamb Pancakes with Herb Sauce

Serves 6
Working time: about 1 hour and 15 minutes
Total time: about 1 hour and 25 minutes

Calories **345**
Protein **26g.**
Cholesterol **85mg.**
Total fat **13g.**
Saturated fat **4g.**
Sodium **270mg.**

1 lb. lean lamb (from the leg), trimmed of fat and ground or very finely chopped (technique, page 43)
1 cup plus 2 tbsp. unbleached all-purpose flour
3/8 tsp. salt
1 egg
1 1/4 cups beer
1 tbsp. olive oil
1 onion, finely chopped
1/4 lb. mushrooms, chopped
6 tbsp. unsalted chicken stock (recipe, page 137)
freshly ground black pepper
2 tbsp. finely sliced scallion for garnish
2 tbsp. finely cut fresh chives for garnish

Herb sauce

2 cups skim milk
1 small onion, peeled
1 bay leaf
1/8 tsp. ground mace
1 sprig parsley
6 black peppercorns
2 tbsp. polyunsaturated margarine
1/4 cup unbleached all-purpose flour
2 tbsp. mixed fresh herbs, or 2 tsp. mixed dried herbs
1/8 tsp. salt
freshly grated nutmeg
freshly ground black pepper

First, make the pancake batter. Sift 1 cup of the flour with 1/8 teaspoon of the salt into a mixing bowl and make a well in the center. Break the egg into the center of the flour, then gradually whisk the egg into the flour. Add the beer a little at a time, beating well after each addition, until the batter is smooth. Cover the bowl, and allow the batter to stand while you make the sauce and the filling.

To prepare the herb sauce, put the skim milk into a heavy-bottomed saucepan, and add the onion, bay leaf, ground mace, parsley sprig, and peppercorns. Scald the milk over medium heat, then remove it from the heat. Cover the saucepan and let the milk infuse for at least 30 minutes.

Meanwhile, make the lamb filling. Heat half of the olive oil in a large, heavy-bottomed frying pan over medium heat. Add the onion, and cook until it is soft but not brown—five to six minutes. Increase the heat to high and add the lamb. Cook the lamb until it changes color—three to four minutes—breaking it up with a wooden spoon as it cooks. Stir in the remaining 2 tablespoons of flour and 1/4 teaspoon of salt, then add the mushrooms, stock, and some black pepper. Bring the mixture to a boil, then lower the heat and simmer, uncovered, for six to eight minutes. Remove the pan from the heat, cover it, and allow the filling to cool while you make the pancakes.

To make the pancakes, heat the remaining 1/2 tablespoon of olive oil in a 6-inch nonstick frying pan or crepe pan set over medium heat. When the oil is hot, pour it out of the pan into a small mixing bowl, leaving just a thin film behind to cover the bottom of the pan. Stir the pancake batter, then ladle just enough batter into the pan to cover the bottom, quickly swirling it over the bottom as you pour it in. As soon as the bottom of the pan is covered with pancake batter, pour the excess batter back into the bowl. Trim off and discard the trail of batter. Cook the pancake until the underside is golden brown—approximately one minute—then turn it over and cook the other side for one minute more. Transfer the pancake to a small plate and cover it with a paper towel. Make 11 more pancakes in the same way.

Preheat the oven to 425° F. Lay the pancakes flat on a work surface and divide the lamb filling among them. Roll each pancake around the filling. Place the filled pancakes in a large, ovenproof dish, or put two per person in individual gratin dishes.

To complete the sauce, strain the milk through a sieve into a bowl; discard the contents of the sieve. Rinse the saucepan. Melt the margarine in the saucepan over medium heat, stir in the flour, and then gradually add the milk. Bring the sauce to a boil, stirring continuously until it thickens. Stir in the mixed herbs and salt, then season with some freshly grated nutmeg and black pepper. Reduce the heat to low and simmer the sauce for two to three minutes.

Pour the herb sauce over and around the pancakes. Cook, uncovered, in the oven until the pancakes are heated through—approximately 10 minutes. Sprinkle them evenly with the scallion and chives, and serve them immediately.

SUGGESTED ACCOMPANIMENT: *mixed green salad.*

Chili Lamb Tortillas

Serves 4
Working time: about 50 minutes
Total time: about 3 hours and 30 minutes (includes soaking)

Calories **385**
Protein **28g.**
Cholesterol **40mg.**
Total fat **12g.**
Saturated fat **4g.**
Sodium **240mg.**

½ lb. lean lamb (from the loin), trimmed of fat and finely chopped
¾ cup dried pinto beans, picked over
1 tbsp. safflower oil
2 onions, chopped
1 sweet red pepper, seeded, deribbed, and chopped
1 garlic clove, chopped
3 tomatoes, peeled, seeded, and chopped
1 green chili pepper, seeded and chopped (cautionary note, page 83)
2 tbsp. tomato paste
½ cup unsalted brown stock (recipe, page 137)
¼ tsp. salt
freshly ground black pepper

Tortilla dough

¾ cup unbleached all-purpose flour
⅛ tsp. salt
1 tbsp. vegetable shortening

Rinse the beans under cold running water, then put them into a heavy-bottomed pan and pour in enough cold water to cover them by about 3 inches. Discard any beans that float to the surface. Cover the pan, leaving the lid ajar, and slowly bring the liquid to a boil. Boil the beans for two minutes, then turn off the heat and soak the beans, covered, for at least one hour. (Alternatively, soak the beans overnight in cold water.)

Discard the soaking liquid and rinse the beans. Pour in enough cold water to cover them by about 3 inches. Boil the beans for 10 minutes, then lower the heat and simmer them until they are tender—one to two hours. Drain the beans and rinse them under cold water.

To make the tortillas, sift the flour and salt into a bowl, and rub in the shortening until the mixture resembles fine breadcrumbs. Add 3 to 4 tablespoons of warm water, enough to form a stiff dough, and mix well. Turn out the dough onto a floured surface and knead until it is smooth—about two minutes. Divide the dough into four equal pieces, form each quarter into a ball with your hands, and roll it out on a lightly floured surface to a 7-inch circle.

Heat a heavy-bottomed frying pan, and cook a tortilla over high heat until its surface bubbles and the underside begins to brown—about 30 seconds. Turn it over and cook the other side until it is pale brown—about 30 seconds more. Remove the tortilla from the pan, and immediately place it over an inverted aluminum or ceramic custard cup so that it will cool and harden in a cupped shape. Cook and shape the remaining tortillas; remove them from the custard cups when they are cool.

To make the chili, heat the oil in a sauté pan over medium heat. Add the lamb and sear it by stirring it until it changes color. Lower the heat, add the onions, red pepper, and garlic, and sauté them until the onions soften—about five minutes. Add the tomatoes, chili pepper, tomato paste, and stock; season with the salt and some black pepper. Cover the pan and cook for 10 minutes. Then stir in the beans and heat them through. Keep the chili warm.

Meanwhile, preheat the oven to 350° F. Fit the tortillas over the cups again and heat them in the oven for 10 minutes. Place the hot tortillas on a serving dish, fill them with the lamb chili, and serve immediately.

SUGGESTED ACCOMPANIMENT: *tomato and avocado salad.*

EDITOR'S NOTE: *Lean ground lamb may be used instead of chopped lamb.*

Sweet Pepper and Lamb Lasagna

Serves 6
Working time: about 45 minutes
Total time: about 1 hour and 45 minutes

Calories **315**
Protein **25g.**
Cholesterol **50mg.**
Total fat **10g.**
Saturated fat **4g.**
Sodium **290mg.**

12 oz. lean lamb (from the leg), trimmed of fat and ground or very finely chopped (technique, page 43)
1 onion, chopped
1 garlic clove, chopped
2 celery stalks, chopped
2 tbsp. tomato paste
½ cup red wine
½ cup unsalted brown or chicken stock (recipes, page 137)
1 bay leaf
½ tsp. salt
freshly ground black pepper
9 lasagna strips
2 tbsp. polyunsaturated margarine
¼ cup unbleached all-purpose flour
1¼ cups skim milk
1 oz. Parmesan cheese, grated (about ¼ cup)
ground white pepper

Sweet-pepper sauce

3 sweet peppers (1 each green, red, and yellow), seeded and sliced
3 medium tomatoes, peeled, seeded, and very finely chopped
2 garlic cloves, crushed
1 tsp. chopped fresh thyme, or ¼ tsp. dried thyme leaves
1 tsp. chopped fresh oregano, or ¼ tsp. dried oregano
½ tbsp. cornstarch

Heat a heavy-bottomed, nonstick sauté pan over medium heat and cook the lamb, stirring, until the meat is seared and separated—three to four minutes. Add the onion and continue stirring until it is soft—about three minutes. Add the garlic, celery, tomato paste, wine, stock, and bay leaf; season with the salt and some freshly ground black pepper. Cover and cook over low heat for 30 minutes.

Meanwhile, make the sweet-pepper sauce. Put the peppers, chopped tomatoes, garlic cloves, thyme, and oregano into a saucepan, cover, and simmer for 15 minutes. Then blend the cornstarch with 2 tablespoons of water, add it to the pepper mixture, and stir until the sauce thickens—one to two minutes. Set the pepper sauce aside.

While the sauce is simmering, bring 3 quarts of water to a boil with 1½ teaspoons of salt. Add the lasagna and boil for seven minutes—the pasta will be slightly undercooked. Drain the pasta and spread it on a dishtowel to dry. Preheat the oven to 375° F.

When the meat mixture is cooked, arrange three strips of lasagna in the bottom of a 12-by-8-inch baking dish. Spread the pepper sauce evenly over the lasagna, then make a second layer of pasta with three more strips of lasagna. Cover this with the lamb mixture and arrange the remaining lasagna on top.

To make a gratin topping, melt the margarine in a saucepan over medium heat. Add the flour and stir for one minute, then gradually add the milk, stirring continuously, and cook for three minutes. Stir in half of the grated Parmesan and season with some white pepper.

Pour the topping evenly over the lasagna. Sprinkle it with the remaining Parmesan and bake until the topping is golden brown—40 to 45 minutes.

SUGGESTED ACCOMPANIMENT: *green salad.*

Mongolian Stuffed Dumplings

Serves 4
Working time: about 1 hour and 15 minutes
Total time: about 2 hours

Calories **390**
Protein **24g.**
Cholesterol **100mg.**
Total fat **8g.**
Saturated fat **3g.**
Sodium **220mg.**

½ lb. lean lamb (from the leg or loin), trimmed of fat and ground or very finely chopped (technique, page 43)
1 tsp. ground allspice, plus a little for garnish
½ tsp. salt
freshly ground black pepper
4 ripe purple plums, pitted
1 tbsp. light brown sugar
1½ tsp. fruit vinegar
½ cup sour cream

Dumpling dough

2 cups unbleached all-purpose flour
⅛ tsp. salt
1 egg, beaten

First, make the dumpling dough. Sift the flour and salt into a mixing bowl, and form a well in the center. Pour the beaten egg and 5 tablespoons of cold water into the well, and gradually incorporate the flour into the liquid to form a stiff dough. You may need an additional tablespoon of water; add just enough to make a ball of dough that is pliable but not crumbly. Knead the dough on a floured surface until it stretches when pulled apart—about 10 minutes. Cover the dough and let it rest in a cool place for 30 minutes.

In a mixing bowl, beat the teaspoon of allspice, the salt, and some black pepper into the lamb. Knead it well and set it aside.

Reserve two of the plums. Simmer the other two, covered, with the sugar and 1 tablespoon of water in a heavy-bottomed, nonreactive saucepan until the fruit is tender and the skins soft—15 to 20 minutes. Purée the cooked plums in a blender or a food processor with the stewing juice and the vinegar. Beat two-thirds of the plum purée into the lamb and set the remainder aside for the sauce.

Divide the dumpling dough in half. Form each piece of dough into a ball. Roll out one ball to a thickness of about 1⁄16 inch on a lightly floured surface. Using a 3-inch circular plain cookie cutter, cut out 12 circles. Repeat the procedure with the second ball of dough. Spoon a little of the lamb filling onto the center of a dough circle. Dampen the edges of the dough, pull them up, and press them firmly together, forming a semicircular dumpling with a scalloped top. Fill and seal all the dough circles in the same way.

Pour enough water into a saucepan to fill it 1 inch deep. Set a steamer over the pan and bring the water to a boil. Brush the bottom of the steamer lightly with oil and add the dumplings, leaving a little space around each one. Cover and steam them for 15 minutes.

While the dumplings are steaming, prepare the dressings. Finely dice the reserved plums, then heat them through on low with the reserved plum purée in a nonreactive saucepan. Heat the sour cream in a bowl set over a saucepan of gently simmering water. Season it with black pepper.

Serve the stuffed dumplings piping hot in heated bowls, dressed with a spoonful each of warm sour cream and hot plum sauce and a light sprinkling of ground allspice.

SUGGESTED ACCOMPANIMENT: *a salad of Belgian endive and watercress.*

Bulgur Layered with Lamb and Fruit

Serves 6
Working time: about 30 minutes
Total time: about 1 hour and 45 minutes

Calories **350**
Protein **30g.**
Cholesterol **75mg.**
Total fat **13g.**
Saturated fat **4g.**
Sodium **335mg.**

1¼ lb. thin lamb slices, (from the sirloin end of the leg), trimmed of fat and flattened into cutlets ⅛ inch thick (technique, page 24)
1 tsp. olive oil
1 small onion, peeled and sliced
1 tsp. salt
freshly ground black pepper
⅓ cup dried apricots, thoroughly rinsed
1 tsp. ground cinnamon
½ tsp. ground coriander
1 cup bulgur
2 tbsp. finely chopped fresh mint
6 tbsp. raisins
⅓ cup fresh or dried dates, pitted and halved

Heat the oil in a large, heavy-bottomed frying pan until it is hot but not smoking. Cook the lamb slices until they are browned—about 30 seconds on each side—and transfer them to a flameproof casserole or saucepan. Lower the heat, put the onion in the frying pan, and cook it, stirring, until it softens—two to three minutes. Season the lamb slices with ½ teaspoon of the salt and some pepper, then add the onion to the casserole, together with the apricots, cinnamon, and coriander. Cover the contents of the casserole with boiling water and simmer until the ingredients are tender—about one hour.

While the meat is cooking, soak the bulgur in twice its volume of cold water for 30 minutes. Strain off any residual liquid, add the mint and the remaining ½ teaspoon of salt to the bulgur, and stir well.

Add the raisins and dates to the casserole, and allow them to warm through—two to three minutes. Strain the stock from the casserole through a sieve into a saucepan. Boil it rapidly until only about ½ cup of liquid remains, then pour the reduced stock back over the meat and fruit.

Layer the soaked bulgur and the lamb mixture in a 1½-quart casserole, beginning and ending with a layer of bulgur. Place a fourfold layer of cheesecloth over the top of the bulgur and seal the top of the casserole with aluminum foil. Put the casserole on a trivet inside a larger pot and pour boiling water into the outer pot to a depth of about 2 inches. Cover the outer pot and steam over low heat for about 30 minutes. Remove the foil and cheesecloth, and serve the dish hot, straight from the casserole.

SUGGESTED ACCOMPANIMENT: *lightly steamed leaf spinach.*

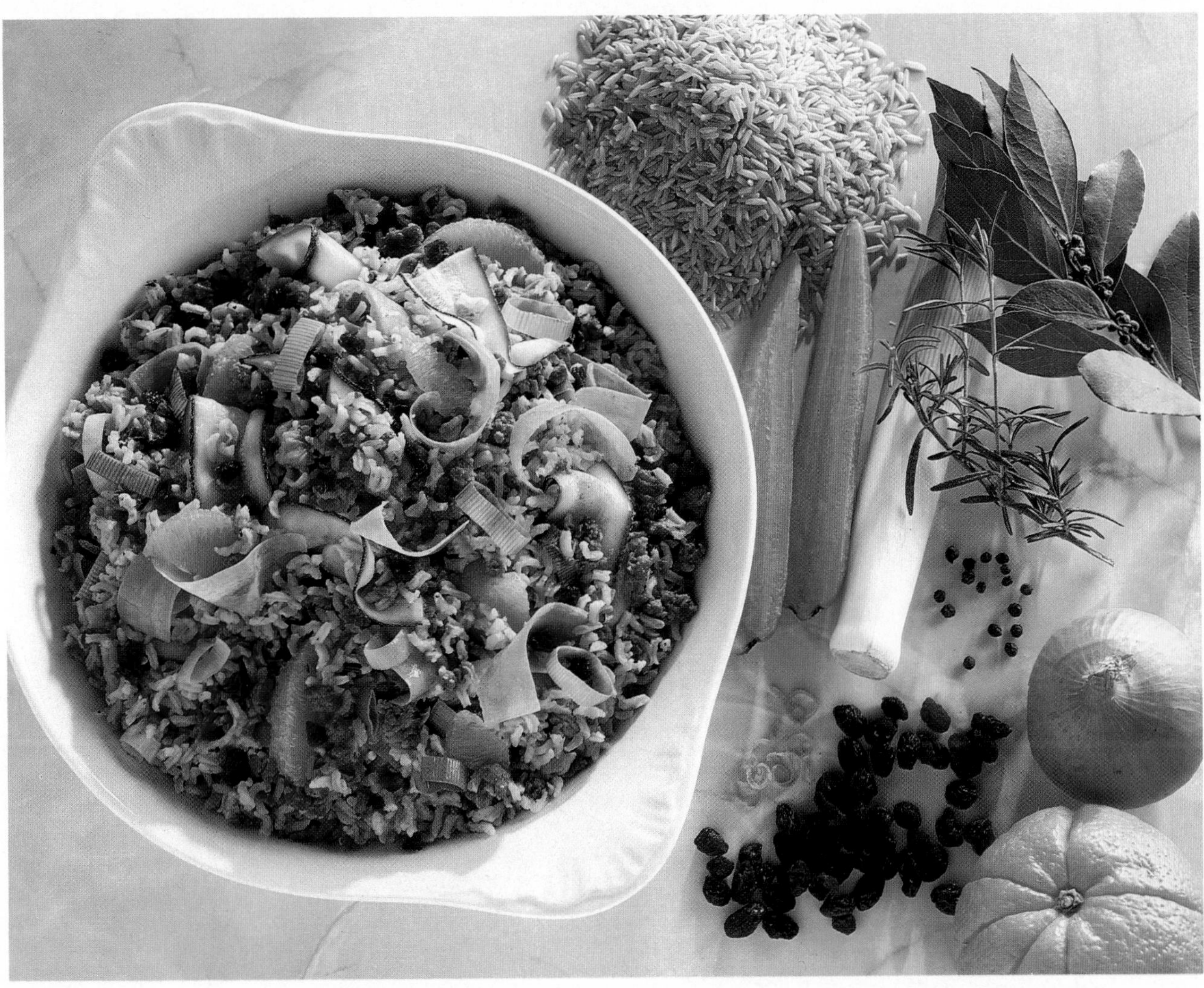

Lamb and Orange Pilaf

Serves 4
Working time: about 30 minutes
Total time: about 1 hour and 25 minutes

Calories **385**
Protein **16g.**
Cholesterol **55mg.**
Total fat **8g.**
Saturated fat **3g.**
Sodium **205mg.**

¾ lb. lean lamb (from the leg or loin), trimmed of fat and finely chopped (technique, page 43)
1 tsp. safflower oil
1 onion, chopped
1 large leek, trimmed, washed, and sliced
1 cup long-grain brown rice
2 cups unsalted brown or chicken stock (recipes, page 137)
1 tsp. chopped fresh rosemary, or ½ tsp. dried rosemary
¼ tsp. salt
freshly ground black pepper
1 orange, zest grated and flesh cut into segments
2 carrots, peeled
1 medium zucchini, trimmed
3 tbsp. raisins

Preheat the oven to 350° F. Heat the safflower oil in a flameproof casserole over high heat. Add the lamb and sear it quickly on all sides. Stir in the onion, leek, and brown rice, and cook them for one minute. Add the stock, rosemary, salt, some black pepper, and the orange zest. Bring the mixture to a boil, then cover the casserole, transfer it to the oven, and bake the pilaf until the rice is almost tender and the liquid virtually absorbed—approximately 40 minutes.

Using a potato peeler, shred the carrots and zucchini into long strips. Reserve a few carrot strips for garnish and stir the remainder into the lamb mixture along with the zucchini strips and the raisins. Return the casserole to the oven and cook, covered, until the rice and carrots are tender—about 20 minutes. Stir in the orange segments and garnish with the reserved carrot ribbons just before serving.

Kibbeh with Coriander Sauce

THE MANY VARIATIONS ON THIS LEBANESE DISH ARE ALL MADE WITH A SPICED CRUST OF BULGUR AND MINCED LAMB.

Serves 4
Working time: about 40 minutes
Total time: about 1 hour and 25 minutes

Calories **335**
Protein **38g.**
Cholesterol **75mg.**
Total fat **14g.**
Saturated fat **5g.**
Sodium **390mg.**

6 oz. lean lamb (from the leg or loin), trimmed of fat and ground or very finely chopped (technique, page 43)
½ cup bulgur
1 onion, quartered
¼ bunch parsley
2 garlic cloves, 1 coarsely chopped, 1 crushed
½ tsp. ground cinnamon
½ tsp. ground allspice
½ tsp. salt
freshly ground black pepper
½ cup plain low-fat yogurt
1 tsp. fresh lemon juice
½ tsp. ground coriander
cilantro sprigs for garnish

Lamb and pine-nut filling

6 oz. lean lamb (from the leg or loin), trimmed of fat and ground or very finely chopped (technique, page 43)
1 tsp. olive oil
1 onion, chopped
1 garlic clove, chopped
2 tbsp. pine nuts
1 tsp. ground cinnamon
½ tsp. ground allspice
2 tsp. fresh lemon juice
¼ tsp. salt
freshly ground black pepper

Put the bulgur into a flameproof bowl and pour 2½ cups of boiling water over it. Let the bulgur soak for 20 minutes, then drain it in a sieve, pressing out as much liquid as possible with the back of a spoon. Put the onion, parsley, and coarsely chopped garlic into a food processor, and process just long enough to chop them up. Add the soaked bulgur and the lamb, along with the cinnamon and allspice, all but a pinch of the salt, and a generous grinding of pepper. Blend until all the ingredients are mixed and well bound together. Set the mixture aside.

To make the filling, heat the oil in a frying pan and cook the onion over medium heat until it is soft—about two minutes. Add the garlic and lamb, and cook, stirring constantly, until the meat begins to brown—four to five minutes. Add the pine nuts and continue to cook for two minutes. Stir in the cinnamon, allspice, lemon juice, salt, and some pepper, and cook for one minute more. Set the filling aside.

Preheat the oven to 375° F.

Lightly oil an 8-inch springform pan, and spread half of the lamb and bulgur mixture smoothly over the bottom of the dish. Cover the mixture with the lamb and pine-nut filling, pressing it down well, then spread the remaining bulgur mixture over the top. Smooth the surface with a spatula and lightly inscribe cutting lines for eight wedge-shaped sections. Brush the surface with a little olive oil and bake the *kibbeh* until it is brown—35 to 45 minutes.

For the coriander sauce, combine the yogurt, lemon juice, crushed garlic, and coriander with some pepper and the remaining pinch of salt. Serve the *kibbeh* hot or cold with the sauce, garnished with cilantro.

SUGGESTED ACCOMPANIMENT: *white cabbage and radish salad in a lemon and cardamom dressing.*

Lamb Loaf Stuffed with Dried Apricots

Serves 6
Working time: about 1 hour
Total time: about 2 hours

Calories **290**
Protein **27g.**
Cholesterol **80mg.**
Total fat **10g.**
Saturated fat **3g.**
Sodium **270mg.**

1 lb. lean lamb (from the leg), trimmed of fat and ground or very finely chopped (technique, page 43)
½ cup split red lentils
¼ cup finely cut fresh dill
2 tbsp. grated onion
3 garlic cloves, crushed
2 tsp. turmeric
¼ tsp. freshly grated nutmeg
1 large egg white, lightly beaten
½ tsp. salt
freshly ground black pepper
½ cup dried apricots, finely chopped
2 tbsp. sunflower seeds
1 tbsp. finely chopped golden raisins
1 tbsp. fresh lemon juice
1 tbsp. safflower oil
1 large onion, finely chopped
1 cup unsalted brown or chicken stock, (recipes, page 137)

Dill sauce

4 tbsp. sour cream
6 tbsp. plain low-fat yogurt
2 tbsp. finely cut fresh dill
⅛ tsp. salt
freshly ground black pepper

Place the lentils in a saucepan and cover them with water; bring the water to a boil, then lower the heat and simmer them until they are tender—about 20 minutes. Drain the lentils thoroughly, then transfer them to a bowl and allow them to cool.

Add the lamb to the lentils, together with the dill, grated onion, garlic, turmeric, nutmeg, egg white, salt, and some pepper. Knead well with your hands until all the ingredients are evenly combined and stick together—about five minutes.

Put the dried apricots, sunflower seeds, golden raisins, and lemon juice into a separate bowl, and mix them well together. Divide the meat mixture in half on a dampened board and flatten each half into an oval about ¾ inch thick. Shape the stuffing into two smaller ovals and place one in the center of each oval of meat. With your hands, shape the meat mixture around the stuffing to cover it completely.

Heat the oil in a deep, nonstick sauté pan. Cook the lamb loaves over medium heat until they are lightly browned all over—about five minutes. Remove them carefully from the pan and set them aside. Wipe the pan clean with a paper towel, then add the chopped onion. Return the pan to the heat and dry-fry the onion until it is browned—about five minutes.

Stir in the stock and bring it to a boil, then lower the heat and add the lamb loaves. Cover and simmer gently for 45 minutes to one hour, carefully turning the loaves once during this time so that they cook evenly.

To prepare the dill sauce, mix together the sour cream and yogurt, stir in the dill, and season with the salt and some freshly ground black pepper.

Remove the lamb loaves from the pan, slice them with a sharp knife, then arrange them on a warm serving platter.

Serve the lamb loaves immediately, accompanied by the dill sauce.

SUGGESTED ACCOMPANIMENT: *watercress, Belgian endive, and orange salad.*

Loin Chop and Artichoke Gratin

Serves 8
Working time: about 25 minutes
Total time: about 50 minutes

Calories **225**
Protein **23g.**
Cholesterol **75mg.**
Total fat **14g.**
Saturated fat **6g.**
Sodium **205mg.**

8 loin chops (about 5 oz. each), trimmed of fat
12 garlic cloves, peeled
1 tbsp. virgin olive oil
1 tsp. fresh thyme, or ½ tsp. dried thyme leaves
½ tsp. salt
freshly ground black pepper
3 large artichokes
1 oz. Parmesan cheese, grated (about ¼ cup)
2 tbsp. fresh white breadcrumbs
1 tbsp. chopped fresh parsley

Preheat the oven to 400° F.

Arrange the chops in the bottom of a shallow, flameproof dish, interspersing them with the garlic cloves. Brush the chops with the oil, sprinkle them with the thyme, and season with the salt and some freshly ground black pepper. Cook, uncovered, in the oven for 15 minutes.

In the meantime, prepare the artichokes. Bring a large saucepan of water to a boil. Break off the stalks from the artichokes and remove the bottom three to four rows of tough outer leaves. Trim off the dark green base of each artichoke using a paring knife. Cut the top 1½ inches off each artichoke and discard, then pull out the densely packed central leaves to expose the hairy choke. Scoop out the chokes with a teaspoon. While working on the artichokes, rub them frequently with the surface of half a cut lemon to prevent them from discoloring. Squeeze the juice remaining in the lemon half into the boiling water. Add the artichokes and cook them until they are tender—15 to 20 minutes. Drain them well and cut them into eighths or slices.

Remove the chops from the oven and increase the temperature to 425° F. Skim off any fat from the juices in the cooking dish. Distribute the artichokes evenly over and around the chops. Combine the Parmesan cheese and the breadcrumbs, then sprinkle this mixture over the chops and artichokes. Return the dish to the oven until the chops are well cooked and the topping is golden brown—20 to 25 minutes.

Sprinkle the parsley over the topping and serve the gratin immediately.

SUGGESTED ACCOMPANIMENTS: *hot French bread; tomato and green bean salad.*

Moussaka

Serves 6
Working time: about 1 hour and 10 minutes
Total time: about 2 hours and 30 minutes

Calories **380**
Protein **30g.**
Cholesterol **90mg.**
Total fat **14g.**
Saturated fat **6g.**
Sodium **370mg**

1 lb. lean lamb (from the leg), trimmed of fat and ground or very finely chopped (technique, page 43)
2 onions, chopped
2 garlic cloves, crushed
3 tomatoes, coarsely chopped
1 cup red wine
2 tbsp. tomato paste
1 green chili pepper, halved, seeded, and finely chopped (cautionary note, page 83)
2 tbsp. chopped fresh parsley
1 tbsp. chopped fresh marjoram, or 1½ tsp. dried marjoram
1 bay leaf
¼ tsp. freshly grated nutmeg
¾ tsp. salt
freshly ground black pepper
1 large eggplant, trimmed and thinly sliced
2 medium potatoes, peeled and thinly sliced
1 oz. Parmesan cheese, grated (about ¼ cup)

White sauce

¼ cup unsalted polyunsaturated margarine
½ cup unbleached all-purpose flour
1¼ cups skim milk
½ tsp. freshly grated nutmeg
⅛ tsp. salt
1¼ cups plain low-fat yogurt

Brush a nonstick frying pan lightly with oil and heat it over medium heat. Add the lamb and cook it, stirring constantly, until it changes color—three to four minutes. Add the onions and continue stirring for five minutes more. Add the garlic, tomatoes, wine, tomato paste, chili pepper, parsley, marjoram, bay leaf, and nutmeg. Season with ¼ teaspoon of the salt and some pepper. Continue stirring until the mixture comes to a boil, then lower the heat, cover, and simmer gently for 40 minutes.

Meanwhile, sprinkle the eggplant slices with the remaining ½ teaspoon of salt. Let them stand for 20 minutes, then rinse them under cold running water to remove the salt.

Pour enough water into a saucepan to fill it 1 inch deep. Set a vegetable steamer in the pan and bring the water to a boil. Put the eggplant slices in the steamer, cover the saucepan tightly, and steam the eggplant until it is tender—about 10 minutes. Meanwhile, boil the potato slices in unsalted water until they are tender—about five minutes. Drain well.

Preheat the oven to 350° F. Cover the bottom of an 11-by-9-inch baking dish with the potato slices. Cover the potatoes with half of the eggplant slices, then add the meat mixture. Arrange the remaining eggplant slices in a layer on top.

To make the sauce, melt the margarine over medium heat in a heavy-bottomed saucepan, add the flour, and stir for one minute. Gradually add the milk, stirring continuously, then add the nutmeg and the salt. Continue stirring the sauce until it thickens—three to four minutes. Remove the sauce from the heat and stir in the yogurt.

Pour the sauce over the moussaka, then sprinkle it with the Parmesan cheese. Bake the moussaka in the oven until it is golden brown and bubbling—40 to 50 minutes. Serve hot, straight from the dish.

SUGGESTED ACCOMPANIMENT: *mixed green salad.*

Lamb and Endive Gratin

Serves 4
Working time: about 45 minutes
Total time: about 1 hour and 30 minutes

Calories **335**
Protein **35g.**
Cholesterol **93mg.**
Total fat **16g.**
Saturated fat **7g.**
Sodium **337mg.**

one 2-lb. lamb loin roast, trimmed of fat and boned
1 tbsp. fresh lemon juice
4 heads of Belgian endive, trimmed
2 tsp. safflower oil
4 shallots, or 1 small onion, thinly sliced
1 tbsp. flour
¾ cup unsalted brown stock or unsalted chicken stock (recipes, page 137)
1 tbsp. Dijon mustard
freshly ground black pepper
½ cup dry breadcrumbs
¼ lb. low-fat mozzarella, grated

Bring 1 quart of water to a boil in a large saucepan. Add the lemon juice and Belgian endive, and cook them for five minutes. Drain the endive and rinse it under cold running water. When the endive is cool enough to handle, squeeze out the liquid with your hands. Quarter each head of endive lengthwise and set the pieces aside.

Preheat the oven to 400° F.

Cut the lamb into eight slices. Place the slices between two pieces of plastic wrap or wax paper, and pound them with a meat mallet or the flat of a heavy knife *(page 24)* until they are only about ¼ inch thick. Heat the safflower oil in a large, nonstick skillet over high heat. Add the lamb slices and cook them for 30 seconds on each side. Remove the slices from the skillet and set them aside.

Lower the heat to medium. Add the shallot or onion slices to the skillet; cook them, stirring continuously, until they have browned—about five minutes. Remove the skillet from the heat and stir in the flour. Whisking constantly, pour in the stock in a slow, steady stream. Return the skillet to the heat and cook the sauce, stirring, until it thickens—about two minutes. Mix in the mustard and a generous grinding of pepper, then simmer the sauce for five minutes more.

Sprinkle 1 tablespoon of the breadcrumbs into a baking or gratin dish. Place the reserved lamb slices on top of the crumbs and spread the endive quarters over the lamb. Pour the sauce over all; sprinkle the mozzarella and the remaining breadcrumbs on top. Bake the gratin until the liquid bubbles and the top has browned—about 40 minutes.

SUGGESTED ACCOMPANIMENTS: *steamed asparagus; toasted French bread.*

Layered Lamb Bake with Fennel

Serves 6
Working time: about 45 minutes
Total time: about 1 hour and 30 minutes

Calories **350**
Protein **29g.**
Cholesterol **75mg.**
Total fat **14g.**
Saturated fat **6g.**
Sodium **390mg.**

6 loin chops (about 5 oz. each), trimmed of fat
6 medium potatoes, peeled and thinly sliced
⅓ cup skim milk
3 medium zucchini, trimmed and thinly sliced
6 medium fennel bulbs, trimmed and thinly sliced, trimmings reserved
½ tsp. salt
¾ tsp. ground nutmeg
freshly ground black pepper
1½ tbsp. polyunsaturated margarine, melted
3 tsp. grated lemon zest
2 tsp. chopped fennel-bulb tops
lemon wedges for garnish
sprigs of fennel-bulb tops for garnish

Preheat the oven to 425° F.

Rinse the potato slices in cold water and pat them dry with paper towels. Pour half of the milk into a shallow 2-quart, ovenproof casserole dish. Arrange one-third of the potato slices over the bottom of the dish. Cover the potato slices with half of the zucchini slices, and top these with half of the fennel. Season with one-third of the salt, half of the nutmeg, and a few generous grindings of black pepper. Over the fennel, layer half of the remaining potatoes and then the remaining zucchini and fennel. Season as before and add the remaining milk. Arrange the remaining potatoes in overlapping slices on the top, brush them evenly with the margarine, and cover the casserole with aluminum foil.

Bake the vegetables in the oven for 30 minutes.

While the vegetables are baking, prepare the chops. Mix together the remaining third of the salt, some freshly ground black pepper, and the lemon zest. Rub a little of this mixture over both sides of the chops. Secure the chops into neat rounds with toothpicks. Chop the reserved fennel trimmings and combine with the chopped fennel-bulb tops. Stuff some into the space between the flap and loin of each chop.

Arrange the lamb chops on top of the vegetables and return the dish to the oven, uncovered, for 20 to 30 minutes for rare to medium meat.

Remove the toothpicks, and serve the chops and vegetables garnished with lemon wedges and sprigs of fennel-bulb tops.

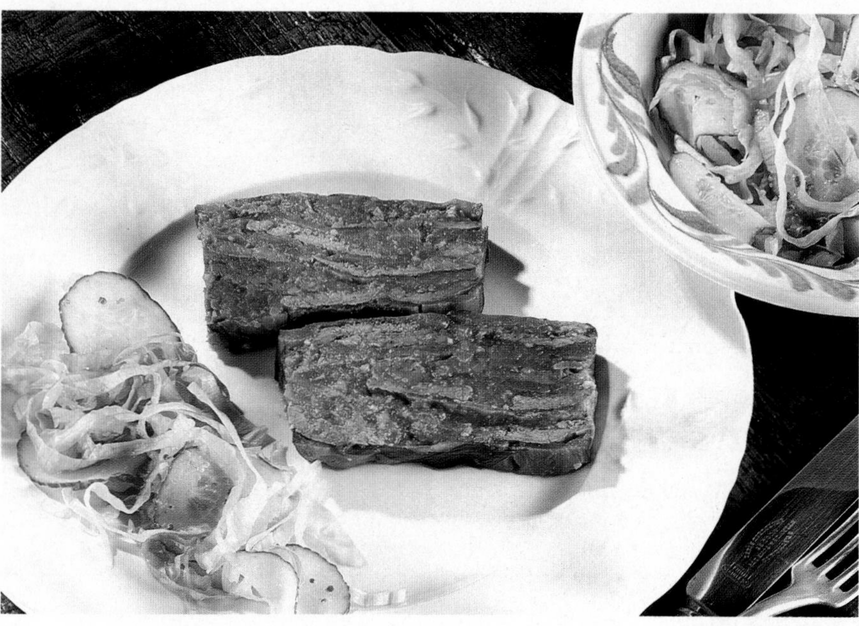

Lamb and Eggplant Terrine

Serves 8
Working time: about 1 hour and 20 minutes
Total time: about 9 hours (includes chilling)

Calories **255**
Protein **31g.**
Cholesterol **75mg.**
Total fat **12g.**
Saturated fat **5g.**
Sodium **170mg.**

one 2½-lb. leg of lamb (loin end), boned, trimmed of fat, and cut into ¼-inch-thick slices
2 sweet red peppers
2 tbsp. virgin olive oil
1 onion, chopped
3 garlic cloves, thinly sliced
½ tbsp. chopped fresh oregano, or ½ tsp. dried oregano
½ tbsp. fresh thyme, or ½ tsp. dried thyme leaves
½ tsp. salt
freshly ground black pepper
28 oz. canned unsalted whole tomatoes, drained, or 4 large ripe tomatoes, peeled, seeded, and chopped
2 tbsp. red wine vinegar
1 large eggplant (about 1¾ lb.)
½ tsp. fresh lemon juice

Broil the peppers, turning them with tongs as they blister, until their skins are blackened all over—about 15 minutes. Transfer the peppers to a bowl and cover it with plastic wrap. When the peppers are cool enough to handle, peel, seed, and coarsely chop them, reserving their juice.

Heat ½ tablespoon of the oil in a heavy-bottomed saucepan over medium-low heat. Add the onion, garlic, oregano, thyme, ¼ teaspoon of the salt, and some black pepper. Cook the mixture, stirring occasionally, until the onion is translucent—about five minutes. Add the tomatoes, the peppers and their juice, and the vinegar. Simmer the sauce until it has thickened—about seven minutes. Purée the sauce in a food processor or a blender, and return it to the pan.

With a small, sharp knife, remove four long strips of skin from the eggplant; each strip should be about ½ inch wide. Set the strips aside. Slice the eggplant lengthwise into ¼-inch slices. Place the slices on a large, nonreactive baking sheet, sprinkle them with the lemon juice and the remaining ¼ teaspoon of salt, and broil them for five minutes. Set the slices aside until you are ready to assemble the terrine.

Place the slices of lamb between plastic wrap or wax paper or parchment paper; pound them with a meat mallet or the flat of a heavy knife *(technique, page 24)* to a thickness of about ⅛ inch.

Heat 1 tablespoon of the remaining oil in a large, nonstick frying pan over high heat. Add one-quarter of the lamb slices and sauté them for 30 seconds on each side. Remove the slices and sauté a second batch; set the second batch aside. Pour the remaining ½ tablespoon of oil into the pan and sauté the remaining lamb slices in two final batches. After removing the last slices from the pan, pour in ¼ cup of water and stir to dislodge any caramelized juices; add this liquid to the tomato sauce.

Preheat the oven to 325° F. Lightly oil a 2-quart, nonreactive loaf pan. Arrange the strips of eggplant skin in a crisscross pattern in the bottom, their shiny sides down. Place a layer of eggplant slices on top, followed by a layer of the lamb slices and about ¼ cup of the sauce. Repeat the layering process until all the slices have been used, topping the terrine with a layer of eggplant. Reserve any remaining sauce.

Cover the top of the terrine with wax or parchment paper, and set the terrine in the oven. To prevent the lamb slices from curling during cooking, weight the top of the terrine by placing another loaf pan filled partway with dried beans on top of the terrine.

Bake the terrine for 45 minutes. Remove the weight from the top and continue baking the terrine until the meat is tender—about 45 minutes more. Remove the terrine from the oven and allow it to stand at room temperature for 30 minutes. Chill for at least six hours.

To unmold the terrine, run a knife around the inside of the pan, then remove the wax paper, and invert a platter over the top. Turn pan and platter over together. Wrap the terrine for a few seconds in a hot, wet dishtowel, then carefully lift away the pan. Serve the terrine in slices, with any reserved sauce.

SUGGESTED ACCOMPANIMENTS: *lettuce and cucumber salad; pita bread.*

Eggplant Fans

Serves 4
Working time: about 25 minutes
Total time: about 1 hour

Calories **200**
Protein **23g.**
Cholesterol **60mg.**
Total fat **10g.**
Saturated fat **6g.**
Sodium **400mg.**

½ lb. lean lamb (from the leg or loin), trimmed of fat and ground or finely chopped (technique, page 43)
2 small eggplants (about ½ lb. each)
1 small fennel bulb, trimmed and finely chopped
½ tsp. dried fennel seeds, lightly crushed
1 tbsp. tomato paste
4 tomatoes, peeled, 2 chopped, 2 sliced
¼ tsp. salt
freshly ground black pepper
¼ lb. low-fat mozzarella, thinly sliced

Halve the eggplants lengthwise. Lay one eggplant half, cut side down, on a board. Using a sharp knife, cut several horizontal slices ¼ inch apart, leaving a hinge of flesh about ½ inch wide at the stalk end. Trim off and discard the top slice. Cut the remaining half eggplants into fans in the same way. Place the fans in a shallow baking dish.

Preheat the oven to 375° F. Heat a nonstick frying pan over medium heat, add the lamb, and cook it for three minutes, stirring to sear it all over. Stir in the chopped fennel and cook for one minute more, then add the fennel seeds, tomato paste, chopped tomatoes, salt, and some pepper. Stir well and remove the pan from the heat.

Using a teaspoon, spoon the lamb mixture between the slices of the eggplant fans, then cover each layer of meat filling with mozzarella or tomato slices, alternating the toppings. Cover the dish with foil and bake for 20 minutes, then bake, uncovered, until the eggplants are tender and the cheese is golden brown—about 20 minutes.

SUGGESTED ACCOMPANIMENT: *steamed snow peas and baby corn.*

Potatoes with a Spiced Lamb Stuffing

Serves 4
Working time: about 40 minutes
Total time: about 1 hour and 40 minutes

Calories **270**
Protein **14g.**
Cholesterol **25mg.**
Total fat **5g.**
Saturated fat **2g.**
Sodium **230mg.**

5 oz. lean lamb (from the leg), trimmed of fat and ground or very finely chopped (technique, page 43)
8 potatoes (about 4 oz. each), scrubbed
1 small onion, finely chopped
1 garlic clove, crushed
1 tbsp. raisins, rinsed and finely chopped
1 tbsp. pine nuts
1 tsp. ground cinnamon
½ tsp. ground allspice
½ tsp. turmeric
2 tbsp. tomato paste
¼ tsp. salt
freshly ground black pepper
6 tbsp. unsalted brown or chicken stock (recipes, page 137)
1 tbsp. sour cream

Preheat the oven to 400° F. Make a ½-inch-deep horizontal slit about one-quarter of the way down each potato. Bake the potatoes until they are tender—about one hour.

Meanwhile, make the stuffing. Brush a nonstick frying pan lightly with oil and heat it over medium heat. Stir-fry the onion until it is brown—about five minutes. Add the lamb and continue stir-frying until it changes color—three to four minutes—then add the garlic, raisins, pine nuts, cinnamon, allspice, turmeric, tomato paste, salt, and some pepper. Stir for one minute, then add the stock and continue cooking the mixture for five minutes more, stirring regularly. Set the stuffing aside.

When the potatoes are cool enough to handle, slice off their tops and hollow out their insides with a teaspoon, taking care not to puncture their skins; leave a shell of about ¼ inch on each potato. Mash half of the scooped-out potatoes with the sour cream. (Reserve the remaining scooped-out potatoes and the tops for another use.) Spoon the mashed potatoes into the potato shells, pressing down in the center to make a well for the stuffing. Fill the shells with the stuffing and return them to the oven to heat through—about 10 minutes. Serve hot.

SUGGESTED ACCOMPANIMENT: *green salad.*

Baked Stuffed Onions

Serves 4
Working time: about 30 minutes
Total time: about 1 hour and 10 minutes

Calories **215**
Protein **25g.**
Cholesterol **75mg.**
Total Fat **10g.**
Saturated fat **3g.**
Sodium **170mg.**

¾ lb. lean lamb (from the leg or loin), trimmed of fat and ground or very finely chopped (technique, page 43)

4 large Spanish onions (about ½ lb. each)

2 medium celeriacs, peeled and finely chopped

2 oz. mushrooms, chopped

1 tsp. chopped fresh marjoram, or ¼ tsp. dried marjoram

¼ lb. grated horseradish

¼ cup cashews, coarsely chopped

¼ tsp. salt

freshly ground black pepper

celery leaves for garnish

Peel the onions, trimming off the root ends, but leaving the tops intact. Place them in a large saucepan of simmering water, and cook until they are soft but still keep their shape—about 10 minutes. Drain and cool. Slice lids off the pointed ends, about one-quarter of the way down each onion. Push out the centers of the onions with a teaspoon, leaving shells about two layers thick. (Save the centers for a soup or stock.)

Preheat the oven to 350° F. Brush a nonstick frying pan lightly with oil and heat it over high heat. Add the lamb, stirring, until it changes color—about two minutes. Add the celeriacs, mushrooms, and marjoram, lower the heat to medium, and cook for two minutes more. Stir in the horseradish, cashews, salt, and some pepper, and remove the pan from the heat.

Place the onion shells in a shallow, ovenproof dish. Using a teaspoon, pack the lamb mixture as tightly as possible into the shells, piling it up above the shells if necessary. Place the lids beside the onions, cover the dish with aluminum foil, and bake the onions until they are tender—about 40 minutes. Replace the lids and serve the onions garnished with celery leaves.

Spinach-Wrapped Chops Stuffed with Shiitake Mushrooms

Serves 6
Working time: about 40 minutes
Total time: about 1 hour and 30 minutes (includes soaking)

Calories **340**
Protein **29g.**
Cholesterol **75mg.**
Total fat **14g.**
Saturated fat **5g.**
Sodium **355mg.**

12 rib chops (about 3 oz. each)
12 large spinach leaves, washed
24 shiitake mushrooms, soaked in 1¼ cups warm water for 20 minutes
one 1½-inch piece fresh ginger, julienned
16 shallots, 12 finely sliced, 4 finely chopped
4 tsp. safflower oil
¾ tsp. salt
freshly ground black pepper
¼ cup dry sherry
2 cups unsalted brown or chicken stock (recipes page 137)

Blanch the spinach leaves in boiling water for two to three seconds. Rinse them immediately in cold water and let them drain on dishtowels.

Squeeze the shiitake mushrooms dry. Strain the soaking liquid through a sieve lined with cheesecloth and reserve it. Reserve the 12 most attractive mushrooms. Remove the stalks from the remaining mushrooms and finely slice the caps; keep the stalks and the sliced caps separate.

Sauté the ginger and the sliced shallots in the oil over low heat for three minutes. Add the sliced shiitake mushrooms and continue to cook for five minutes more. Season the mushroom stuffing with ⅛ teaspoon of the salt and some black pepper, and allow it to cool while you prepare the chops.

Trim the chops of all fat and loose bones, so that you are left with an eye of meat attached to a long rib bone. Using a small, sharp knife, scrape the exposed rib bones clean of meat and fat. Lay the chops flat on a work surface and make one horizontal slit in the side of each chop to form pockets about 1 inch deep by 1 inch wide for the mushroom stuffing.

Season the trimmed chops with ⅛ teaspoon of the salt and some black pepper. Place a spinach leaf, vein side up, on the work surface and pare away a thin slice of the center rib of the leaf, taking care not to cut through it. Divide the mushroom stuffing into 12 portions. Spoon half of one portion in the center of the leaf; push the remaining half portion of stuffing into the pocket of a chop. Place the chop on the stuffing in the center of the leaf so that the rib bone protrudes beyond the edge of the leaf. Wrap the ends of the leaf over the chop to enclose it, then fold over any loose edges to make a neat parcel. Fill and wrap the remaining chops and set them aside.

To prepare a sauce, put the chopped shallots and the sherry into a small saucepan, cover, and simmer for five minutes. Add the stock and the mushroom soaking liquid, return the mixture to a boil, add the reserved mushrooms and stalks; then lower the heat and simmer for 10 minutes. Remove the whole mushrooms with a slotted spoon and keep them warm. Increase the heat and boil, reducing the sauce until only 1 cup of liquid remains. Strain the sauce, season it with the remaining salt, and keep it warm.

In the meantime, pour enough water into a saucepan to fill it to a depth of 1 inch. Set a steamer in the pan and bring the water to a boil. Place the prepared chops, seam side down, in the steamer, cover the pan tightly, and steam them for 8 to 10 minutes.

To serve, place two chop parcels on each plate, surround them with sauce, and garnish them with the whole mushrooms.

SUGGESTED ACCOMPANIMENT: *broiled sweet peppers tossed with sesame oil and toasted sesame seeds.*

Lamb and Leek Parcels

Serves 4
Working time: about 45 minutes
Total time: about 1 hour

Calories **215**
Protein **30g.**
Cholesterol **75mg.**
Total fat **9g.**
Saturated fat **4g.**
Sodium **265mg.**

1 lb. lean lamb (from the loin), trimmed of fat

1 lime, juice and grated zest

1 tsp. virgin olive oil

1 tbsp. chopped fresh oregano

½ tsp. salt

freshly ground black pepper

4 leeks, trimmed and the tough outer layers discarded

1¼ cups unsalted chicken stock (recipe, page 137)

Cut the lamb into 12 strips, each about 5 inches long by ½ inch wide. Put the meat into a small bowl along with the lime juice and zest, the olive oil, two-thirds of the oregano, ¼ teaspoon of the salt, and some freshly ground black pepper. Stir the strips to coat them evenly and let them marinate at room temperature while you prepare the leeks.

Make a slit down the length of the three outer layers of each leek and remove these layers. Slice the leeks into rounds, wash them well, and put them into a flameproof casserole; set the leek rounds aside. Thoroughly wash the detached layers and cook them in boiling water until they are tender—three to five minutes. Refresh them in cold water and spread them on a dishtowel to dry.

Preheat the oven to 450° F.

Cut four of the cooked leek layers in half lengthwise. Spread one of the intact layers flat on a work surface. Lift a strip of lamb out of the marinade and lay it along the center of the layer. Cover the lamb with one of the half-leek layers, place a second strip of lamb on top, then another half layer, and finally a third strip of lamb. Bring up the sides of the whole-leek layer, place another whole-leek layer on top, and fold down its sides to form a neat open-ended parcel. Make up three more parcels in the same way. Reserve the marinade.

Place the lamb and leek parcels on top of the sliced leeks in the casserole. Add the chicken stock and the marinade, cover with aluminum foil, and bake the parcels for 10 to 12 minutes for rare to medium meat.

Turn off the oven and transfer the leek parcels to a chopping board. Remove the leek slices from the casserole with a slotted spoon and put them into a warm serving dish. Cut each parcel into three pieces and place them on top of the leek slices. Put the serving dish in the oven to keep warm.

Set the casserole over high heat and boil the cooking juices until only ½ cup of liquid remains—about two minutes. Add the remaining oregano and ¼ teaspoon of salt and some black pepper. Pour the sauce over the leek parcels and serve.

SUGGESTED ACCOMPANIMENTS: *broiled tomatoes with breadcrumbs and garlic; pureéd potato.*

Acorn Squash with Lamb and Vegetable Stuffing

Serves 4
Working time: about 1 hour
Total time: about 2 hours and 30 minutes

Calories **325**
Protein **26g.**
Cholesterol **71mg.**
Total fat **11g.**
Saturated fat **4g.**
Sodium **315mg.**

1 lb. lean lamb (from the leg or loin), trimmed of fat and ground or very finely chopped (technique, page 43)
4 acorn squash (about 1 lb. each)
1 tsp. safflower oil
½ cup green beans, trimmed and cut into ¼-inch pieces
½ cup fresh corn kernels (cut from 1 small ear) or frozen corn kernels, thawed
1 onion, chopped
⅓ cup freshly grated Parmesan cheese (about 1 oz.)
¼ tsp. salt
freshly ground black pepper

Preheat the oven to 400° F.

Cut a ½-inch-thick slice from the bottom of each squash so that it will stand upright. Cut a 1-inch-thick slice from the stem end of each squash and scoop out the seeds with a spoon. Set the squash, stem sides down, in a baking dish. Pour 1 cup of water into the dish, then cover it tightly with aluminum foil. Bake the squash until they are tender when pierced with the tip of a sharp knife—about one hour.

While the squash are baking, make the lamb and vegetable stuffing. Heat the oil in a large, nonstick skillet over medium-high heat. Add the beans, corn, and onion, and sauté them until the onion is soft and lightly browned—about five minutes. Transfer the vegetables to a large bowl. Increase the heat under the skillet to high; add the lamb and cook it, stirring and breaking it up with a wooden spoon, until it is evenly browned—about five minutes. Pour off any fat. Add the meat to the vegetables, and stir in half of the Parmesan cheese, the salt, and a generous grinding of pepper. Set the stuffing aside.

Remove the squash from the baking dish and discard the water. Place the squash upside down on a towel to drain. When they are cool enough to handle, scoop out the flesh with a spoon, forming shells with walls approximately ¼ inch thick. Add the squash flesh to the stuffing and stir to mix it in thoroughly.

Divide the stuffing among the four squash shells. Sprinkle a little of the remaining Parmesan cheese on top of each squash. Return the squash to the baking dish and bake them until they are hot—about 30 minutes. Serve the stuffed squash immediately.

SUGGESTED ACCOMPANIMENTS: *tomato and lettuce salad; sourdough rolls.*

Patterning Sauces

1 *POURING THE SAUCES. Prepare two sauces of contrasting color. Just before serving the dish, pour one of them into the center of a flat-bottomed plate. Tip and swirl the plate to cover the bottom evenly. Carefully spoon the sauce of a contrasting color onto the first sauce; move your hand to elongate the shape slightly.*

2 *FEATHERING THE SAUCES. Place the tip of a fine skewer in the contrasting sauce, and draw it through the first sauce and back into the contrasting sauce to create a loop. Repeat the process to form a feathered pattern.*

Lamb Stuffed with Chicken and Wild Mushroom Mousse

Serves 4
Working time: about 1 hour
Total time: about 2 hours (includes chilling)

Calories **400**
Protein **40g.**
Cholesterol **105mg.**
Total fat **15g.**
Saturated fat **7g.**
Sodium **235mg.**

one 1-lb. rack of lamb, boned, the fatty flap of meat that extends from the loin removed
1/8 tsp. salt
freshly ground black pepper
1/2 tbsp. unsalted butter
4 cherry tomatoes
parsley sprigs for garnish

Chicken and mushroom mousse

1/3 oz. dried wild mushrooms such as porcini or shiitake
1/4 lb. breast of chicken, cut into chunks and chilled for at least 40 minutes
1 egg white, chilled for at least 40 minutes
1/8 tsp. salt
1 tbsp. sour cream, chilled
freshly ground black pepper
1/2 tsp. chopped fresh flat-leaf parsley

Morel sauces

24 small dried morels
1 cup unsalted chicken stock (recipe, page 137)
2 tbsp. dry sherry
1/2 tsp. cornstarch
3 tbsp. plain low-fat yogurt

Put the mushrooms for the mousse and the morels for the sauce into a bowl together, and cover them with 1 cup of lukewarm water. Set the bowl aside for 20 minutes while you prepare the meat.

Remove any tough membrane left on the lamb, then make a horizontal slit lengthwise, cutting from the thinner edge, about three-quarters of the way through the meat. Open the meat like a book, and flatten it between two sheets of plastic wrap with a meat mallet or a rolling pin to a thickness of about 1/4 inch. Season the meat with the salt and some pepper, and chill it, still in the plastic wrap, while you prepare the mousse.

Strain the mushroom liquid through cheesecloth; reserve the morels and the liquid. Squeeze the porcini or shiitake dry, rinse to remove any grit, squeeze them dry again and finely chop them. Set them aside.

To make the mousse, put the chicken into a chilled food processor with the egg white and salt. Process the chicken until it forms a smooth paste—one to two minutes. Press the mixture through a fine sieve into a chilled bowl to remove any sinew. Beat the sour cream into the chicken paste, then add the chopped porcini or shiitake, some pepper, and the parsley, stirring gently until they are evenly distributed. Cover and chill the mousse in the refrigerator for at least 30 minutes.

Preheat the oven to 325° F. Unwrap the flattened meat, and spoon the chilled mousse along its center in a sausage shape. Wrap the meat around the mousse, overlapping the two long edges by about 1 inch. Tie the rolled meat in three or four places with string. Melt the butter in a frying pan and brown the meat evenly over medium heat, then wrap it in a sheet of aluminum foil and bake it in the oven for 15 minutes. Turn off the oven, remove the meat, and pour off and reserve the juices collected in the foil. Cover the meat loosely with the foil again and return it to the oven for 10 minutes before slicing. Place the cherry tomatoes in the oven to warm them through and loosen their skins.

To make the sauce, put the stock, sherry, and reserved mushroom soaking liquid into a saucepan. Boil gently until only half the liquid remains. Add the morels and poach them for 10 minutes, then remove them with a slotted spoon and keep them warm. Add the reserved meat juice to the sauce. Blend the cornstarch with a tablespoon of water and stir it into the pan. Bring the sauce back to a boil, turn the heat down, and simmer for two to three minutes, stirring constantly, until it thickens and clears. Place the yogurt in a bowl over a pan of simmering water to warm it through. Blend one-third of the sauce into the yogurt and whisk until it is smooth. Keep the plain sauce and the yogurt sauce warm in separate containers.

Carefully peel the cherry tomatoes.

To serve, cut the stuffed lamb diagonally into 16 slices with a sharp knife. Pour one-quarter of the plain sauce to one side of each of four warmed plates, then one-quarter of the yogurt sauce on top. Feather the edge of the yogurt sauce with a skewer *(technique, opposite).* Arrange four slices of meat on the edge of the sauce, and garnish with the parsley, cherry tomatoes, and morels.

SUGGESTED ACCOMPANIMENT: *green beans.*

EDITOR'S NOTE: *If dried morels are unavailable, porcini, shiitake, or other dried wild mushrooms can be substituted.*

Roast Five-Spice Leg of Lamb

FIVE-SPICE POWDER IS A TRADITIONAL CHINESE SEASONING. THE ACTUAL SPICES USED TO MAKE IT UP VARY FROM REGION TO REGION, BUT THREE OF THEM ARE ALWAYS PRESENT: CASSIA BARK (CHINESE CINNAMON), STAR ANISE, AND SICHUAN PEPPER.

Serves 8
Working time: about 45 minutes
Total time: about 16 hours (includes marinating)

Calories **225**
Protein **32g.**
Cholesterol **75mg.**
Total fat **9g.**
Saturated fat **4g.**
Sodium **140mg.**

one 3-lb. half leg of lamb, shank end, trimmed of fat
1 tbsp. apple jelly
1¼ lb. small carrots, peeled
32 pearl onions, blanched and peeled
½ tsp. arrowroot

Five-spice marinade

¾ oz. cassia bark (Chinese cinnamon), or 6 cinnamon sticks
12 star anise
12 cloves
1½ tsp. Sichuan peppercorns
3 strips fresh orange zest
1 or 2 dried chili peppers (cautionary note, page 83)
¼ cup low-sodium dark soy sauce
¼ cup low-sodium light soy sauce
2 cups Chinese rice wine or dry sherry
2 tsp. brown sugar
4 garlic cloves, unpeeled
one 1-inch piece fresh ginger, unpeeled and cut into quarters
½ tsp. arrowroot

To make the marinade, put the cassia bark or the cinnamon sticks, star anise, cloves, Sichuan peppercorns, orange zest, and chili peppers into a small piece of cheesecloth, and tie it up with cotton string, leaving one long end. Mix the dark and the light soy sauce, the rice wine or sherry, and the sugar with 2 cups of water in a large saucepan. Bring the liquid to a simmer, stirring to dissolve the sugar, then add the garlic, ginger, and the spice bag, tying its string to the handle of the pan. Cover the pan and let the marinade simmer for 30 minutes, skimming off any scum from time to time. At the end of this period, add the leg of lamb and boil it, uncovered, for six to seven minutes, turning it once. Reduce the heat to very low and skim the marinade, then cover the pan and simmer the lamb for 30 minutes. Turn the meat after 15 minutes and skim again if necessary. Let the lamb cool in the liquid, then marinate it in the refrigerator for 12 to 24 hours, turning it several times.

Preheat the oven to 450° F. Remove the leg of lamb from the pan, reserving half of the marinade for basting and deglazing, and the other half for the sauce. Place the meat on a rack over a roasting pan and roast it for 10 minutes. Lower the heat to 350° F., put a pan of cold water on the bottom shelf, and continue cooking for one hour to one hour and 20 minutes for medium to well-done meat; baste the meat several times with the marinade. Ten minutes before the end of roasting time, glaze the meat: Mix the apple jelly with 1 teaspoon of boiling water, brush this solution evenly over the leg, and return it to the oven.

While the lamb is roasting, begin to make the sauce. Strain the remaining half of the marinade into a saucepan through a fine sieve, bring it to a boil, and add the carrots. Let the liquid return to a boil, lower the heat, and simmer the carrots for five minutes; then add the onions and simmer the vegetables until they are tender—about 15 minutes. Remove the pan from the heat and leave the vegetables in the liquid for 10 minutes to absorb its color. Remove them with a slotted spoon and keep them warm. Strain the liquid into a saucepan and set it aside.

When the meat is cooked, turn off the oven and transfer the leg to a large platter. Let it rest for 15 minutes in the oven with the door slightly ajar. Meanwhile, skim off any fat from the roasting pan, set the pan over high heat, and add about 3 tablespoons of the marinade. Stir the liquid as it comes to a boil, scraping off any browned bits from the bottom of the pan. Strain the pan juices and add them to the vegetable cooking liquid. Boil the liquid rapidly for one to two minutes. Add ½ cup of water. Mix the arrowroot with 1 tablespoon of water and add it to the sauce. Return it to a boil, and cook until the sauce thickens and clears—two to three minutes. Transfer it to a serving bowl.

Arrange the vegetables around the meat and carve at the table.

SUGGESTED ACCOMPANIMENTS: *rice; apple jelly.*

EDITOR'S NOTE: *All the spices required for this recipe can be purchased in Asian markets.*

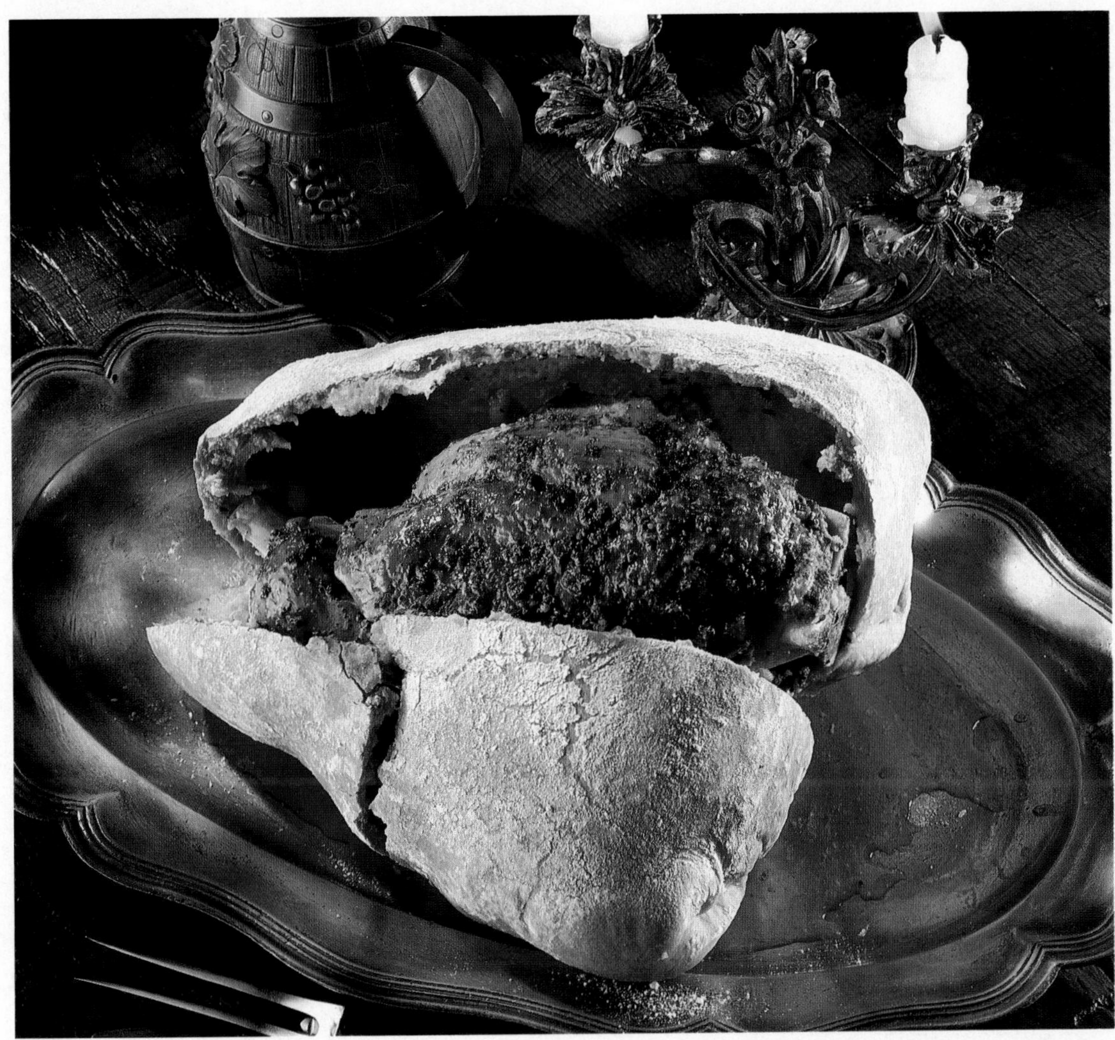

Parslied Leg of Lamb Baked in a Casing of Dough

IN THIS RECIPE, A PASTE OF FLOUR AND WATER WORKS IN THE SAME WAY THAT A CLAY OVEN DOES, SEALING IN THE FLAVORS AND KEEPING THE MEAT MOIST AND TENDER.

Serves 10
Working time: about 30 minutes
Total time: about 2 hours and 30 minutes

Calories **210**
Protein **30g.**
Cholesterol **80mg.**
Total fat **10g.**
Saturated fat **4g.**
Sodium **185mg.**

one 5-lb. leg of lamb, trimmed of fat
6 garlic cloves, peeled
¾ tsp. salt
freshly ground black pepper
¼ cup chopped fresh parsley
1 tbsp. virgin olive oil
6 cups unbleached all-purpose flour

Preheat the oven to 400° F.

Work the garlic cloves and salt into a creamy paste with a mortar and pestle. Mix in some freshly ground black pepper, the parsley, and the oil. Rub this mixture evenly all over the leg of lamb.

Put the flour into a large mixing bowl and make a well in the center. Add 2 cups of cold water and mix to make a soft dough. Lightly knead the dough on a floured work surface until it is smooth, then roll it out into a rectangle large enough to completely encase the leg of lamb.

Place the lamb upside down in the center of the dough. Bring the short sides of the rectangle up and over each end of the leg, then fold in the long edges to encase the lamb completely. Mold the dough neatly around the leg and press the edges well together to seal the casing.

Place the lamb in a large roasting pan with the seams in the dough underneath. Sprinkle the dough lightly with flour. Cook the lamb for two hours.

To serve, break open and discard the casing, by now baked to hardness, then carve the leg in the usual way.

SUGGESTED ACCOMPANIMENTS: *braised leeks; glazed carrots; creamed potatoes.*

4 Neat grape-leaf packages, stuffed with spiced lamb and rice, need only half the traditional cooking time when prepared in a microwave (recipe, opposite).

Microwaving Lamb

Stuffed Grape Leaves

Quick and inexpensive to run, a microwave offers undoubted convenience. It is also versatile for cooking lamb, as demonstrated in the following recipes, which range from a traditional cottage pie *(page 132)* to satisfy robust appetites, to lamb timbales *(page 124)* that will gladden the eye as well as the palate of the most sophisticated diner.

To get the best results from your microwave, you should understand its strengths. Because the microwaves generated penetrate only about 2 inches into the food, the microwave oven is ideal for dishes in which the meat is diced or cut into strips. To ensure that the meat cooks evenly, simply stir it from time to time. Recipes for ground lamb are also very successful; the meat loaf on page 129 requires only 10 to 12 minutes in the oven.

But large cuts of lamb that are generally roasted can also be cooked successfully in a microwave, provided they are turned and repositioned on the roasting dish halfway through the cooking period. The 4-pound boned leg of lamb on page 127 cooks in just over half an hour; a roasting bag helps to seal in the moisture and preserve the meat's natural succulence. Chops also lend themselves to the microwave process. Never salt cuts of lamb before microwaving them; salting tends to dry out and toughen the meat.

A crucial element in microwave cooking is the "standing time"—a period after the food has been removed from the oven but continues to cook. This can account for up to half of the total cooking time. Test food for doneness only at the end of standing time. With a roast, testing is simplified by using a meat thermometer inserted into the thickest part, as in the roast with winter vegetables *(page 127)*.

The power at which you microwave lamb depends upon the quality of the meat. Tender cuts—including ground meat—are best cooked on high (100 percent power). Less tender cuts should be covered and cooked in liquid on medium (50 percent power). When cooking a dish covered in plastic wrap, remember to pull back one corner so that steam can escape.

Microwave cooking does not brown meat, but other ingredients often compensate; lamb baked in saffron yogurt *(page 127)*, for instance, assumes the vivid color of its sauce. A few of the recipes, however, call for a browning dish—a dish specifically designed for the microwave with a special coating on its base. Used as directed, a browning dish gives lamb cooked in the microwave the seared and browned surface normally associated with roasting, broiling, or frying.

Serves 6
Working (and total) time: about 1 hour

Calories **190**
Protein **16g.**
Cholesterol **35mg.**
Total fat **8g.**
Saturated fat **3g.**
Sodium **50mg.**

½ lb. lean lamb (from the leg or loin), trimmed of fat and ground or very finely chopped (technique, page 43)
⅓ cup brown rice
30 fresh grape leaves, or 30 preserved grape leaves rinsed under cold running water
1 small onion, finely chopped
¼ cup pine nuts
¼ cup currants
1 tsp. ground cinnamon
1 tsp. ground allspice
2½ tbsp. fresh lemon juice
freshly ground black pepper
1 egg white, lightly beaten
6 garlic cloves, thinly sliced
1¼ cups puréed tomatoes
1 tsp. brown sugar
6 tbsp. plain low-fat yogurt for garnish

Put the rice into a bowl with 1 cup of boiling water. Cover the bowl loosely and microwave on high for five minutes. Reduce the power to medium and cook for five minutes more. Let the rice stand for five minutes, then drain off any liquid and allow the rice to cool.

If you are using fresh grape leaves, put them into a bowl and cover them with water. Microwave on high until the water boils—about five minutes. Let them stand for 10 minutes, drain, and trim off the stalks.

Combine the lamb in a bowl with the rice, onion, nuts, currants, cinnamon, allspice, 1 teaspoon of the lemon juice, and some pepper. Mix in the egg white.

Lay a grape leaf, vein side upward, on a work surface. Place one heaping teaspoon of filling near the bottom of the leaf and fold the sides of the leaf toward the center. Roll up the leaf into a neat cigar shape. Stuff the remaining grape leaves in the same way. Place the packages, seam side down, in a baking dish and tuck the slivers of garlic between them.

Mix together the tomatoes, the remaining lemon juice, the sugar, and some pepper, and pour the mixture into the baking dish. Cover the dish with a lid or with plastic wrap, pulling one corner back for venting. Microwave on high for 10 minutes. Reduce the power to medium and cook for another 15 minutes, turning the dish every three minutes. Allow the grape leaves to stand for five minutes, then serve with the yogurt.

SUGGESTED ACCOMPANIMENT: *salad of tomatoes, cucumber, onion, and olives.*

Lamb Timbales

THIS RECIPE IS IDEAL FOR USING UP LAMB LEFT OVER FROM BONING A LOIN FOR DISHES CALLING FOR EYE OF LOIN ONLY.

Serves 6
Working (and total) time: about 1 hour and 15 minutes

Calories **150**
Protein **17g.**
Cholesterol **40mg.**
Total fat **7g.**
Saturated fat **3g.**
Sodium **145mg.**

6 oz. lean loin of lamb, all fat and connective tissue removed, ground 3 times, and well chilled
¼ lb. lamb slices from the sirloin end of the leg, trimmed of fat and flattened (technique, page 24)
1 large sweet red pepper
3 large zucchini (about 10½ oz.), ends trimmed
¼ cup fresh fine breadcrumbs
4 tbsp. skim milk
1 tsp. arrowroot
6 tbsp. sour cream
1 tsp. finely chopped fresh marjoram, or ¼ tsp. dried marjoram
1 tbsp. tomato paste
½ tsp. salt
ground white pepper
1 tsp. virgin olive oil

Prick the pepper several times with a fork or a skewer, place it on a double layer of paper towels, and microwave it on high until it is soft—about five minutes—turning it once. Place the pepper in a bowl and cover it with plastic wrap. After 5 to 10 minutes, skin, halve, derib, and seed the pepper. Using a 1½-inch-diameter cookie cutter, stamp out six rounds from the pepper and set them aside.

Cut two thin slices from one end of each zucchini, then cut the zucchini into thin strips by running the full width of a potato peeler along their lengths. Place the slices and strips in a shallow microwave dish, add 2 tablespoons of water, and cover with plastic wrap, lifting one corner slightly to allow excess steam to escape. Microwave on high for two minutes, carefully turning the slices and strips with a slotted spatula after one minute. Lift the softened strips onto a double layer of paper towels and let them drain.

Place a zucchini slice followed by a pepper round in the bottom of each cup of a 6-cup microwave muffin tray; the cups used here are 2½ by 1¾ inches. Then line the cups with slightly overlapping zucchini strips, allowing 1½ inches of each strip to hang over the rims of the cups. Set the lined cups aside.

To make the mousse, soak the breadcrumbs in the

milk for two minutes. In a small bowl, blend the arrowroot with 1 tablespoon of the sour cream, then stir in the remaining sour cream. In a large bowl, combine the ground lamb and soaked breadcrumbs, then stir in the sour cream, marjoram, tomato paste, salt, and some white pepper. Place all the ingredients in a food processor and process until the mixture is smooth—about two minutes. Spoon half of the lamb mousse into the cups to fill them halfway.

Preheat a browning dish according to the manufacturer's instructions. Using a 2¼-inch round cutter as a guide, cut six round shapes from the cutlets with a sharp knife. Pour the oil into the dish and immediately arrange the rounds of meat in the dish in a single layer. Microwave on high until the meat is browned—about one minute—turning once after 30 seconds. Remove the cutlets and gently place one round on top of the mousse mixture in each cup. Distribute the remaining mousse among the cups—it will mound up about ½ inch above the rims. Fold the ends of the zucchini strips over the mousse to enclose it.

Cover the cups loosely with plastic wrap and cook the timbales on medium high for four minutes, turning them once. Remove the cups from the microwave and allow them to rest, still covered, for four minutes more. Turn the timbales out of their cups and serve them hot.

SUGGESTED ACCOMPANIMENTS: *tomato concassé; salad.*

EDITOR'S NOTE: *For a smooth mousse, it is essential to grind the meat in this recipe by passing it through a grinder three times; a food processor will not remove the connective tissue.*

Sage-Marinated Lamb Chops

Serves 4
Working time: about 25 minutes
Total time: about 1 hour and 20 minutes
(includes marinating)

Calories **235**
Protein **25g.**
Cholesterol **75mg.**
Total fat **12g.**
Saturated fat **6g.**
Sodium **175mg.**

8 lamb loin chops (about 4 oz. each), trimmed of fat
2 tsp. chopped fresh sage, or ¾ tsp. crumbled dried sage
3 garlic cloves, finely chopped
grated zest of 1 lemon
2 tbsp. balsamic vinegar, or 1½ tbsp. red wine vinegar mixed with ½ tsp. honey
1 tbsp. dark brown sugar
1 tbsp. brandy
¼ tsp. salt
freshly ground black pepper

Mix the sage, garlic, lemon zest, vinegar, brown sugar, brandy, salt, and some pepper in an 8-inch-square glass dish. Add the lamb chops to the dish and turn them to coat them with the marinade. Let the lamb chops stand for one hour at room temperature; turn the chops every 15 minutes while they marinate.

Microwave the chops, uncovered, on high for two minutes. Rotate the dish 180 degrees. Turn the chops over, rearranging them so that the chops that were on the outside are now in the center. Cook the chops on high for three minutes more. Remove the dish from the oven and loosely cover it with aluminum foil. Let the lamb chops stand for five minutes before serving them.

SUGGESTED ACCOMPANIMENTS: *stewed tomatoes; steamed new potatoes.*

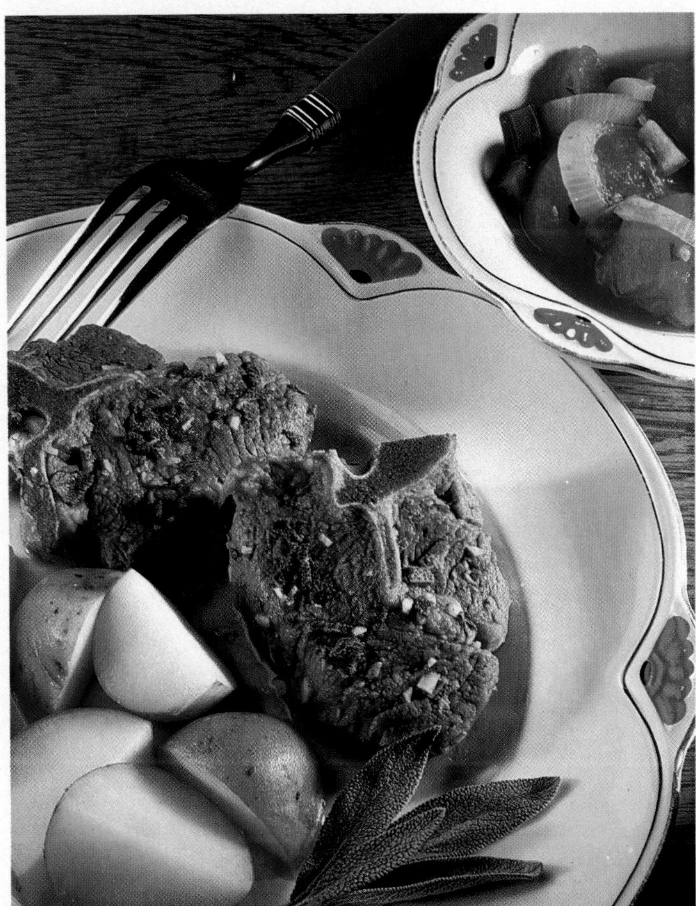

Lamb Roast with Winter Vegetables

Serves 8
Working time: about 30 minutes
Total time: about 1 hour

Calories **220**
Protein **26g.**
Cholesterol **75mg.**
Total fat **8g.**
Saturated fat **3g.**
Sodium **175mg.**

one 4-lb. leg of lamb, sirloin half, trimmed of fat and boned
2 tsp. chili powder
1 tbsp. chopped fresh rosemary, or 2 tsp. dried rosemary, crumbled
freshly ground black pepper
1 small cauliflower (about 1¼ lb.), trimmed and divided into florets
3 carrots, sliced on the diagonal into 1-inch pieces
1 lb. Brussels sprouts, trimmed
⅔ cup unsalted brown stock or unsalted chicken stock (recipes, page 137)
¼ tsp. salt
1 tbsp. cornstarch, mixed with 2 tbsp. water

With your fingers, rub the chili powder over the outside of the roast, then sprinkle it with the rosemary and a generous grinding of pepper. Place the lamb in an oven cooking bag, and loosely tie the bag with string or a strip of plastic wrap, leaving an opening for steam to escape. Make sure that the opening faces upward so that the cooking juices do not run out. Place the roast in a shallow dish.

Microwave the roast on medium (50 percent power) for 16 minutes. Rotate the dish 180 degrees, then turn the lamb over, taking care to keep the juices in the bag; cook the lamb for 16 minutes more.

While the lamb is roasting, pour enough water into a large pot to fill it about 1 inch deep. Set a vegetable steamer in the pot; put the cauliflower, carrots, and Brussels sprouts into the steamer, and cover the pot. Set the pot aside.

Remove the lamb from the oven and take it out of the roasting bag. Let the roast stand for 10 minutes. Pour the juices that have collected in the bag into a 1-quart bowl. Set the bowl aside. (At this point, an instant-reading meat thermometer inserted into the center of the roast should register 145° F.; if it does not, microwave the lamb for another five minutes at medium power.)

While the roast is resting, bring the water in the pot to a boil on the stovetop and steam the vegetables until they are tender—7 to 10 minutes.

To make the sauce, skim the fat off the top of the liquid in the bowl. Stir the brown or chicken stock, the salt, and the cornstarch mixture into the juices. Microwave the sauce on high until it has thickened—about two minutes. Stir it once again.

Slice the meat, arrange it on a platter surrounded by the vegetables, and pour the sauce over all.

SUGGESTED ACCOMPANIMENT: *whole-wheat dinner rolls.*

Lamb Baked in Saffron Yogurt

Serves 4
Working time: about 30 minutes
Total time: about 4 hours and 45 minutes (includes marinating)

Calories **195**
Protein **25g.**
Cholesterol **78mg.**
Total fat **8g.**
Saturated fat **3g.**
Sodium **90mg.**

1¼ lb. lean lamb (from the leg or loin), trimmed of fat and cut into 1-inch cubes
3 garlic cloves, finely chopped
2 tbsp. finely chopped fresh ginger
¼ tsp. saffron threads or turmeric
1 tbsp. cornstarch
1 jalapeño pepper, seeded, deribbed, and finely chopped (cautionary note, page 83)
¾ cup plain low-fat yogurt
4 radishes, thinly sliced, for garnish
2 scallions, trimmed and thinly sliced, for garnish

Mix the lamb cubes, chopped garlic and ginger, saffron or turmeric, cornstarch, jalapeño pepper, and low-fat yogurt in a baking dish. Cover the dish and refrigerate it for four hours.

Microwave the lamb and its marinade, covered with wax paper, on medium (50 percent power) for 15 minutes, stirring the mixture every five minutes. Let the dish stand for five minutes; stir it once again before serving. Garnish the lamb with the radishes and scallions before serving.

SUGGESTED ACCOMPANIMENTS: *yellow rice; green beans.*

EDITOR'S NOTE: *Do not marinate the lamb cubes for more than six hours; they will become too soft.*

Chili Meatballs with Two Pepper Sauces

Serves 4
Working time: about 30 minutes
Total time: about 40 minutes

Calories **225**
Protein **25g.**
Cholesterol **60mg.**
Total fat **8g.**
Saturated fat **3g.**
Sodium **175mg.**

¾ lb. lean lamb (from the leg or loin), trimmed of fat and ground or very finely chopped (technique, page 43)
1 celery stalk, finely chopped
½ cup whole-wheat breadcrumbs
2 small hot chilies, finely chopped (cautionary note, page 83)
2 tbsp. finely cut chives, plus a few chives for garnish
1 tsp. anchovy paste
¼ tsp. salt
1 tsp. virgin olive oil

Pepper sauces

1 sweet red pepper
1 sweet yellow pepper
2 tsp. white wine vinegar
2 tbsp. sour cream

First, make the sauces. Prick the sweet peppers in several places with a fork or a skewer, place them on a double layer of paper towels, spaced well apart, and microwave them on high until they are soft, turning them once—about five minutes. Place the peppers in a bowl, cover them with plastic wrap, and set them aside for 5 to 10 minutes. Peel off their skins and remove the seeds. Coarsely chop the red pepper, and purée it in a blender or a food processor with 1 teaspoon of the vinegar and 2 tablespoons of water until the mixture is smooth. Transfer the purée to a small bowl and stir in 1 tablespoon of the sour cream. Process the yellow pepper in the same way. Transfer it to a separate bowl and stir in the remaining sour cream.

To make the meatballs, mix together the lamb, celery, breadcrumbs, chilies, cut chives, anchovy paste, and salt. Using your hands, form the mixture into 20 balls, each about 1 inch in diameter.

Preheat a browning dish following the manufacturer's instructions. Immediately add the olive oil and meatballs, turning the meatballs until they stop sizzling. Cover them with a lid, or with plastic wrap with one corner pulled back for venting, and microwave them on high for five minutes, turning them once. Let the meatballs stand for three minutes.

Meanwhile, heat the red- and yellow-pepper sauces on medium for one and a half minutes; if the bowls are small enough, they should fit in the microwave oven together. Spoon the red-pepper sauce around the edges of four warmed serving plates, and spoon the yellow-pepper sauce into the center of each plate. Use a skewer to draw a pattern in the pepper sauces (technique, page 118). Distribute the meatballs among the plates and serve immediately, garnished with the reserved chives.

SUGGESTED ACCOMPANIMENT: *rice pilaf.*

Meat Loaf with Olives

Serves 6
Working time: about 15 minutes
Total time: about 30 minutes

Calories **275**
Protein **32g.**
Cholesterol **85mg.**
Total fat **12g.**
Saturated fat **5g.**
Sodium **320mg.**

1¾ lb. lean lamb (from the leg or loin), trimmed of fat and ground or very finely chopped (technique, page 43)
1 egg white, lightly beaten
1 tbsp. chopped fresh oregano, or 1 tsp. dried oregano
¼ tsp. cayenne pepper
2 garlic cloves, finely chopped
¼ cup finely chopped onion
¼ cup chopped parsley
6 oil-cured black olives, pitted and finely chopped
⅔ cup dry breadcrumbs
¼ cup freshly grated Parmesan cheese
1 tbsp. red wine vinegar
1½ tbsp. tomato paste

In a bowl, combine the egg white, oregano, cayenne, garlic, and onion. Add the lamb, parsley, olives, breadcrumbs, cheese, vinegar, and 1 tablespoon of the tomato paste; mix well with a wooden spoon.

Shape the meat mixture into a log about 3 inches in diameter. Place the log in a shallow baking dish and spread the remaining ½ tablespoon of tomato paste over the meat. Cook the meat loaf, uncovered, on high for 10 to 12 minutes, rotating the dish a half turn midway through the cooking time. Let the loaf stand for 10 minutes before slicing it into 12 pieces.

SUGGESTED ACCOMPANIMENTS: *mashed rutabaga; steamed shredded spring greens.*

Diced Lamb with Pink Grapefruit and Tarragon

Serves 4
Working (and total) time: about 50 minutes

Calories **340**
Protein **35g.**
Cholesterol **75mg.**
Total fat **11g.**
Saturated fat **6g.**
Sodium **310mg.**

1 lb. lean lamb (from the leg or loin), trimmed of fat and cut into ½-inch cubes
1½ pink grapefruits
1 bunch scallions, trimmed and cut diagonally into 1-inch pieces
3 tbsp. dry white vermouth
1 tbsp. chopped fresh tarragon, or 1 tsp. dried tarragon
1½ lb. spinach, washed, stems removed
2 tbsp. cornstarch
1 tsp. honey
¼ tsp. salt
freshly ground black pepper
¼ cup sour cream

Squeeze out and reserve the juice from the half grapefruit. Using a sharp knife, remove the skin and white pith from the remaining grapefruit, then carefully cut out the flesh from between the membranes, and reserve the segments.

Put the lamb cubes, grapefruit juice, scallions, white vermouth, and tarragon into a 2½-quart casserole dish, and stir. Cover with a lid or with plastic wrap, pulling one corner back to vent, and microwave on medium for 15 minutes, stirring every five minutes. Remove the casserole from the oven and let it stand while you prepare the spinach.

Shake any excess water off the spinach and put it into a large bowl. Cover with plastic wrap, pulling back one corner, and cook on high until the spinach is wilted and tender—five to six minutes. Drain the spinach well, squeeze out as much water as possible, and coarsely chop it. Arrange the spinach around the edge of a microwave-safe serving dish.

Mix the cornstarch with 2 tablespoons of water and stir it into the lamb, together with half of the grapefruit segments and the honey. Cook the mixture, uncovered, on high for five minutes, stirring twice, then stir it well once more. Season the lamb with the salt and some pepper, add the remaining grapefruit segments, and stir in the sour cream. Spoon the lamb mixture into the center of the spinach-rimmed dish and reheat on high for two minutes. Serve immediately.

SUGGESTED ACCOMPANIMENT: *boiled rice.*

Butterfly Chops with Barbecue Sauce

BECAUSE METAL MUST NOT BE USED IN THE MICROWAVE, THE BONED CHOPS IN THIS RECIPE ARE SECURED WITH WOODEN TOOTHPICKS INSTEAD OF METAL SKEWERS.

Serves 6
Working (and total) time: about 1 hour

Calories **270**
Protein **28g.**
Cholesterol **80mg.**
Total fat **12g.**
Saturated fat **5g.**
Sodium **280mg.**

6 double loin butterfly chops (about 6 oz. each), boned and trimmed of fat (technique, page 32), secured with wooden toothpicks

unpeeled pineapple wedges for garnish

Barbecue sauce

½ fresh pineapple, coarsely chopped, or 8 oz. unsweetened canned pineapple chunks, drained and coarsely chopped

7 oz. canned tomatoes, drained and sieved

3 tbsp. low-sodium soy sauce

3 tbsp. honey

2 tbsp. red wine vinegar

2 garlic cloves, crushed

¼ tsp. cayenne pepper

2 tsp. paprika

freshly ground black pepper

To make the sauce, purée the pineapple in a blender or a food processor, then press the purée through a fine sieve into a large, clean bowl to remove any stringy pieces. Add the remaining sauce ingredients to the pineapple purée and stir well. Microwave, uncovered, on high for 10 minutes, stirring every two minutes. Set the sauce aside.

Heat a browning dish for the maximum time allowed in the instruction manual. Brown the chops on both sides in the dish, then cover and microwave on high for three minutes; turn and rearrange the chops after one and a half minutes. Skim off any fat.

Pour the barbecue sauce over and around the meat. Microwave, uncovered, for four minutes—turning and rearranging the chops after two minutes. Serve the chops garnished with pineapple wedges.

SUGGESTED ACCOMPANIMENTS: *red potatoes roasted in their skins; green salad.*

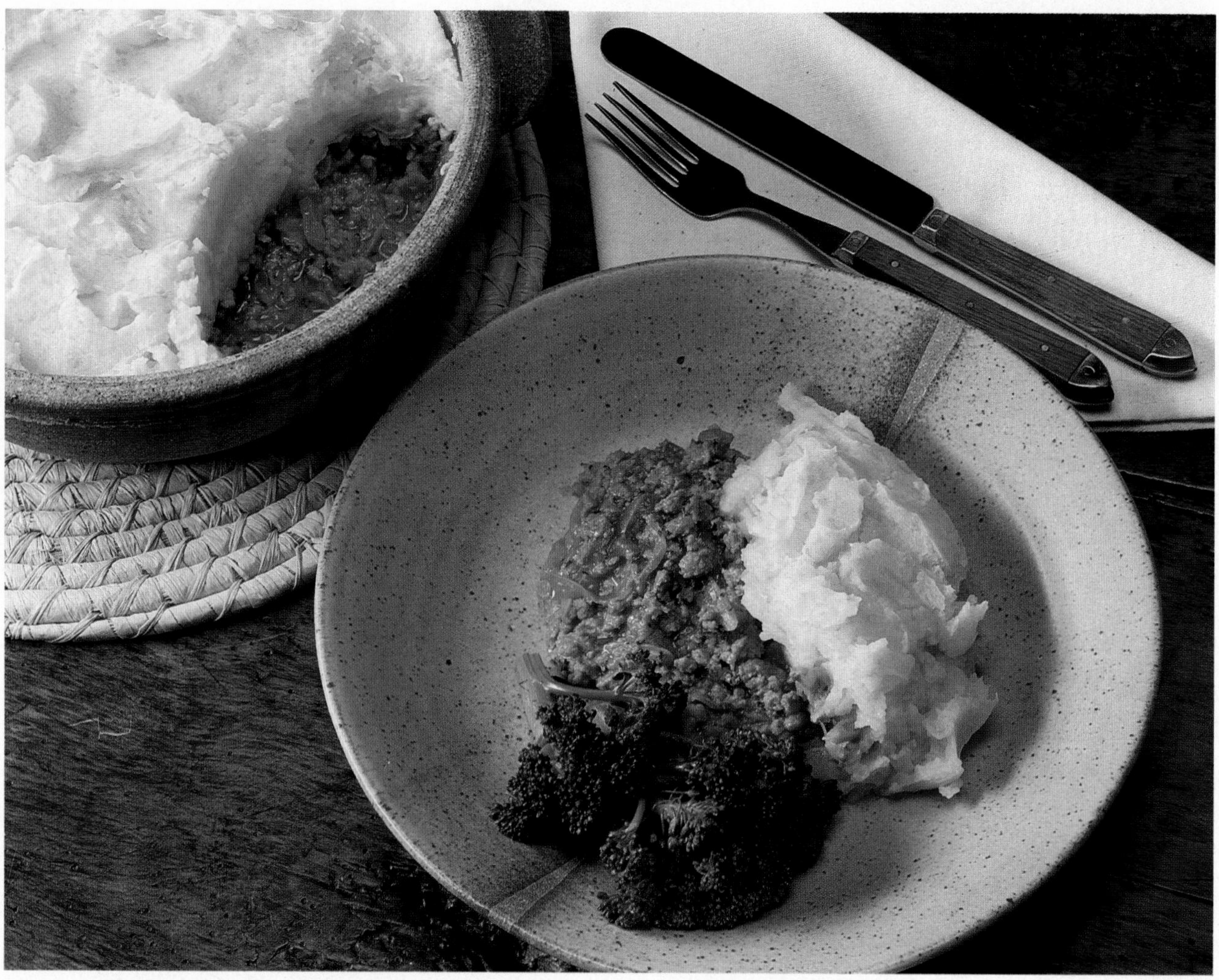

Cottage Pie

Serves 6
Working (and total) time: about 1 hour and 30 minutes

Calories **250**
Protein **22g.**
Cholesterol **55mg.**
Total fat **8g.**
Saturated fat **3g.**
Sodium **240mg.**

1 lb. lean lamb from the loin end of the leg, trimmed of fat and ground or very finely chopped (technique, page 43)
4 medium potatoes, peeled and sliced
3 medium carrots, peeled and sliced
1 medium rutabaga, peeled and sliced
1 tbsp. safflower oil
1 large onion, halved and thinly sliced
3 tbsp. unbleached all-purpose flour
½ cup unsalted brown stock (recipe, page 137)
freshly ground black pepper
½ tsp. salt
2 tbsp. chopped parsley

Put the sliced potatoes, carrots, and rutabaga into a microwave-safe mixing bowl with 6 tablespoons of cold water. Cover the bowl with plastic wrap and pull one side back to vent. Microwave the vegetables on high, stirring every five minutes, until they are soft—about 20 minutes. Remove the dish from the oven and allow the vegetables to stand for five minutes.

Meanwhile, heat a browning dish on high for the maximum time allowed in the manufacturer's instructions. Add the oil and the onion. Cover the dish and microwave on high for two to three minutes, until the onion is soft. Add the lamb and cook, uncovered, on high for two minutes, stirring every 30 seconds with a fork to break up the meat. Stir in the flour and add the stock. Microwave on high for three minutes, stirring every minute. Season with black pepper and half of the salt; stir in the parsley. Spoon the meat into a microwave-safe serving dish.

Using a vegetable masher, mash the potatoes, carrots, and rutabaga, together with any liquid left in the bowl, to create a creamy purée. Season with black pepper and the remaining salt. Spoon the vegetable purée evenly over the meat. Mark swirls on the surface of the purée with a small metal spatula.

Microwave the cottage pie on high for 15 minutes, giving the dish a quarter turn every five minutes. Serve the pie immediately.

SUGGESTED ACCOMPANIMENT: *steamed broccoli or spinach.*

Mediterranean Zucchini

Serves 4
Working (and total) time: about 45 minutes

Calories **160**
Protein **20g.**
Cholesterol **50mg.**
Total fat **5g.**
Saturated fat **2g.**
Sodium **240mg.**

½ lb. lean lamb (from the leg or loin), trimmed of fat and ground or very finely chopped (technique, page 43)
4 zucchini (about 3½ oz. each), ends trimmed
1 tsp. virgin olive oil
½ garlic clove, peeled
¼ cup sun-dried tomatoes, drained of any oil and chopped
1 tbsp. tomato paste
½ tsp. ground cinnamon
3 tbsp. raisins
2 tbsp. pine nuts
1½ tsp. balsamic vinegar, or 1 tsp. red wine vinegar mixed with ⅓ tsp. honey
2 tbsp. finely chopped fresh basil, or 2 tsp. dried basil
½ tsp. salt
freshly ground black pepper

Halve the zucchini lengthwise and arrange them in a single layer in a shallow dish, cut sides upward. Add 1 tablespoon of water and cover the dish with plastic wrap, pulling back one corner to allow excess steam to escape. Cook the zucchini on high for eight minutes; halfway through the cooking time, rearrange them to move the inside pieces to the edges of the dish. Drain the zucchini well. Scoop out the pulp, taking care to leave the skins intact, and place the pulp in a sieve to drain.

Put the oil into a shallow dish and heat on high for 15 seconds. Spear the garlic on a fork and wipe it around the hot dish to infuse the oil. Discard the garlic. Break up the ground lamb with a fork and add it to the dish, along with the sun-dried tomatoes, tomato paste, and cinnamon. Cook on high until no pink meat is visible—three to four minutes—stirring and breaking up the meat thoroughly with a fork every minute. Drain off any fat after cooking.

Add the raisins and pine nuts to the meat, along with the zucchini pulp, and stir in the vinegar, basil, salt, and some pepper. Pile the mixture into the zucchini skins and arrange them in a single layer in the shallow dish. Cover the dish with plastic wrap, leaving one corner loose for venting. Cook on high until the zucchini are tender—four to six minutes—rearranging once halfway through the cooking. Let the zucchini rest, covered, for two minutes before serving them.

SUGGESTED ACCOMPANIMENT: *arugula and radicchio salad.*

EDITOR'S NOTE: *For this dish, tender young zucchini are needed. If you can obtain only mature zucchini, precook them whole in boiling water containing 1 teaspoon of salt for two minutes to remove any bitterness in the skins.*

Techniques

Boning a Loin of Lamb

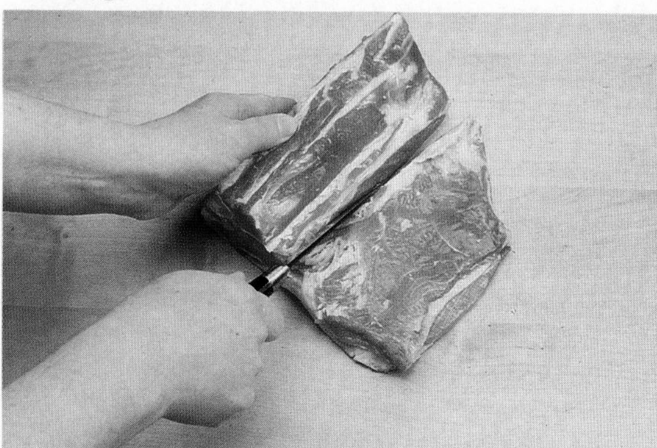

1 *REMOVING THE FATTY FLAP. A loin is generally sold with a flap of fatty meat attached to it. Cut off the flap where it joins the loin and then discard the flap.*

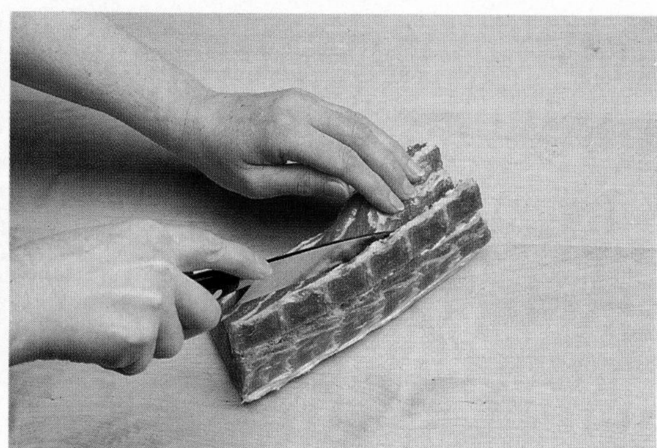

2 *STARTING THE BONING. With the fatty layer of the loin facing down, insert the tip of a sharp, pointed knife between the meat and the backbone, and use short, slicing strokes to separate one from the other.*

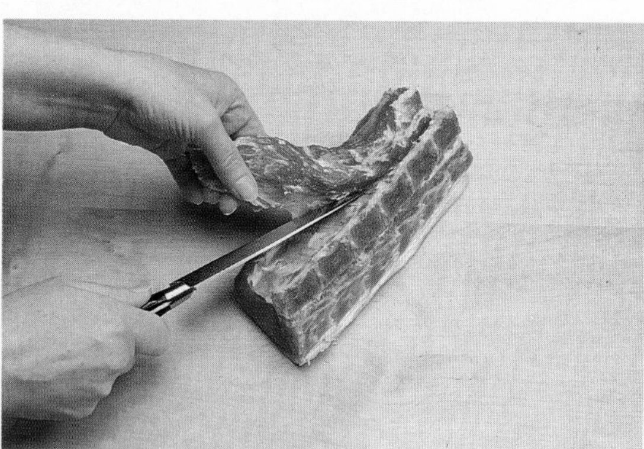

3 *REMOVING THE TENDERLOIN. Carefully pulling away the meat with one hand, continue cutting along the ribs until the tenderloin is freed.*

4 *REMOVING THE LOIN. Flip the rib bones over to expose the underneath. Again, carefully cut the meat from the bones, using the same technique as demonstrated in Steps 2 and 3.*

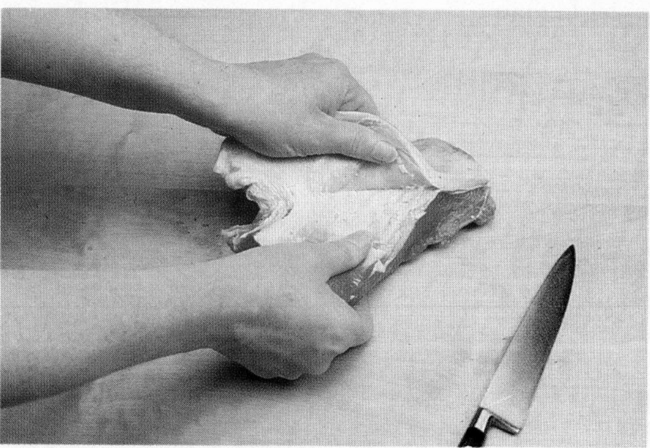

5 *PEELING OFF THE FATTY LAYER. Pick up the loin in your hands and remove the thick layer of fat from the meat by gently pulling it off. If this is done carefully, the whole layer should come away in one piece.*

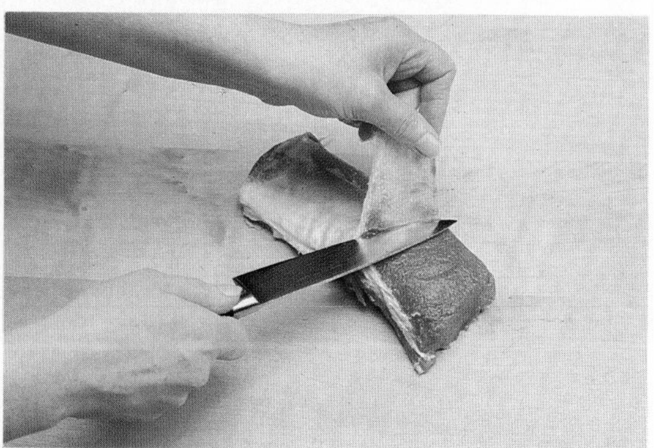

6 *STRIPPING OFF THE SILVER SKIN. With the knife tip, cut under the whitish membrane of the loin to form a tab. Pull the tab taut, insert the knife under it, and remove the silver skin.*

Preparing a Loin Chop

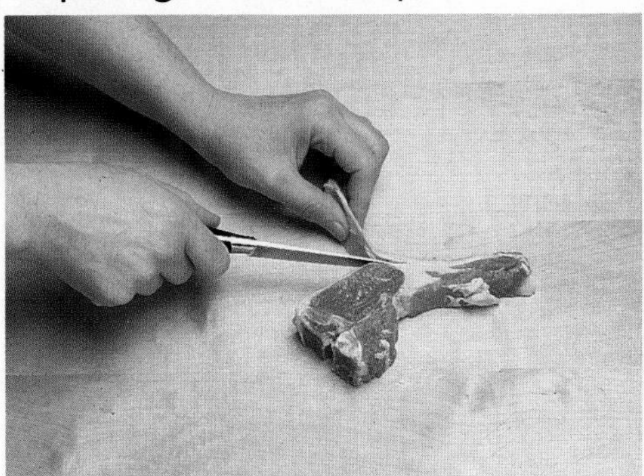

1 REMOVING THE SKIN. *Place the chop on a wooden board. Insert the tip of a sharp knife in the small channel across the base of the bone and pry out the piece of white spinal cord. Then trim the skin and underlying fat from the convex side of the meat.*

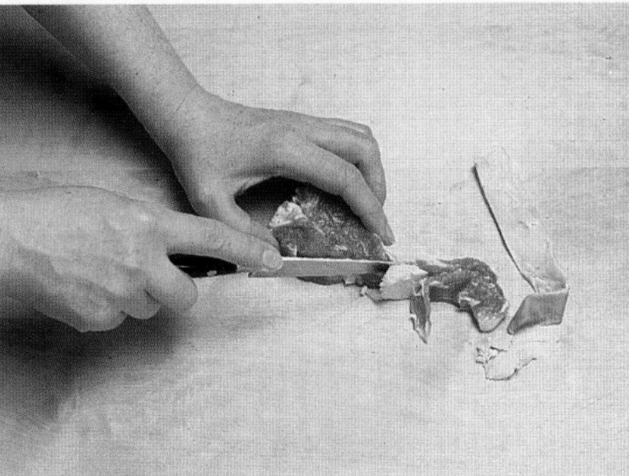

2 TRIMMING EXCESS FAT. *Cut away most of the fat between the loin and flap, leaving enough tissue to keep the chop intact.*

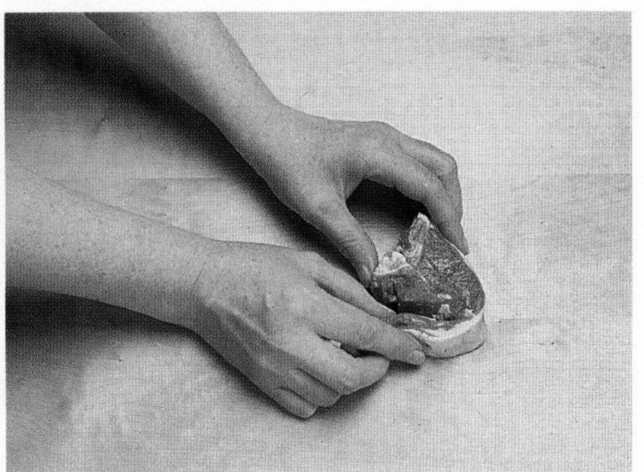

3 SHAPING THE CHOP. *Curl the flap around the tenderloin to form a neat shape. Insert a skewer or a wooden pick through the flap to keep it in place.*

Preparing Racks for Roasting

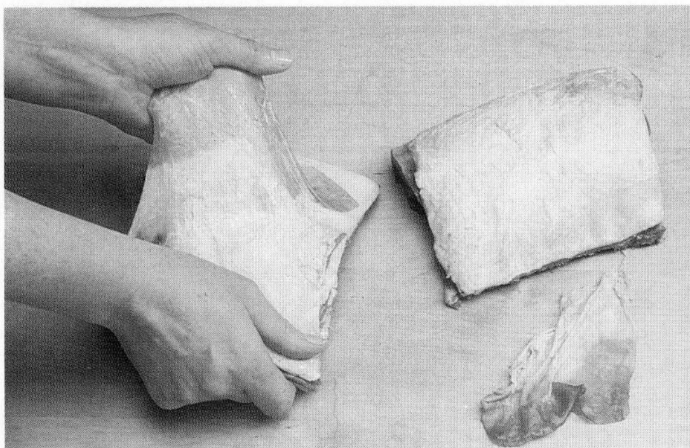

1 STRIPPING OFF THE OUTER MEMBRANE. *Remove any remnant of the shoulder blade, Step 1, page 136. With the rack's convex side up, peel the membrane away from the fat and meat. Start at one corner, and when you have loosened enough membrane, grasp it with one hand, and hold down the fat and meat with the other as you strip it off.*

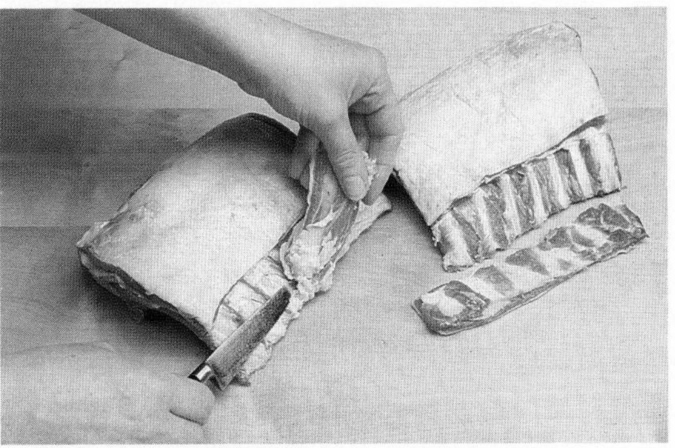

2 EXPOSING THE RIB ENDS. *Score a straight line across the rack, about 2 inches from the tips of the ribs. Pull and cut off the layer of fat and meat between the line and the rib tips to expose the ends of the bones.*

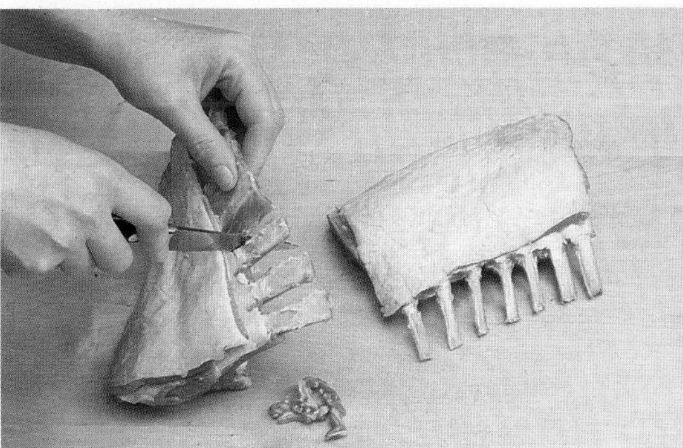

3 CLEANING THE RIB TIPS. *With a knife, cut out the meat and fat from between the bared rib ends. (Save these strips of meat to use in stews.) Holding the rack firmly, scrape the exposed bones with the knife to remove any remaining bits of meat and fat. Be careful not to split the fragile bones.*

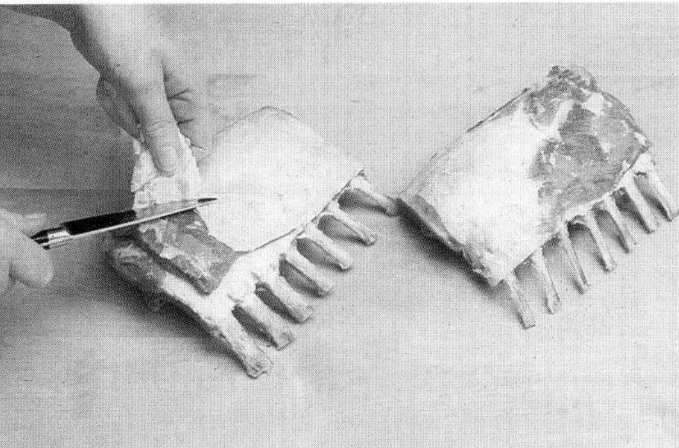

4 REMOVING EXCESS FAT. *Holding the knife blade almost parallel with the meat, pare any excess fat from the meat.*

Preparing Noisettes from a Rack

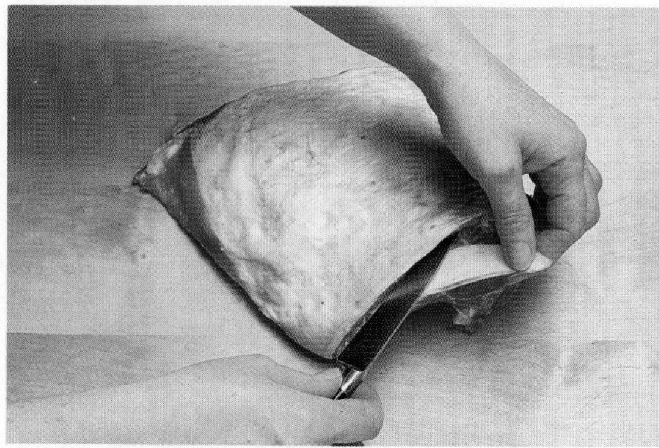

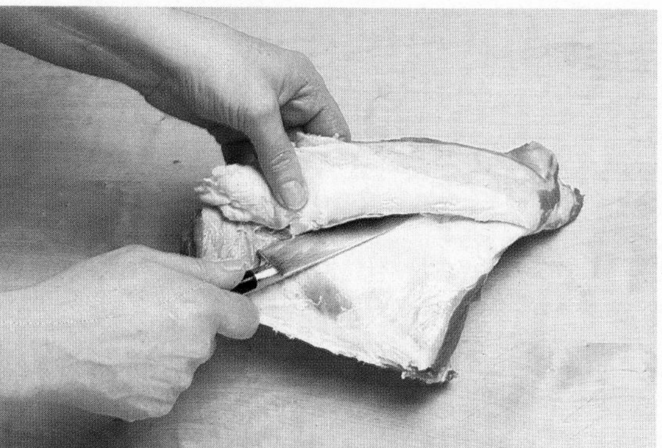

1 *REMOVING THE SHOULDER-BLADE REMNANT. Place the rack, concave side down, on a wooden board. Slit open the shoulder end with a small, pointed knife and cut out any remnant of the shoulder blade.*

2 *STRIPPING OFF THE FAT. Insert the knife blade between the outer layer of fat and the lean meat. Keeping the blade as close to the meat as possible, work it to loosen the fat and attached outer membrane, taking care not to cut into the flesh. Peel back the fat as you loosen it. Trim any remaining fat, keeping the knife blade parallel to the meat.*

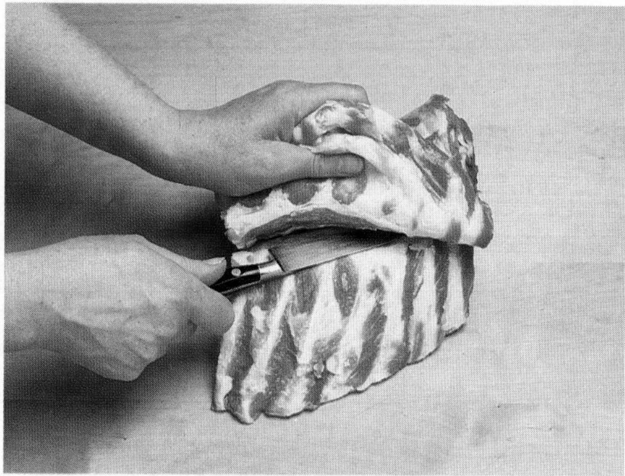

3 *FREEING THE MEAT FROM THE RIBS. Insert the knife blade between the meat and the tips of the rib bones. Keeping the blade parallel with the rib bones, work the knife along the bones to free the meat. Pull the meat back as you release it and take care that the knife does not cut into it (above, left). Continue working the knife between the loin and the base of the rib bones until the blade reaches the backbone (above, right).*

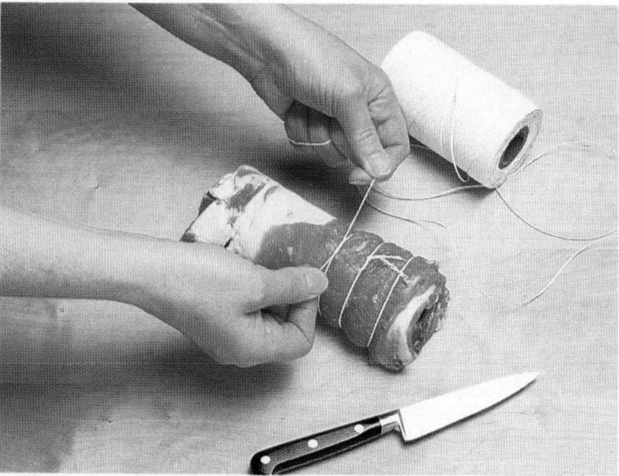

4 *CUTTING THE MEAT FROM THE BACKBONE. Turn the meat around, insert the blade between the loin and the backbone, and detach the loin and attached flap of meat. Then cut away the gristle from the loin.*

5 *ROLLING UP THE LAMB. Starting at the loin end, roll up the meat into a compact cylinder. Pull free about 36 inches of string and tie it around the meat at 1-inch intervals, cutting the string after each knot. Slice the meat into noisettes.*

Brown Stock

Makes about 3 quarts
Working time: about 40 minutes
Total time: about 6 hours

3 lb. veal breast (or veal-shank or beef-shank meat), cut into 3-inch pieces
3 lb. uncooked veal or beef bones, cracked
2 onions, quartered
2 celery stalks, chopped
2 carrots, sliced
3 unpeeled garlic cloves, crushed
8 black peppercorns
3 cloves
2 tsp. fresh thyme, or ½ tsp. dried thyme leaves
1 bay leaf

Preheat the oven to 425° F. Place the meat, bones, onions, celery, and carrots in a large roasting pan, and roast them in the oven until they are well browned—about one hour. Transfer the contents of the roasting pan to a stockpot. Pour 2 cups of water into the roasting pan, scrape up the browned bits from the bottom, and add the liquid to the pot.

Add the garlic, peppercorns, and cloves. Add enough water to cover the contents by about 3 inches. Bring the liquid to a boil, then lower the heat to maintain a simmer, and skim any scum from the surface. Add the thyme and bay leaf, then simmer for four hours, skimming occasionally. Strain the stock; discard the solids. Let the stock stand until tepid, then refrigerate it overnight or put it in the freezer long enough for the fat to congeal. Spoon off and discard the fat.

Tightly covered and refrigerated, the stock may be safely kept for two or three days. Stored in small, tightly covered freezer containers and frozen, the stock may be kept for as long as six months.

EDITOR'S NOTE: *Thoroughly browning the meat, bones, and vegetables in the oven should produce a rich mahogany color. If your stock does not seem dark enough, cook 1 tablespoon of tomato paste in a small pan over medium heat, stirring constantly, until it darkens—about three minutes. Add this to the stock about one hour before the end of cooking. Any combination of meat and bones may be used. Ask your butcher to crack the bones.*

Chicken Stock

Makes about 2 quarts
Working time: about 20 minutes
Total time: about 4 hours

5 lb. uncooked chicken trimmings and bones, the bones cracked with a heavy knife
2 carrots, cut into ½-inch-thick rounds
2 celery stalks, cut into 1-inch pieces
2 large onions (about 1 lb.) cut in half, 1 half stuck with 2 cloves
2 sprigs fresh thyme, or ½ tsp. dried thyme leaves
1 or 2 bay leaves
10 to 15 parsley stems
5 black peppercorns

Put the chicken trimmings and bones into a heavy stockpot; pour in enough water to cover them by about 2 inches. Bring the liquid to a boil over medium heat, skimming off the scum that rises to the surface. Lower the heat and simmer the liquid for 10 minutes, skimming and adding a little cold water to help precipitate the scum.

Add the vegetables, herbs, and peppercorns, and submerge them in the liquid. If necessary, pour in enough additional water to cover the contents of the pot. Simmer the stock for two to three hours, skimming as necessary to remove the scum.

Strain the stock and discard the solids. Allow the stock to stand until it is tepid, then refrigerate it overnight or put it in the freezer long enough for the fat to congeal. Spoon off and discard the layer of fat.

Tightly covered and refrigerated, the stock may be safely kept for two or three days. Stored in small, tightly covered freezer containers and frozen, the stock may be kept for as long as six months.

EDITOR'S NOTE: *The chicken gizzard and heart may be added to the stock. Wings and necks—rich in natural gelatin—produce a particularly gelatinous stock, ideal for sauces and jellied dishes. The liver should never be used for stock.*

Glossary

Allspice: the dried berry of a member of the myrtle family. Used whole or ground, it is called allspice because its flavor resembles a combination of clove, cinnamon, and nutmeg.
Arrowroot: a tasteless, starchy white powder refined from the root of a tropical plant; it is used to thicken purées and sauces. Unlike flour, it is transparent when cooked.
Aspic: a clear savory jelly made from reduced stock. It is used for coating meat, fish, or vegetables, or for encasing them in decorative molds.
Balsamic vinegar: a mild, extremely fragrant wine-based vinegar made in northern Italy. Traditionally, the vinegar is aged for at least seven years in a series of casks made of various woods.
Basil: a leafy herb with a strong, spicy aroma when fresh, often used in Italian cooking. Covered with olive oil and refrigerated in a tightly sealed container, fresh basil leaves may be kept for up to six months.
Baste: to help brown and flavor a food, and keep it from drying out, by pouring pan drippings or other liquid over it during cooking.
Bâtonnet (also called bâton): a vegetable piece that has been cut in the shape of a stick; bâtonnets—usually about 1½ inches long and ¼ inch square—are slightly larger than julienne.
Bay leaves: the aromatic leaves of *Laurus nobilis*—a Mediterranean evergreen—used fresh or dried to flavor stocks and stews; also available in powder form. Dried bay leaves when broken have very sharp edges and can injure internally, so they should be removed before serving.
Bean curd: see Tofu.
Belgian endive: a small, cigar-shaped vegetable, composed of many tightly wrapped white to pale yellow leaves that have a pleasant bitter flavor.
Blanch: to partially cook food by briefly immersing it in boiling water. Blanching makes thin-skinned fruits and vegetables easier to peel; it can also mellow strong flavors.
Braise: to cook meat, vegetables, or a combination of the two with liquid over low heat. Braising can be done in the oven or on top of the stove. It helps to moisten and tenderize the food.
Buckwheat groats (also called kasha): the nutty-tasting seeds of the buckwheat plant, hulled, steamed, dried, and sometimes ground; often also toasted to intensify flavor.
Bulb fennel: see Fennel.
Bulgur: whole-wheat kernels that have been steamed, dried, and cracked.
Calorie (or kilocalorie): a precise measure of the energy food supplies when it is broken down for use in the body.
Cardamom: the bittersweet, aromatic dried seeds or whole pods of a plant in the ginger family. Cardamom seeds may be used whole or ground.
Caul: a weblike fatty membrane that lines a pig's intestines. When wrapped around a lean ground-meat filling, it melts during cooking and moistens the meat.
Cayenne pepper: a fiery powder ground from the seeds and pods of red chili peppers; used in small amounts to heighten other flavors.
Chervil: a lacy, slightly anise-flavored herb often used as a companion to other herbs, such as tarragon and chives. Because long cooking may kill its flavor, chervil should be added at the last minute.
Chili peppers: hot or mild red, yellow, or green members of the pepper family. Fresh or dried, most chili peppers contain volatile oils that can irritate the skin and eyes; they must be handled carefully *(cautionary note, page 83).*
Chine: the backbone of an animal.
Cholesterol: a waxlike substance that is manufactured in the human liver and also found in foods of animal origin. Although a certain amount of cholesterol is necessary for proper body functioning, an excess can accumulate in the arteries, contributing to heart disease. See also Monounsaturated fat; Polyunsaturated fat; Saturated fat.
Cilantro (also called fresh coriander and Chinese parsley): the fresh leaves of the coriander plant; cilantro imparts a lemony, pleasingly pungent flavor to many Latin American, Indian, and Asian dishes.
Concassé: a sauce of a crushed or chopped vegetable, usually tomato; from the French word for crush or chop.
Cornstarch: a starchy white powder made from corn kernels and used to thicken many puddings and sauces. Like arrowroot, it is transparent when cooked. When cooked conventionally, a liquid containing cornstarch must be stirred constantly in the early stages to prevent lumps from forming.
Coulis: a sieved vegetable or fruit purée.
Couscous: a fine semolina grain, traditionally served with the classic North African stew of the same name.
Crème de cassis: a black-currant liqueur.
Cumin: the aromatic seeds of an umbelliferous plant similar to fennel, used whole or powdered as a spice, especially in Indian and Latin American dishes. Toasting gives it a nutty flavor.
Cutlet: in this volume, an adaptation of the traditional veal cutlet. A thin slice of lean lamb is cut from the sirloin end of the leg, then flattened out and tenderized with a mallet before frying or broiling.
Dark sesame oil: a dark seasoning oil made from toasted sesame seeds, high in polyunsaturated fats, with a nutty, smoky aroma. Because the oil has a relatively low smoking point, it is rarely heated.
Deglaze: to dissolve the brown particles left in a pan after roasting or sautéing by stirring in wine, stock, water, or cream.
Degrease: to remove the accumulated fat from cooking liquid by skimming it off with a spoon or blotting it up with paper towels. To eliminate the last traces of fat, draw an ice cube through the warm liquid; the fat will cling to the cube.
Dijon mustard: a smooth mustard once manufactured only in Dijon, France; it may be flavored with herbs, green peppercorns, or wine.
Escarole: a broad-leafed green with a pleasantly bitter flavor; escarole is best used in combination with sweeter greens.
Fat: a basic component of many foods, comprising three types of fatty acid—saturated, monounsaturated, and polyunsaturated—in varying proportions. See also Monounsaturated fat; Polyunsaturated fat; Saturated fat.
Fennel (also called Florence fennel or *finocchio):* a vegetable with feathery leaves and a thick, bulbous stalk having a mild licorice flavor. It can be eaten raw or cooked. The leaves are used both as a garnish and as a flavoring.
Fenugreek: a plant native to Asia. The seeds are highly aromatic with a bitter aftertaste and are normally used as a flavoring in Indian cuisine.
Fermented black beans: soybeans that have been cured in salt, sometimes with citrus peel; used in Chinese dishes. To remove their excess salt, rinse the beans before use.
Feta cheese: a salty Greek and Middle Eastern cheese made from goat's or sheep's milk. The curds are ripened in their own salted whey.
Five-spice powder: a pungent blend of ground Sichuan pepper, star anise, cinnamon, cloves, and fennel seeds; available in Asian groceries.
Ginger: the spicy, buff-colored rhizome, or rootlike stem, of the ginger plant, used as a seasoning either in fresh form or dried and powdered. Dried ginger makes a poor substitute for fresh ginger.
Grape leaves: the tender, lightly flavored leaves of the grapevine, used in many Mediterranean cuisines as wrappers for savory mixtures. Fresh grape leaves should be cooked for five minutes in boiling water before being used in a recipe; grape leaves packed in brine should be thoroughly rinsed.
Gratin: a baked dish with a crunchy topping of breadcrumbs or grated cheese browned in the oven or under the broiler.
Green peppercorns: the green, unripened berries from the pepper vine. Sold fresh, dried, or preserved in brine, the same berries are used to make black, red, and white pepper.
Hazelnut: the fruit of a shrublike tree found primarily in Turkey, Italy, and Spain, and in the United States.
Horseradish: a plant native to Eastern Europe and Asia. Its cylindrical root is grated for use as a pungent flavoring.
Hot red-pepper sauce: a hot, unsweetened chili sauce. A similar Asian version is the Thai *sriracha* sauce.
Julienne: the French term for vegetables or other food cut into matchstick-size pieces.
Juniper berries: the berries of the juniper tree, used as the key flavoring in gin. They lend a resinous tang to marinades and sauces.
Kasha: see Buckwheat groats.
Kohlrabi: a cruciferous vegetable with an enlarged stem in the form of a light green or lavender bulb.
Loin: the tender strip of lean meat from the rib. Also the larger of the two tender strips that make up a loin. (The other strip is the tenderloin.)
Madeira: a fortified wine from the island of Madeira. It has an underlying burnt flavor, which is the result of heating the wine after fermentation.
Mango: a fruit grown throughout the tropics, with sweet, succulent, yellow-orange flesh that is

extremely rich in vitamin A. It may cause an allergic reaction in some individuals.
Marinade: a mixture of aromatic ingredients in which meat is allowed to stand before cooking to enrich its flavor. Some marinades will tenderize meat, but they do not penetrate deeply.
Medallion: in lamb cooking, a round or oval slice of lean lamb for frying or broiling.
Mirin: a sweet Japanese cooking wine that is made from rice. If mirin is unavailable, substitute white wine or sake mixed with a little sugar.
Mixed spices: a mixture of spices and herbs, including several of the following: nutmeg, mace, cinnamon, cayenne pepper, white pepper, cloves, ground bay leaf, thyme, marjoram, and savory.
Monounsaturated fat: one of the three types of fats found in foods. Monounsaturated fats are believed not to raise the level of cholesterol in the blood. Some oils high in monounsaturated fats—olive oil, for example—are thought to lower blood-cholesterol levels.
Morels: wild mushrooms with brown, pitted caps. Dried morels should be soaked in hot water before they are used.
Mozzarella: a soft kneaded cheese from southern Italy, traditionally made from buffalo's milk, but now also made from cow's milk. Full-fat mozzarella has a fat content of 40 to 50 percent, but lower-fat versions are available. The low-fat mozzarella used in the recipes in this book has a fat content of only about 16 percent.
Nappa cabbage (also called Chinese cabbage): an elongated cabbage resembling romaine lettuce, with long, broad ribs and crinkled, light green to white leaves.
Noisettes: boned lamb from the rib or loin, rolled, tied, and cut into rounds for broiling or frying.
Nonreactive pan: a cooking vessel whose surface does not chemically react with food. This includes stainless steel, enamel, glass, and some alloys. Untreated cast iron and aluminum may react with acids, producing discoloration or a peculiar taste.
Nori: paperlike dark green or black sheets of dried seaweed, often used in Japanese cuisine as a flavoring or as wrappers for rice and vegetables.
Okra: the green pods of a plant indigenous to Africa, where it is called gumbo. In stews, okra is prized for its thickening properties.
Olive oil: any of various grades of oil extracted from olives. Extra virgin olive oil, which has a full, fruity flavor and the lowest acidity level, and virgin olive oil come from the first pressing of the olives. Pure olive oil, a processed blend of olive oils, has the lightest taste and the highest acidity.
Paprika: a slightly sweet, spicy, bright red powder produced by grinding dried red peppers. The best type of paprika is Hungarian.
Paupiettes: very thin slices of meat that are stuffed and rolled.
Phyllo (also spelled filo): a paper-thin flour-and-water pastry popular in Greece and the Middle East. It can be bought, fresh or frozen, from delicatessens and shops specializing in Middle Eastern food.
Pilaf: a dish of rice or other grains, heated in a little oil, then simmered in water or stock. Meat or vegetables are often added to turn a pilaf into a main course.
Pine nuts (also called *pignoli):* seeds from the cones of the stone pine, a tree native to the Mediterranean. Toasting brings out their buttery flavor.
Poach: to cook over low heat in simmering liquid. The temperature of the poaching liquid should be approximately 200° F., and its surface should merely tremble.
Polyunsaturated fat: one of the three types of fats found in foods. Polyunsaturated fats exist in abundance in such vegetable oils as safflower, sunflower, corn, and soybean. Polyunsaturated fats lower the level of cholesterol in the blood.
Pomegranate: a red-skinned fruit with succulent seeds that are picked out and eaten; the bitter white membranes are discarded. Pomegranates are in season in the autumn.
Porcini (also called cepes): wild mushrooms with a pungent, earthy flavor that survives drying or long cooking. Dried porcini should be soaked in hot water before they are used.
Prosciutto: an uncooked, dry-cured, and slightly salty Italian ham, sliced paper thin.
Purée: to reduce food to a smooth, even, pulplike consistency by mashing it, passing it through a sieve, or processing it in a food processor or a blender.
Reduce: to boil down a liquid in order to concentrate its flavor and thicken its consistency.
Refresh: to rinse a briefly cooked vegetable under cold water to arrest its cooking and set its color.
Rice vinegar: a mild, fragrant vinegar that is less assertive than cider vinegar or distilled white vinegar. It is available in dark, light, seasoned, and sweetened varieties; Japanese rice vinegar generally is milder than the Chinese version.
Rice wine: Chinese rice wine *(shao-hsing)* is brewed from rice and wine. Japanese rice wine (sake) has a different flavor but may be used as a substitute. If rice wine is not available, use sherry in its place.
Saddle: a roast consisting of a pair of whole loins. A "long" saddle includes the pair of sirloin ends and sometimes the kidneys and tail, as well as the loins.
Safflower oil: the vegetable oil that contains the highest proportion of polyunsaturated fats.
Saffron: the dried yellowish red stigmas (or threads) of the crocus flower, saffron yields a pungent flavor and a bright yellow color. It is available in thread or powdered form.
Sake: see Rice wine.
Saturated fat: one of the three types of fats found in foods. Found in abundance in animal products and coconut and palm oils, saturated fats raise the level of cholesterol in the blood. Because high blood-cholesterol levels contribute to heart disease, saturated-fat consumption should be restricted to less than 10 percent of the calories provided by the daily diet.
Sauté: to cook a food quickly in a small amount of oil, usually in an uncovered frying pan.
Sear: to brown the surface of meat by a short application of intense heat; searing adds flavor and color, but it does not seal in meat juices.
Sesame oil: see Dark sesame oil.
Shallot: a refined cousin of the onion, with a subtle flavor and papery, red-brown skin.
Shank: the lower end of a leg. The foreshank, or knuckle, is the equivalent cut from a shoulder.
Shiitake mushrooms: a variety of mushroom, originally cultivated only in Japan, sold fresh or dried. The dried form should be soaked and stemmed before it is used.
Sichuan pepper (also called Chinese pepper, Japanese pepper, or anise pepper): a dried shrub berry with a tart, aromatic flavor that is less piquant than black pepper.
Simmer: to maintain a liquid at a temperature just below its boiling point so that the liquid's surface barely ripples.
Skim milk: milk from which almost all the fat has been removed.
Snow peas: flat green pea pods eaten whole, with only stems and strings removed.
Sodium: a nutrient essential to maintaining the proper balance of fluids in the body. In most diets, a major source of the element is table salt, which contains 40 percent sodium. Excess sodium may contribute to high blood pressure, which increases the risk of heart disease. One teaspoon of salt, with 2,132 milligrams of sodium, contains about two-thirds of the maximum daily amount recommended by the National Research Council.
Soy sauce: a savory, salty brown liquid made from fermented soybeans and available in both light and dark versions. One tablespoon of regular soy sauce contains 1,030 milligrams of sodium; lower-sodium variations, such as naturally fermented shoyu, may contain half that amount.
Star anise: a woody, star-shaped spice, similar in flavor to anise. Ground star anise is a component of five-spice powder.
Steam: to cook food in the steam created by a boiling liquid. The food is placed in a covered container with a perforated base through which the steam rises from the liquid below. Steaming vegetables preserves the vitamins and flavors that are ordinarily lost in boiling.
Stir-fry: to cook cubes or strips of meat or vegetables, or a combination of both, over high heat in a small amount of oil, stirring constantly to ensure even cooking in a short time. The traditional cooking vessel is a Chinese wok; a heavy-bottomed frying pan may also be used for stir-frying.
Stock: a savory liquid prepared by simmering meat, bones, trimmings, aromatic vegetables, herbs, and spices in water. Stock forms a flavor-rich base for sauces and stews.
Sun-dried tomatoes: tomatoes that have been dried in the open air to concentrate their flavor; some are then packed in oil.
Tahini (also called sesame paste): a nutty-tasting paste made from ground sesame seeds that are usually roasted.
Tarragon: a strong herb with a sweet anise taste. In combination with other herbs—especially

rosemary, sage, or thyme—it should be used sparingly to avoid a clash of flavors. Because heat intensifies tarragon's flavor, cooked dishes require smaller amounts.
Tenderloin (also called fillet): the most tender muscle of the carcass, located inside the loin.
Thyme: a versatile herb with a zesty, slightly fruity flavor and strong aroma.
Timbale: a creamy mixture of vegetables or meat baked in a mold. The term, French for "kettle-drum," also denotes a drum-shaped baking dish.
Tofu (also called bean curd): a dense, unfermented soybean product with a mild flavor. It is rich in protein, relatively low in calories, and free of cholesterol. Lightly pressed silken tofu is used for blending into other ingredients; heavily pressed firm tofu, which has a texture similar to cheese, may be cubed or sliced. Soft tofu, with a texture midway between the two, is also available.
Tomato purée: a purée made from peeled fresh or canned tomatoes. Available commercially, tomato purée should not be confused with the thicker, concentrated tomato paste sometimes labeled tomato purée.
Total fat: an individual's daily intake of polyunsaturated, monounsaturated, and saturated fats. Nutritionists recommend that total fat constitute no more than 30 percent of the energy in the diet. The term as used in this book refers to the combined fats in a given dish or food.
Turmeric: a spice used as a coloring agent and occasionally as a substitute for saffron. It has a musty odor and a slightly bitter flavor.
Virgin olive oil: see Olive oil.
Water chestnut: the walnut-size tuber of an aquatic Asian plant, with rough brown skin and white, sweet, crisp flesh. Fresh water chestnuts may be refrigerated for up to two weeks; they must be peeled before use. To store canned water chestnuts, first blanch or rinse them, then refrigerate them for up to three weeks in fresh water changed daily.
White pepper: a powder ground from the same dried berry as that used to make black pepper. Unlike black pepper, the berries are allowed to ripen and are ground without their shells. Used as a less visible alternative to black pepper in light-colored foods.
Wild rice: the seeds of a water grass native to the Great Lakes region of the United States. Wild rice is appreciated for its robust flavor.
Yogurt: a smooth-textured, semisolid cultured-milk product. The low-fat yogurt used in this book contains about 1 percent fat.

Picture Credits

Credits from left to right are separated by semicolons, from top to bottom by dashes.

Cover: Renée Comet. 4: Chris Knaggs—Andrew Whittuck; Ian O'Leary. 5: Graham Kirk; Andrew Whittuck—John Elliott. 6: David Johnson. 9: Art by Brian Bott, London. 10, 11: Chris Knaggs. 12: Ian O'Leary. 13: Chris Knaggs. 14: Graham Kirk. 15: Andrew Whittuck. 16: Renée Comet. 17: John Elliott. 18: Graham Kirk. 19, 20: Renée Comet. 21: Andrew Whittuck. 22: Jan Baldwin. 23: Chris Knaggs. 24: Ian O'Leary—John Elliott. 25: John Elliott. 26: Ian O'Leary. 27: Renée Comet. 28: Chris Knaggs. 29: Graham Kirk. 30, 31: Ian O'Leary. 32: Graham Kirk—John Elliott. 33: Chris Knaggs. 34: Renée Comet. 35: Graham Kirk. 36, 37: Renée Comet. 38: John Elliott. 39: Andrew Whittuck. 40, 41: Renée Comet. 42: Jan Baldwin. 43: Ian O'Leary—John Elliott. 44: Jan Baldwin. 45: John Elliott. 46-49: Renée Comet. 50: Andrew Whittuck. 51: Chris Knaggs. 52, 53: John Elliott. 54: John Elliott. 55: Graham Kirk. 56, 57: John Elliott. 58: Chris Knaggs. 59: Andrew Whittuck. 60, 61: Ian O'Leary. 62, 63: Renée Comet. 64, 65: Chris Knaggs. 66, 67: Ian O'Leary. 68: Graham Kirk. 69: Ian O'Leary. 70, 71: Graham Kirk. 72: Jan Baldwin. 73, 74: Renée Comet. 75: Graham Kirk. 76, 77: Jan Baldwin. 78, 79: Renée Comet. 80: Ian O'Leary. 81, 82: Renée Comet. 83: Chris Knaggs. 84: Ian O'Leary. 85: Renée Comet. 87-89: Chris Knaggs. 90: John Elliott. 91: Ian O'Leary. 92, 93: Renée Comet. 95: Graham Kirk. 96: Jan Baldwin. 97: Andrew Whittuck. 98: Jan Baldwin. 99: Renée Comet. 100: Chris Knaggs. 101, 102: Andrew Whittuck. 103, 104: Chris Knaggs. 105: Jan Baldwin. 106, 107: Andrew Whittuck. 108: John Elliott. 109: Andrew Whittuck. 110: Renée Comet. 111, 112: Chris Knaggs. 113: Jan Baldwin. 114: Chris Knaggs. 115: Jan Baldwin. 116: Graham Kirk. 117: Chris Knaggs. 118: Renée Comet—John Elliott (2). 119: Andrew Whittuck. 120, 121: Chris Knaggs. 122: Graham Kirk. 124: Ian O'Leary. 125-127: Renée Comet. 128: Jan Baldwin. 129: Chris Knaggs. 130, 131: Andrew Whittuck. 132: John Elliott. 133: Ian O'Leary. 134-136: John Elliott.

Props: The editors wish to thank the following outlets and manufacturers; all are based in London unless otherwise stated. 16: Ginza, Washington, D.C. 19: Joan Tapper, U.S.A. 20: Cobweb, New York. 24: napkin, Ewart Liddell. 26: napkin, Kilkenny. 30: platter, Thomas (London) Ltd.—platter, Inshop. 32: cloth, Ewart Liddell. 34: Fitz and Floyd, Inc., Dallas. 35: napkin, Kilkenny. 36: Williams-Sonoma, Washington, D.C. 37: China Closet, Kensington, Md. 40: Steven Hill, Kansas City, Mo. 41: Stephen Kilborn, Jackie Chalkley; bowl, Ron Bower, Jackie Chalkley, Washington, D.C. 43: marble, W. E. Grant & Co. (Marble) Ltd. 47: Sandra Selesnick, Full Circle, Alexandria, Va. 48: background, Michael Latil, U.S.A. 54: marble, W. E. Grant & Co. (Marble) Ltd. 55: carvers, Mappin & Webb Silversmiths. 58: cloth, Ewart Liddell. 59: plate, Rosenthal (London) Ltd.; cloth, Ewart Liddell. 62: plate, Preferred Stock, Washington, D.C.; bowl, The Flower Designer, Washington, D.C.; place mat and napkin, Abrielle Fine Linens & Lingerie, Washington, D.C. 63: plates, Gwathmey/Siegel for Sind, Powell and Alessi, U.S.A.; bowl, The American Hand Plus, Washington, D.C. 68: rice dish, Mary Wondraush; large dish, Derek Emms, The Craftsmen Potters Shop. 72: plate, Hutschenreuther (U.K.) Ltd. 73: Cobweb, New York. 74: Ruff & Ready Furnishings, Washington, D.C. 75: napkin, Kilkenny; cloth, Ewart Liddell; knife and fork, Mappin & Webb Silversmiths. 76: marble, W. E. Grant & Co. (Marble) Ltd. 77: plates, Villeroy & Boch; napkin, Ewart Liddell. 78: Peter Kaizer, The American Hand Plus, Washington, D.C. 84: rice dish, Tony Gant; large dish, Winchcombe Pottery, The Craftsmen Potters Shop. 92: bowls, Nora Pate Studio, San Francisco. 93: Cobweb, New York. 95: plate, The Reject China Shop. 96: plate, Royal Worcester, Worcester. 97: pie dish, Winchcombe Pottery, The Craftsmen Potters Shop. 98: china, Inshop. 99: Sasaki Crystal, Inc., New York. 103-104, 109: marble, W. E. Grant & Co. (Marble) Ltd. 117: fork, Mappin & Webb Silversmiths. 127: Wilton Armetale, New York. 132: plate, Tony Gant; pie dish, Mike Dodd, The Craftsmen Potters Shop. 133: salad bowl, Clive Bowen, The Craftsmen Potters Shop.

Index

Acknowledgments

The editors would like to thank: I. A. Bell and O. Kadlecek, Wiener Porzellanmanufaktur Augarten, Gesellschaft MBH, Vienna, Austria; Paul van Biene, London; René Bloom, London; Maureen Burrows, London; David Donaldson, ADAS, Chichester, West Sussex; Jonathan Driver, London; Bruce Horn, Hellet's Butchers, Kimbolton, Huntingdon; Lidgates of Holland Park, London; Meat & Livestock Commission, Milton Keynes; Perstorp Warerite Ltd., London; Sharp Electronics (U.K.) Ltd., London; Jane Stevenson, London; Toshiba (U.K.) Ltd., London.